A Badge, a Gun, an Attitude

25 Years as a Los Angeles County Deputy Sheriff

DEAN SCOVILLE

Exposit

Jefferson, North Carolina

Frontispiece: The author, "Lean Dean," 1983.

LIBRARY OF CONGRESS CATALOGUING-IN-PUBLICATION DATA

Names: Scoville, Dean, 1960– author.
Title: A badge, a gun, an attitude : 25 years as a Los Angeles
County deputy sheriff / Dean Scoville.
Description: Jefferson, North Carolina : Exposit Books, 2017 | Includes index.
Identifiers: LCCN 2017036819 | ISBN 9781476670454
(softcover : acid free paper) ∞
Subjects: LCSH: Scoville, Dean, 1960– | Sheriffs—California—Los Angeles
County—Biography. | Law enforcement—California—Los Angeles
County—Biography. | Crime—California—Los Angeles County.
Classification: LCC HV7911.S365 A3 2017 | DDC 363.28/2092 [B]—dc23
LC record available at https://lccn.loc.gov/2017036819

BRITISH LIBRARY CATALOGUING DATA ARE AVAILABLE

ISBN 978-1-4766-7045-4 (print)
ISBN 978-1-4766-3078-6 (ebook)

Front cover images © 2017 iStock

Printed in the United States of America

Exposit is an imprint of McFarland & Company, Inc., Publishers
Jefferson, North Carolina

Exposit

*Box 611, Jefferson, North Carolina 28640
www.expositbooks.com*

A Badge, a Gun,
an Attitude

Dedicated to the love of my life and the mother
of my talented and compassionate son.
I'd hate to contemplate where I would be
without your support, patience, and forgiveness.

Acknowledgments

Thanks to Jolynn Coronel, Elena Smith, Lynn Helbing, and Michele Carey for their invaluable assistance in midwifing this book. And to all the good cops I have worked with and known for inspiring me to start it in the first place.

Table of Contents

Preface

It's been said that there should be no such things as laws—that good men don't need them, and bad men won't abide by them.

As the sentiment sums up my own take on the matter, it also marks my career as an administrator of the California Penal Code as a damn curious one. Yet how, why and whether one should be pounding the streets (or felons) are necessary concerns for those who don a uniform, badge, and firearm. In wrestling with these questions, answers can be more difficult to pin down than suspects.

My experiences in law enforcement helped shape not only my perceptions of the vocation, but also my perceptions of those with whom I came in contact through my work. The ambassadorships of those individuals disabused certain personal prejudices, even as they helped to reinforce others. More than a few of my conclusions regarding the profession and its liabilities are equally owed to them.

Those conclusions—and many of the factors that precipitated them—are the primary focus of this memoir.

Experience should be the trump card in commentary proceedings on law enforcement. Not the Monday-morning quarterbacking of what some cop did by journalists, nor whether those actions conformed to the expectations of some self-proclaimed community activist. Just a knowledgeable assessment of what actually occurred within the context of any peculiar episode associated with the profession, and of the performance executed by the person trained to do it.

Throughout my career, I was witness to situations that ranged from humorous to heartbreaking, salacious to gory, and none that left me lacking for subjects to write about. In writing this memoir, I have strived to use archetypal incidents to illustrate my personal viewpoints and to offer ammunition to those who would rebut law enforcement's critics.

What follows is my summation of a profession that affords "trial by fire" baptisms from an officer's first day to his last—it is the nature of this career that no segment of society is immune from contact with law enforcement, and there is no volatile social issue that does not impact it.

Looking back on generations of law enforcement practitioners, mine was the first to get accustomed to the near universal deployment of ballistic vests, portable radios, and mobile digital transmitters; the one responsible for changing things for the worse (Rodney King), and the better (less lethal weaponry); the last to perform the job without its every move being tracked or recorded. If I could have chosen, I might well have preferred to have started my career a decade or so before—in an era that had its own unique threats, but still afforded the good, aggressive street cop the opportunity to perform the job as his conscience saw fit.

But even within the 25-year span of my career, I found enough wiggle-room to make the challenge work—which is more than I could anticipate if I were to start the job now. Still, I revisit that period with as much objectivity and candor as possible. I suspect few will find fault with my honesty.

Chronologically, my story begins with my joining the Los Angeles County Sheriff's Department as a cadet in its Training Academy in the early 1980s. It follows my graduation to custody; tracks my subsequent transfer to patrol; then charts the balance of my career as I work a variety of assignments thereafter before being promoted to supervisor, where I spend the last 15 years flitting against the unreasonable person's glass ceiling like some brain-fried moth. It wraps with my time at *POLICE* magazine, after my retirement from the sheriff's department, a period when I authored the highly successful "Shots Fired" column that profiled officer-involved shootings as experienced by the officers themselves.

In some instances, I have lost contact with former co-workers and was unable or unwilling to secure permission to use their names. In others cases, I was reticent to mention names for fear of stigmatizing their family members. For this reason, I have changed the names of the vast majority of people mentioned in this book. Two notable exceptions are my second training officer, Lynn Helbing, and Deputy Brad Higgins, who helped save my ass in a shooting. Both have given permission to use their names.

Spiritually and philosophically, this memoir finds me transitioning from a slacker critic of law enforcement to an admirer of its more ardent practitioners. It also details how along the way I found myself bitten, punched, shot, and backstabbed—more often than not in the literal sense. And while I might piss and moan along the way, I ultimately come to appreciate how I have profited from my misadventures more often than not.

And that is perhaps the main thing that I want the reader to consider: The silver linings that we encounter, not just within our beleaguered careers, but in life in general.

Because without them, we'd really be screwed.

1

Sympathy for the Poor Bastards of the World

"Be Someone's Hero"
—Los Angeles County Sheriff's
Department recruiting slogan

I don't recall any youthful fantasies of becoming a cop. Sure, I'd played cops and robbers as a kid. I'd also played cowboys and Indians—but nobody was going to find my ass falling off a horse at a dude ranch anytime soon. This, coupled with questionable childhood associations, generally maladaptive behavior, and an inability to function as a team player, marked that choice of profession a low-percentage gamble for me.

But I am nothing if not a gambler, and so it was that shortly after entering college I began to give law enforcement serious consideration.

Dad had planted the seed sometime earlier, his only child's spotty work history no doubt the basis for the recommendation. While a career in law enforcement would save him the aggravation of firing me from his sign shop every other week, his pitch relied on two salient points: namely that police work would offer me some badly needed discipline, and let me see what the real world was like.

"After all, you can't live here forever," noted my nominee for Father of the Year.

Normally, I was one to take the hint. At the first sign that someone wants their space, my inclination has always been to make them feel like Neil Armstrong.

It wasn't as though finding another job hadn't been on the table before. I'd spent a year at the Covina Book Store, where I'd worn out my welcome by punching out a co-worker. I did a three-week stint with

Orange Julius before I was let go for dropping a tray of 40 hotdogs onto the floor (apparently, they weren't edible after). I spent two days at a sporting goods store before my total ignorance of all things sports-related became painfully obvious and they, too, showed me the door.

No, dealing with fickle employers who didn't owe me a damn thing was always doable. But moving out of my parents' home? Too much work. Besides, most of my under-the-table pay was going right back into Dad's pocket as rent.

Given these realities, I felt comfortable handing Dad a written reply wherein I outlined the many reasons I didn't want to be part of a "fascist state." Worse than the cliché of my principled rebuttal was the fact that it was also entirely disingenuous.

The truth was that I was more sympathetic to cops than not. Sure, the popular films of the previous decade had exposed me to *Dirty Harry*, *The French Connection*, and many other celluloid cops that could charitably be characterized as conflicted. However, Joseph Wambaugh had presented a contrasting image of cops, given them flesh and bone, put me in their cars, their homes, their addled heads. And let's face it—I'd always been a softie for the poor bastards of the world.

Cultural indoctrination aside, the job had undeniable appeal. The opportunity to take bad guys to jail. A chance to save lives. The happiness of pursuit.

Then there was the economy.

The stagflation of the seventies had led to inflation in the eighties. Unemployment was jumping off like my fellow students from the Humanities building at Cal State University–Fullerton, and banks were going tits up. By 1981, the recession was getting worse and however self-actualizing a creative job such as screenwriting might have been, my priority was to make sure I could eventually put a roof over my head and keep it there.

When it came to my college major—psychology—I was increasingly pessimistic about its long-term prospects. In class, I'd noticed that if the disorder in question didn't speak to Dad's emotional problems, it almost certainly spoke to mine. There were other concerns as well. The profession had not been a particularly well paying one even in better economic times and its practitioners were prone to suicide (physician heal thyself, indeed). And while I was open to hearing people discuss their fears, I wondered how many would feel comfortable opening up to me.

Even my declared minor—journalism—was losing its appeal. I'd simply be doing post mortems on what others had accomplished. Fluff pieces on people who were making millions selling my generation pet rocks suggested the demise of hard-hitting journalism.

Becoming a law enforcement officer would at least allow me to insinuate myself into many a news story, and have some say in how it played out. And while I had little desire to bust my ass, I wasn't above busting someone else's. Perhaps most important, while I'd been present for many a criminal act, I'd usually been prudent enough to refrain from active participation.

I'd seen my neighbor, James, shoot out the streetlight with a BB gun when I was 11.

I'd gone joyriding with my best friend, Ray, in his dad's car when I was 12.

I knew who burned down our sixth grade classroom (Ray again).

But none of these misdeeds had come about through my own initiative. The few crimes for which I was solely culpable—breaking into the piggy bank of my babysitter's daughter; entering the unlocked rear door of another friend's house and helping myself to some Morgan silver dollars I found atop a dresser—had either gone undetected, or someone else took the fall.

This confluence of dumb luck and smart execution had spared me a criminal record—which was more than many of Los Angeles County's sons and daughters could claim.

Most of my crimes—save for a minor hit-and-run stemming from underage drinking and certain statutory matters—had been committed well before my 14th birthday. From that time on, I'd pretty much remained on the right side of the law.

But in analyzing law enforcement's offerings, my young self saw as many pitfalls as perks.

Sure, I'd get to wear a uniform, a gun, and a badge, and to extract an overdue pound of flesh from an occasional world-class predator. I wouldn't have to put up with any more "don't let the door hit you in the ass" parting shots from my on-again/off-again boss-father. No longer would I sweat getting pulled over for some chicken-shit traffic violation.

I could also get my ass shot and killed.

But then the fear-fantasies would morph into something more

seductive. Imagined scenarios of running headlong into harm's way to save the lives of others appealed to the more gallant aspects of my nature. Daydreams wherein my Holmes-like acumen tripped up some ne'er-do-well Moriarty gave me an intellectual rush. Reveries of frustrated felons being dragged off to the hoosegow had me believing that if my becoming a cop didn't wipe clean the slate of my pubescent transgressions, it might at least tilt the scales a little more in my favor.

Finally, I was an adult—at least physically if not mentally, and in the eyes of the law I was thinking of enforcing, culpably so. Perhaps it was time to get serious and strike out on my own.

Hearing that I'd been contemplating his advice, Dad repeatedly drove one point home.

"It's a civil service job, numb nuts: Once you're in, you're in," he postulated. "It's not like around here where I get to fire your ass every other month. It'll take an act of Congress to get rid of you. Just keep your nose clean and you'll be okay."

And so I celebrated my 21st birthday in East Los Angeles taking the entry exam for the Los Angeles County Sheriff's Department.

The next few months were a series of downtown commutes for physical and endurance examinations and oral interviews. Meanwhile my background investigator visited my neck of the woods, speaking with former co-workers, employers, and friends. About the only oversights in my hiring process were my inexplicably being spared polygraph and psych examinations, but I prudently refrained from mentioning them to anyone.

As winter and spring came and went, things quieted down. Communications with the sheriff's department dwindled and other things occupied my mind and time.

That spring, I'd messed around on my girlfriend and by summer she'd broken up with me. Dad finally had enough of my revolving door employment and I ended up taking a part-time job doing janitorial and security work at Little Tokyo's Weller Court in downtown Los Angeles. Attacking unsuspecting cigarette butts with a push broom, I'd ask myself if I'd been unduly optimistic in switching my major to criminal justice.

By late July, I'd pretty much forgotten about the Sheriff's Department and was looking at Daryl Gates' LAPD. True, I'd be confined to working the city limits, but I would also be spared the aggravation of working custody and I'd have a uniform that looked sharp.

Then one day my stepmother, Judy, took a call at Dad's shop and then handed the phone to me. Part of me hoped it was my ex-girlfriend. It wasn't.

"How'd you like to come work for the Los Angeles County Sheriff's Department?" a jaunty voice asked.

Months had gone by without a word from the Department. Now, out of the blue, my background investigator was offering me the job.

If the words out of my mouth weren't, "Hell, yes!" I'm pretty sure he got some sense of my enthusiasm.

I gave notice to a visibly relieved Ron Yasuda, the man who'd hired me only weeks before for the Weller Court job. No longer would I be obliged to show up every Saturday and Sunday night at the tri-level plaza located next to the New Otani Hotel to relieve my cousin Bob. Ended were long nights of collecting cigarette butts from ash tray urns, washing down the court's three levels with a hose, replacing the liners in trash cans, and conducting security rounds of the court and its perimeter. The elderly folks, drug addicts, and prostitutes who inhabited the dilapidated motel across the street would no longer be subject to my voyeuristic pere-grinations about the Weller rooftop. Ron would no longer have to re-trace my footsteps at 4:30 a.m. and point out every janitorial oversight.

No, I was going from amateur nosy bastard to pro. I'd be able to legally carry a firearm, and not have to sweat getting caught with the .25 caliber semi-auto I'd been carrying since Dad had found out about my first citizen's arrest of a strong-arm robbery suspect at Weller Court.

I could hardly wait.

Shortly after I'd graduated from high school in 1979, and possibly under the influence of the Village People's hit that year, I'd taken a writ-ten exam for the Navy. I figured that if I couldn't get into college—a rea-sonable concern, given my 2.2 high school GPA—the military would be my fallback. Uncle Sam might be looking for a few good men, but would probably settle for me all the same.

But a letter of acceptance from Cal State Fullerton arrived in the mail and I never looked back or answered any of the poor naval recruiter's calls to my home.

The promise of a job with the sheriff's department summoned forth all manner of emotions. Feelings of validation, charged-up optimism, and low-level anxiety descended on me, as well as a determination to make the most of the two weeks that separated the background investigator's call and my appointed date with the Hall of Justice.

To celebrate, I accompanied my friends, Harold Dubois and Matt McDonald, to Hollywood. Normally, Whittier Boulevard was my choice for Friday night cruising, despite the city's lack of affinity for out-of-town punks like me. But Harold and Matt wanted to try something new and I didn't object, particularly as the three of us were now old enough to get into the local strip clubs.

We were stopped for a red light as we cruised Hollywood Boulevard when my attention was drawn to a car in the lane next to us. In the back seat, a young man with a punk haircut stared at me intently.

When eye contact is made between strangers, it is common for one party to politely avert his gaze. Elsewhere in the animal kingdom, it is simply a matter of seeing who'll blink first.

I met the stranger's gaze and held it with my own.

His expression dissolved into a "What the fuck are you staring at?" glare.

I returned the look.

He flipped me off.

I mouthed the words, "*Fuck you,*" to him.

Our mutual contempt ratified, he suddenly jumped out of the car and darted towards me. As he cleared the rear bumper of his ride, a switchblade knife popped into view.

This was no shit-house theater dramatics. The guy was closing the gap between us as quickly as possible so as to strike with the knife before our car could move or I could roll up my window. From his perspective, I no doubt appeared a sitting duck.

Little did he know that I had the blessed peace of mind of a man holding four aces.

Against my passenger-side door and below his line of sight, the .25 caliber automatic I'd been carrying with me on my weekend treks to Weller Court was clenched in my right hand.

As he came within 25 feet of my car door, I started to raise the gun and flicked off the safety.

This bastard is about to get shot and is going to have nobody to blame but himself.

But before I could squeeze the trigger, I found myself suddenly thrust back against my seat from the forward momentum of the car. Harold had hit the gas of his VW, veering into the lanes of oncoming traffic, blowing a red light at the intersection, and damn near getting us T-boned in the process, as he made a sharp left onto a side street.

As he slowed and looked in his rearview mirror for the would-be slasher or the cops, I found myself getting pissed.

"What the hell did you do that for?" I asked, putting the gun away. "I had his ass!"

"I don't want any trouble," Harold said.

Disgusted, I sulked for the rest of the night. We didn't even hit the strip club.

Running around the Workman High School track and listening to my Walkman cassette player at night, I got to thinking long and hard about how shit-stupid my behavior had been. If anything, I was indebted to Harold for preventing me from shooting that knife-wielding moron.

Sure, the shooting would have been justified, but my carrying a loaded firearm would have been prosecutable and, like subway shooter Bernard Goetz a couple of years later, I doubtless would have been charged. Conviction or no, an arrest would have effectively killed any chance of becoming a deputy sheriff.

And there was another thing on my mind: I didn't like how much I *wanted* to pull the trigger that night. How much I wanted to kill another human being. Whatever sense of security carrying a firearm might have given me, becoming an even bigger asshole was a real risk I had to assess.

It was one thing to know how to pull the trigger—any idiot could do that, and plenty had. It was another to know when you really had to, and to recognize the grievous implications of that action.

He never received a medal for it, but Harold had saved two idiots' lives that night.

At 9:30 a.m. on August 11, 1982, 11 young men—six white males, four Latinos, one black, all appropriately respectful of their situation if not of one another—were ushered into an office at the Hall of Justice to swear an oath to protect the citizens of Los Angeles County.

As I stood in an administrative office, I thought of childhood superheroes who'd invoked similar oaths, who by lanterns and rings swore to defend the weak and strike against evil wherever it might lurk.

And that covered a lot of territory.

Had I actually considered the import of the oath being administered to us—that this subsidiary form of allegiance was to some five million citizens whose interests often ran at cross purposes with one another, that making the pledge would oblige me to enforce laws that I often opposed at a philosophical level—I might have questioned how effective I'd be in fulfilling that pledge.

But such thoughts never crossed my mind. It was merely one more formality toward becoming a deputy sheriff, and that was what mattered.

So I took the County's oath with all the sincerity I'd mustered as a child when I'd first said the Pledge of Allegiance.

And having taken this oath, I wasn't ever asked to repeat it.

Deputy Hanson, our orientation officer, gave us a tour of the building and told us what to expect in the weeks ahead. As he conducted us through the hallowed halls, we found ourselves issued both a flat badge to carry in our wallets and a regular one to go on our uniform, along with a picture ID and business cards that read "Deputy Sheriff." No civilians were ever more apathetic than those handing out these trinkets, nor more dependent upon muscle memory for their ministrations.

No sooner were the business cards in our hands when Hanson cautioned us against showing them off, reminding us that as cadets we were not full-fledged deputy sheriffs and therefore had no arrest powers beyond those of any other citizen. If our lack of arrest powers weren't enough to deter us, the horror story of a cadet who played cop was. As Hanson explained soberly, the cadet ended up getting shot and his car was stolen.

"Oh, and he was fired from the Department."

I stared at my badge. "4950" gleamed back at me, an easy enough number to remember.

Our next stop would be across town at the Academy, but only after we'd made sure that forms reflecting our emergency care and mortuary preferences were filled out.

For the second time that morning, and in a manner portending extended ETAs in patrol later, I got lost. Eventually my circumnavigation found me at the well-manicured Academy grounds on Eastern Avenue in East Los Angeles.

The inmates lived in a County jail situated next to the Sheriff's Academy, a facility named in honor of former Los Angeles County Sheriff Eugene Biscailuz. Inside its administrative offices, I found my fellow cadets already being introduced to the facility by its watch commander, Lt. Marcus Nakamura.

Situated atop a hill, Biscailuz facility's two-floored bungalows housed primarily pre-sentenced "low risk" offenders, inmates who by and large wouldn't escape simply because they didn't have any cause to. Just down the street was the County's correctional facility for women, Sybil Brand Institute.

With the start of the Academy still six weeks away, the 11 of us were split up among these custody facilities, as well as the Hall of Justice Jail and Men's Central Jail, to work as "off-the-streeter" jailers, thereby abetting the ratio of deputies to inmates while giving us a look at the nature of what would be our first Department assignment.

From the Admin office, we marched to the nearby Logistics office where they issued us our regulation gear: handcuffs, whistle, and a cheap plastic flashlight. My love life was looking up.

The administration deputy asked which of us would like to work the 3:00 to 11:00 p.m. shift. Figuring the next shift would probably be worse, I volunteered. Everyone else ended up on day shift, but they also got the traffic that went with it.

My consolation prize? Weekends off. It was the last time I volunteered for anything on Eastern Avenue.

Released at noon and told to pick up our uniforms, I headed for Keystone Uniform in West Covina where a seamstress measured me for alterations and said the uniforms could be picked up the next day.

That weekend I could hardly wait to get to my aunt's house where my cousin Rick was back home over the weekend from University of Nevada–Las Vegas.

The yin to my yang, Richard Alexander Yamada had been my childhood terror, rival, and hero. When we were boys, his bite marks had adorned my arms and his gloved hand had landed many a punch upside my head in "boxing matches" refereed by his father, Richard Sr., in the Yamada's back yard. As young men, we faced off over a girl—I told him that I had more brains than he ever would.

"Yeah?" he'd asked. "And how would you like me to knock them out?"

That summed up our lifelong relationship, constituted of equal parts jealousy and respect on both sides. But my feelings about him went unspoken—Rick was hands down the bravest man I knew, and had taken on multiple assailants on more than one occasion.

So here I finally had something redolent of manhood that I could flaunt at the 6'3", 240 lb. triathlete and UNLV football defensive lineman, something to elicit the kind of envy I'd so often felt for him.

I flashed my badge.

He summed up his newfound impression of me in one word.

"Pig."

Nothing so surprised me during my time at Biscailuz Jail as the inmates I found myself supervising.

I was well aware that these were low-level offenders. Nonetheless, their largely deferential attitudes and compliant natures contrasted sharply with the hardened criminals I imagined. My anxieties about the kind of head-chopping horrors associated with the New Mexico prison riots two years earlier immediately dissipated.

And it wasn't just the charges they were facing that kept them in line. Almost to a man, they made a conscious effort to not offend anyone wearing the uniform. None of this respect had anything to do with my skinny 21-year-old ass and I knew it. It had everything to do with the men who'd donned the uniform before me and the inmates' collective desire not to be transferred to Men's Central Jail.

"Don't fuck with deputies—they'll fuck you up!"

Recidivists who wouldn't blanch at the prospect of breaking the law would think twice before having a second go-round with the County's finest, and that I was now guardian to men who pretty much abided by that wisdom was nothing short of a blessing.

My lowly status of "off-the-streeter" suggested to me a steady diet of dismissive attitudes, calls of "fish on the line," and lonely lunches for the foreseeable future.

But those same badass deputies proved not only welcoming, but downright friendly, taking the time to explain the nuances of the job and give my fellow cadets and me helpful tips about what to expect in the Academy and how to get through it. No counsel registered more than that summed up by the Japanese adage, "The nail that sticks out gets hammered." I was determined to keep as low a profile in the Academy as my 6'3" frame would allow.

Such wisdom was shared over lunch or by prowlers—roaming support deputies—who'd stop by my booth during security checks of my dorm. It was there that I came to appreciate another of their virtues: their sense of protectiveness.

It happened one night as I was walking count—checking inmates' names on the dorm board against their wristbands—that I found men missing from their bunks.

Just because most Biscailuz inmates didn't have a good reason to escape didn't mean the more shit-stupid among them didn't try. On this occasion two had done just that, using bedding to fashion two "bodies" under their blankets prior to walking out an unsecured door. The deceit didn't quite rise to *Escape from Alcatraz* levels, but it was good enough that a less vigilant soul might have bypassed them.

I got on my radio and requested a prowler to respond to my dorm. That radio was part of the reason the men had been able to escape. Earlier, its battery had died and in the absence of an available deputy to shuttle a new one to me, I'd been obligated to leave my monitoring booth to retrieve a fresh radio from the administrative office myself.

During my short absence, the downstairs dorm deputy heard an alarm indicating that a door had been opened. He hadn't thought anything of it, but later realized that it must have been when the defiant ones had fled.

I was worried to death that I'd just lost my job, although for the life of me I couldn't see where I'd done anything other than by the numbers. Fortunately, the deputies working that night felt likewise and helped me with the necessary documentation.

The net effect of the escape was that one inmate was able to enjoy a few days' liberty before getting corralled near his home.

The other fared less favorably, running over the hill and straight to where Special Enforcement Bureau deputies happened to be conducting canine training that very night.

He ended up being treated at a local hospital for dog bites.

2

Academy

The more time one spends living life, the less time one has to write about it. So it was that the journal entries I'd started about a year before getting hired ceased shortly after my being hired.

But whatever was not recorded by hand was embedding itself in my memory—so many new faces, new places, and new experiences.

And nothing became more entrenched than our second day in the Academy. The first day, we'd been welcomed to the Hill with warm and courteous smiles. The next day, the drill instructors barked orders and intimidated us.

The first of these barked orders had us lining up in two long rows atop the asphalt. Called out alphabetically, we then were split into platoon formations: five across, four deep. Divide and conquer was on, and row by row cadets labored using their peripheral vision to maintain an arm's distance from their peers in front and to the side of them in a bid to establish some uniformity to the proceedings.

Aiding us to that end were our mercurial drill instructors: Wayne Lightner, Tim Macy, Wanda Morse, Todd Hanson, Larry Haskell, John Beasley, and John Garcia. The seven stood before us, equidistant from one another and in front of their adopted platoons save for when they would suddenly swoop upon some poor bastard and start yelling or laughing at him for whatever came to mind.

The person on the receiving end of this spittle and chortle was often an odds-on favorite to get appointed platoon sergeant, expected to make sure that all cadets in their respective platoons had their shit together.

Getting our shit together was a cagey mix of not stepping on one another's toes, anticipating the DI's demands, and somehow remaining inoffensive to the powers that be.

And so it was that the male and female cadets obediently marched to and fro across the "grinder"—that portion of asphalt that stretched from the Academy bungalows to the Biscailuz administration office—for hours on end.

Einstein said, "That a man can take pleasure in marching in fours to the strains of a band is enough to make me despise him."

I never understood the whole $E=mc^2$ thing, but at some level I related to him regarding this marching shit—and didn't even have the pleasure of a goddamned band, only sideways glances at one another, communicating the same unspoken thoughts: When are we going to go in the classroom? When are we going to start learning about the job?

When not marching, we stood at parade rest, legs spread shoulder width apart and hands clasped behind our backs. Intended to give us a rest, we were nonetheless expected to remain still in this position. I blinked my eyes to minimize the sting of Brylcreem that seeped down my forehead as sweat cascaded down my inner arms and torso. As the perspiration stained my $200 suit and compromised my grip on my briefcase, one omnipresent thought kept me company: *This is stupid. If they want us to be uncomfortable, they need only put us in sweats and coats.*

This was only one of numerous objectionable routines we became accustomed to. The grinder soon lived up to its name. As cadets rotated in and out of the class sergeant position, obliged to memorize commands, reciting those same commands to fellow cadets, and acting upon those they were given, their best efforts often reflected a kind of confused compliance.

Told to retrieve some test forms from the logistics office up the hill, I paused long enough on the way back to stare at my fellow cadets on the grinder, little more than a series of vertical lines, bowling pins really, all waiting to be knocked down by the ever-willing DIs.

I wondered if I was to become one of the casualties.

Next to squared-away cadets, about the only thing in short supply at the Academy were parking spaces, a reality that translated to our being assigned carpools.

"You'd better get used to hanging with people you probably wouldn't socialize with otherwise," we were told. "You're not going to be picking your partners in the field for some time. You're all in this together, sink or swim. Get used to it."

Our residential proximity to one another found Damion Simmons, Charles Street, and myself commuting to the Academy together.

Simmons was black, a reservist in the military, and endowed with the deepest baritone I'd ever heard. Red-haired and freckled Street I recognized as a fellow alumnus of Workman High School. These were the two guys with whom I'd spend the next four and a half months commuting in a silent stupor, half-drowsy, half-listening to Rick Dees in the Morning on KIIS-FM.

That second day was the start of our physical agility training and the first of three physical agility exams. After a battery of push-ups, sit-ups, pull-ups, and sprints of various distances, I found that for all my pre–Academy training I was hurting.

As much as I resented all the calisthenics, the DIs did not spare themselves of them. Indeed, their arrival invariably preceded ours, a conscientious display of professional decorum that only irked my fatigued ass all the more. Given a few minutes to shower and change, we were sent home, our first true Academy day behind us.

Over the following days and weeks, we cadets found ourselves standing on the grinder, elbows akimbo with hands clasped behind our backs, chests inflated outward, doing little more than monitoring our steamy breaths in the morning air, and listening to the whispered jokes of our representative class jokesters while the DIs tore into the target of the hour. Each platoon had a joker, and Dan Robles was Platoon Six's. More than once he provided the only smile I could muster before noon.

The rest of the time I stood brooding, sullenly resentful of what I'd subjected myself to and wondering how I could get by without attracting notice. The only solace available to me—that I could simply drop out at any time—was no less a torment as it portended only more proof of my indefatigable willingness to give up at the first sign of opposition. And so, every hour I vacillated between "Screw this, I'll *quit*" and "Screw *them*, I won't quit."

Some cadets were similarly constituted, but I was surprised by how many actually seemed to be enjoying themselves. They were really fired up for everything the DIs threw at them: role playing ... verbal Q and As.... Scantron quizzes and tests. For them, it was all good.

While none of it turned me on, I recognized the need for most of it and was dedicated to putting up with all of it, including the occasional snide aside of a fellow cadet.

If there was one thing that literally chafed my hide, it was the amount of running they made us do.

The DIs were always talking it up with a kind of "pinch me, I'm dreaming" rhetoric: "Can you believe that they're actually paying us to get into shape? Where else in the world can you do this?"

And many of the cadets did, in fact, love it. These masochists would go on to score perfect 500s in the physical exams and become honor guards on our runs.

But I hated it, and the only person who possibly hated it more was Cadet Schneider, who daily ran in front of me sweating the prospect of his feet being swept from under him by mine.

If there was a silver lining to the running it was the occasional relief they offered from a certain olfactory offensiveness owed to the methane gas deposits beneath our feet. On hot days when the odors became more pronounced, we moved from the track to the city streets where we jogged through the hilly "Alps" of East Los Angeles.

Rainy days offered an alternative torture. Congregated in the gymnasium, we went through a series of "stress-recovery-stress" exercises that somehow managed to ignore the recovery part.

We'd been issued our uniforms well before the Academy, but were told we couldn't wear them until the drill instructors gave the approval. By the time we were given the okay, the shines I'd administered to my Sam Browne (belt) and shoes were piss-poor no matter how much work I'd put into them. And despite my best and most cautious efforts at using tweezers to remove portions of the newspaper that had adhered to the belt during shining, flecks of white appeared here and there.

Somehow my uniform appearance was deemed passable, an amnesty I could only attribute to the fact that the fashion police couldn't come down hard on you when you were obliged to wear Class B khaki shirts and forest green pants all the time.

It made me wonder if I should have gone with LAPD. Those guys looked sharp in their dark blue uniforms.

We looked like a bunch of damned forest rangers.

A month into the Academy, we were told that our service revolvers would be issued to us on the morning of November 2nd. Those of us not at Logistics by 0530 would be "shit out of luck."

It was well before 0500 when Simmons, Street, and I arrived. Shivering with the morning cold, we waited in line as each preceding cadet walked off in a trance, a blue steel .38 revolver in tow. Our envy was short-lived as we each received our own Smith and Wesson Model 15.

Back in the classroom, we admired our new toys, half afraid their distribution would prove just the latest cruelty perpetrated by our drill instructors, who at any moment would take them away.

But our fears proved ill-founded. We had to deposit the firearms inside our vehicles until the end of the day, but at 1700 we found ourselves back in the parking lot, standing before a parade of saluting trunk lids, and again fondling the objects of our admiration.

Climbing into the backseat of Charles Street's car, I cradled the tool of my trade, that I would theoretically use to protect the lives of innocent civilians, as well as my own, in the years to come. Street steered onto the eastbound 10 Freeway and everything was fine until we neared the Edgewood Drive-In in Baldwin Park. As we passed its double-bill marquee, a claustrophobic bubble seemed to descend over me. It lasted only a couple seconds, but sucked the air out of me so that I felt a sense of incipient panic. The sensation passed as suddenly as it started, so that by the time I was dropped off at my house, I was again at ease and whistling as I walked up the driveway.

As I walked in the front door, I noticed an absence of familial sounds—Mom cooking in the kitchen, Dad strumming his guitar or reading aloud from some World War II book. The eerie silence overwhelmed me.

Just beyond the front door I found my parents waiting, neatly dressed and ready to step out. My own jacket was half off, and Dad waved me to put it back on.

"Rick's shot himself," he said bluntly. "We're going to meet Mary at the hospital."

I accompanied my parents to Queen of the Valley Hospital in West Covina and reflected on the odd sensation that had washed over me only minutes earlier. Had I had some terrible premonition after all? (If so, why then? Why not earlier?).

At the hospital, Rick's family and friends congregated about an ICU corridor—except his father, Richard, who stood characteristically off to the side alone. I hugged my Aunt Mary and placed a cautious hand on my uncle's shoulder, then walked into the hospital room. Beyond a curtain, Rick lay in bed.

My eyes were no less red-rimmed and bloodshot than those congregated about me. But the sight of Rick flooded my vision still further. Cousin, hero, tormentor, friend, and enemy, he was the nearest thing to a brother I'd ever had.

I dabbed at my eyes repeatedly, but neither sorrow nor tears blinded me to what the bullet had done to him and part of me was sickened at the morbid fascination with which I regarded his state.

Save for the tubes, IVs, and other medical intrusions that marked it, Rick's body looked as I remembered it: enviably powerful with a musculature that belied his youth, a physique honed by years playing football, basketball, and baseball. But his head was grotesquely misshapen. Dark circles lined eyes that bulged beneath eyelids as the machines that anchored him to this plane monitored and assisted his breathing.

About me, Bob and others were crying. Save for Richard Sr., everyone seemed to want to reach out and be reached out to. They were mostly Rick's friends, guys with whom I'd played tackle football and baseball on weekends. As such, I felt a kinship with them as well. Our leader had fallen.

Two hours of muted commiserations passed without any change in Rick's prognosis.

Told that the next 24 hours were critical and there was nothing more any of us could do, most of us returned home.

Back at home, I went to my room. On the turntable of my stereo was the 45 single that I'd borrowed from Rick the Saturday before. I pressed PLAY.

"Time for Me to Fly" by REO Speedwagon began. Knowing that Rick had appropriated the song's title for his suicide note, part of me resented his plagiarism. The bastard could've been a little more original.

As the song began, my eyes clouded over again. What the hell had happened? My chat with him at his home three days before had betrayed no hint of imminent self-destruction. If anything seemed unusual it was the remarkably even-tempered manner in which he'd conducted himself, and how typically intimidated I'd felt upon hearing his contemplated entry into law enforcement and working with kids: *Terrific—just one more thing for Rick to outshine me on.*

As much as I wanted to wash that thought from my memory, there was no denying the parsimony in my heart and that the lip-service encouragement I'd given him on his porch had been that and nothing more. I hadn't wanted him to be a cop. No way.

Seated atop my bed, I let the record replay repeatedly.

... I have to set myself free ...

Free from what?

Plainly, something had broken Rick's spirit long before the bullet had shattered his brain. Conversations with Bob and others over the days that followed offered glimpses into the last weeks of Rick's life, stories of his having gotten his UNLV football college scholarship at the same moment he learned his girlfriend was pregnant.

But nothing offered any clarity, and decades later his actions remain inexplicable.

In recent years, I have found myself attuned to studies of athletes who suffered from CTE, chronic traumatic encephalopathy. Though only recently recognized by the medical field, I've wondered what role, if any, it might have played in Rick's death. Between an assault at a convenience store where he'd worked, multiple car accidents, innumerable collisions on the football field, could some aggregate affliction have been responsible?

I don't know. When 21-year-old Penn State Football player Owen Thomas shot and killed himself, an autopsy revealed that he'd suffered previous brain damage. Having committed suicide at the same age three decades before, might Rick have been suffering from similar trauma?

I will never know. But being only 21 at the time, I was at a loss to see how Rick's actions could have helped anything. All that I could see on the horizon were new and far greater problems for his family. Shocked, saddened, and scared, even the atheists among us prayed.

The following day I reported to the Academy staff and advised them of what had happened and that, depending on changes in Rick's condition over the following days, I might have to leave early or call in.

The DIs displayed nothing but compassion. Still, I wondered if they would now look askance at me and ask themselves if there was room in their ranks for someone whose lineage merited a second glance.

I got through the day and returned home to find that the hospital was pressuring Mary to allow them to harvest organs from Rick. She refused.

Rick hung on for one more day.

He died on November 4, 1982.

His funeral was well attended. Three hundred friends and acquaintances paid their respects. UNLV's basketball coach, Jerry Tarkanian, wrote a nice column about Rick's death. Tears were shed, promises to keep in touch were made, and phone numbers exchanged to be disposed of later.

The damage one hollow-point bullet did was considerable. The Yamada family would eventually fragment, like the bullet itself. Mary would die less than a decade later. Richard would pass in 2008.

I found myself re-evaluating my hero as more revelations began circulating, including Rick's having collided with a number of cars and not always remaining at the scene. At one point Bob had taken a call from the aggrieved owner of one of these vehicles, an angry man who was threatening to sue. "Hey, have at it," Bob had said. "My brother's dead."

No longer did I see Rick to be the strong man I'd thought him to be, but a weak and crippled soul whose facade had melted away with the growing apprehension of responsibility.

I still dreamed about him. In one, he'd made good on his intent to become a cop and we were working together on patrol when we made a traffic stop on some gangsters. He was about to lecture them when a shot rang out and I woke up.

The odds of even getting hired by the sheriff's department were 100 to one. It would seem likely that having survived the hiring process, those hires would be vigilant against missteps. But then some cadet from North Carolina got fired after DIs found pot in his ashtray during a random search of our personal vehicles.

Others apparently didn't have that much to sweat, no matter the offense. And no "get out of jail free" card carried more clout than political connections.

To amp up his score on the firing range, one cadet had punched holes in his target with a mechanical pencil. In theory, the transgression was grounds for automatic termination. In reality, his father was a councilman for one of the Department's contract cities and the cadet went on to graduate, eventually working two separate assignments with me and validating my every suspicion that he should never have been allowed to graduate, let alone promote.

Other cadets without such insulating buffers were occasionally called to the back of the room and told to pack their shit and leave.

But nothing thinned the herd so much as stress.

More often than not, the cadets decided they'd had enough of the yelling and quit, the rest of the class moving forward one desk to fill each vacated seat.

One ancillary benefit of having been raised by a temperamental artist of Sicilian descent was my acclimation to getting yelled at. If anything, the DIs were pikers compared to Dad. And yet the prospect of hearing my name and getting called to the back of the class or getting chewed out in the front stressed me out; an idle contemplation of being made platoon sergeant—or, worse still, class sergeant—would send me into an emotional tailspin.

It was more than just the additional stress that the collateral responsibilities would assume. It ran the risk of my being discovered as the immature and undisciplined person I was. And it would almost surely mean the end of my Academy stay.

I may have been emotionally retarded, but that didn't mean I was stupid. As became apparent that both the class all-stars and the flunkies received special attention from the DIs, it became equally obvious that I should strive to end up in the middle of the pack, be it academically, physically or socially.

Whether or not the DIs were onto my game plan for getting through the Academy was up in the air. I could not say as much about my fellow cadets, as their comments left little doubt as to how they regarded me.

Between the funeral and daylight savings time, I didn't get much sleep over the following weeks. Those weeks were a blur of radio and penal codes, physical conditioning, report writing, use-of-force procedures, and much more. But throughout there was one unifying theme to the proceedings: officer survival.

Nothing was drilled into us more. In the gym above our exhausted and supine bodies loomed a sign: "The More You Sweat Here, the Less You Will Bleed in the Street." In the classroom, officer-involved shootings were dissected and Monday-morning quarterbacked with the omnipresent reminder to "Never Give Up."

"Look around you," the DI said. "Odds are that someone in this room will die in the line of duty. It may be in a traffic accident because you or your fellow motorist is driving with their head up their ass. It may be from a heart attack because you've let yourself go to seed visiting those infamous donut shops that we're known for congregating at. But, most likely, it'll be at the hands of some murdering bastard who doesn't give a rat's ass about who you are—you just stand to prevent him a moment's freedom. There are people out there who will beg you not to go to jail. They'll make you all kinds of offers. Really far-out offers. They'll offer you their car, their kids, and the Cowboys in the Super Bowl and 20 points, in which case you've damned near got a bribery."

There was nervous laughter in the classroom.

"But then there are those who aren't much for bartering. In fact, they'd love nothing more than to get a piece of your ass. And if they can blow your ass away, well that's just icing on the cake."

The DI stopped next to a cadet whose expression suggested that the idea of going to the back of the room had growing appeal.

"Well, we're here to decrease those odds. You are an important investment to this Department. The County has a stake in you. Before you've worked one day in patrol or in the jails, the Department has better than $50,000 invested in each and every one of you. You're more than just a name and a badge number."

On cue, another DI walked from the rear of the classroom and handed a stack of pictures to the cadet sitting in the last seat of the extreme left row of the classroom.

"But a name and a badge number are all there'll be to remember you by. A name and a badge number on the memorial wall. Oh, the Department will do the right thing. It'll make sure that two deputies respond to your home to notify your family before any news crews get there. And they'll have the honor guard at your all-expenses-paid funeral. And if it's an election year, you can bet your ass that no less than the governor himself will be there."

The DI took his eyes off the cadet and stared at the back of the classroom.

"There are some pictures being circulated throughout the class-room now. They're of people such as yourselves who sat in this same classroom and listened to this same lecture."

I felt a tap on my shoulder and reached back to retrieve the stack that had worked its way up to me.

"Right now, there's only one significant difference between you and them," the DI asserted. "They're dead."

The pictures before me underscored the man's assertion. I took in the images of uniformed young men who had been shot and killed, stabbed and disemboweled. Their bodies lay in residential hallways, on oil-soaked streets, and atop beds of bright green grass.

The DI's baleful tone continued. "And while I don't like to speak ill of the dead, we should try to learn by their example, even if it's only by their mistakes. The fact remains that in most of these shootings, there were mistakes made by either themselves or their partners that resulted in their getting killed."

I'd read of several of these officer-involved shootings, and so was familiar with many of the scenarios that the DI communicated to us. The trainee who split from his partner and was later shot and killed by a suspect who'd taken his gun. The deputy who'd been shot and killed while investigating an open door at an otherwise closed business. The deputy who'd been shot just as he exited his car on a traffic stop.

But all I'd known came from bland news articles filled with purported facts and sketchy details relayed to the public in the hours immediately following any shooting, so I had no idea of the true carnage involved. Brains, viscera, and powder burns soaked and stained the uniforms of these dead men. Their faces were death masks of shock, dismay, and horror. If the DI's intentions were to scare us with the photos, they could claim an unqualified success with me.

I contemplated the pictures with an agnostic's resignation, wondering if this was all these young men had to show for their existence on this planet, just these pictures and some names on the wall. The DI clarified the matter.

"Between them, these eight men left behind six wives, two fiancées, and 17 sons and daughters. Not to mention a lot of heartbroken friends and other relatives. I take offense to this. I've gone to too many of these damned funerals, and frankly, can go the rest of my life without hearing another goddamned set of bagpipes. But rest assured, the odds are good that at least one of you might well die within the next ten years."

The DI proved prescient in his prediction. In fact, the first fellow cadet to die would do so in less than 18 months.

He was a friend of mine.

There would be one conspicuous difference between his fate and that of the fallen deputies under discussion—he would not die a hero.

As things settled into a routine at the Academy, cadets continued to wash out, albeit at a slower rate. Occasionally, the DIs would offer lip service to the importance of independent thought and decisive action. But the class proved to be a quick study: To act independently or decisively was to tempt fate. The reality was that individualism was out and uniformity was in and we were increasingly in sync with one another in mood, manner, and movements.

Despite the DI's promises that we were more than names and badge numbers, I thought that Bob Seger had it right with *Feel Like a Number.* Outside of our DIs, who relied on the names that adorned our uniforms and gym shirts, everyone else—e.g., range and tactical defense instructors—simply called out our numbers. The number we responded to depended upon which squad, platoon, role-playing scenario team, or target we were assigned. This at least afforded a degree of anonymity that facilitated my desire to remain low profile, a mission that was compromised when I distinguished myself by joining the remedial relay team at the Wayside Training Range in Newhall.

My geographic bearing for the area surrounding Wayside was that four California Highway Patrol officers had been shot and killed nearby during a robbery in 1970. Of the shootings covered in our lectures, none were more detailed. Indeed, the incident had been recognized as having implications on the national level when it came to the development of sound officer survival practices.

More than our DI's words, it was the pictures of the fallen officers' bodies, laid out on slabs, that stuck with me. Their images rode shotgun with me as I watched my range instructors, veterans of innumerable firefights with inanimate objects, decimate paper targets.

"I know that wazoo shit looks really good in the movies when you shoot the gun out of the guy's hand," said one range master. "That's what the public expects of us too. The truth is, you can consider yourself lucky to get a hit on him in a fluid firefight. That's why we aim for center body mass. We don't shoot at arms or legs, although given the option of time, we may go for a head shot.

"The news media isn't shy about showing those instances where some sniper knocks the gun out of a guy's hand at 500 feet, but those Annie Oakley shots are the exception. The fact remains that in the vast majority of firefights, you're shooting at a distance of around 10 to 15 feet and it's all over in less than three seconds. In those three seconds, you two can kill one another. That's why it's imperative that you're first on the draw and first on target to make sure that son-of-a-bitch shows up at death's door alone."

The range staff confidently loaded our weapons for us and helped us take aim, before less confidently backing off a considerable distance and telling the cadets to fire away. A row of targets was lined up 25 yards down range, one of which had my name on it. One need only to look at the bottom of any casino urinal to realize that, no matter how big the target, there will be those unable to hit it. After the expenditure of some 30 rounds, my target still had my name on it, but remained pretty much otherwise unmarred. I could not be sure where most of my rounds had gone, but judging by the amount of landscape chewed up in front of my target, I figured that at least there wouldn't be any gophers fucking with me anytime soon.

Unimpressed with my innovative spray and pray tactics, the range instructors introduced me to concepts such as "sight alignment" and "trigger control." On the one hand, they weren't shy about letting us know that they would not put up with any crap. On the other, they could be forgiving if we couldn't shoot out of the gate. So long as we didn't do anything shit stupid, they'd work with us. The atmosphere was sort of Mr. Rogers meets Rambo, and the heroic patience with which these expert shooters mentored us would stick with me for years.

Their efforts—and ours—eventually paid off. To the best of my recollection, nobody washed out of the Academy for lack of range success.

And I didn't have to resort to upping my scores with a mechanical pencil.

Armed with some confidence that we could manage our firearms, we got our first glimpses of patrol as we began our patrol station ride-alongs.

My first ride was with Franklin Styles, a black East Los Angeles deputy who was blessed with the even temperament of Kanye West. When my inexperience at dismantling a shotgun became evident, Styles berated me to no end and later took the time to pencil-fuck me by painstakingly documenting this deficiency.

Perhaps this would have had the desired effect of screwing me, save for the time a far more compassionate East LA deputy spent writing a separate evaluation based upon my ride-along with him. Fred Mulcahy had been impressed with the initiative I'd displayed in helping County Fire unload hoses from their engine at the scene of a commercial fire.

After reviewing the two critiques, DI Lightner concluded they were mutually offsetting and gave me a much-appreciated reprieve.

The following Saturday found me riding a busy night shift at Carson Station. We rolled on multiple shootings, the scene of one at which I was tasked with maintaining part of a containment search for an outstanding suspect.

An Aero Unit circled above, violating a fundamental precept of officer survival by backlighting my paranoid silhouette for the benefit of the suspect—who I was positive was about to light it up, too. The adrenaline rush I felt at that moment reminded me of my first ride-along at ELA.

The ELA deputy received a call regarding a dispute over trash. Just hearing that initial call was enough to belatedly engage my faculties to wonder: who ever thought inserting a strange, uniformed presence into situations rife with high emotions, low self-esteem and boiling tempers could be a good thing? My heart racing, I wondered, *My God, what awaits us? Will things have escalated between the call and our arrival? Am I to die over a matter of haphazardly deposited waste?*

Well, I didn't die. In fact, there wasn't much to do other than warn some guy to be more vigilant in his dumping.

And that proved the case on my other ride-alongs at San Dimas, Altadena, and Crescenta Valley stations. I'd accompany the deputy who'd handle the call and we'd be off again. Not only were things relatively uneventful, but my contacts with the deputies were such that I could envision finding some that I might actually enjoy working with.

All of the ride-alongs proved enjoyable, but none were more memorable than the back-to-back nights I spent in West Hollywood.

The first night was my introduction to the world of young gay hustlers. San Vicente Boulevard and its side streets were packed with gays of all races who would either affect disinterest in our presence or disappear around a corner when we came into view. The local restaurants featured some of the best free food I would ever enjoy on patrol. The women were seemingly all fashion models (although the first 927-S "screaming woman" call I got turned out to be a male who'd been beaten with a phone receiver).

The next night, I was assigned to ride with an imposing female deputy who, while brusque with everyone we came in contact with, was at least nice enough to me. It wasn't Halloween, so I wasn't treated to West Hollywood's world famous annual extravaganza, but it was December 31st and things were busy enough that I asked to stay on an additional two hours with her to catch the scene at midnight.

As the hour drew near, so did many of the festive and flirtatious locals who cajoled us to "Have a Happy New Year!"

My partner, not yet exposed to the concepts of political correctness, community policing, or tactical diplomacy, returned the amenities through her open driver's window with, "Fuck you, faggots."

As the Academy progressed, I did not experience a change of personality so much as a change of presence. I continued to keep my mouth shut—at least around the DIs—but found myself standing more erect as my physical and emotional stamina improved. I was feeling tall and lean but was still somehow able to fly below the radar.

That I had lucked out in getting Wayne Lightner as my DI was not lost on me. More than once he'd caught me sleep-deprived and unshaven, only to shake his head in wonder and say, "Cadet Scoville, I don't know what I'm going to do about you," before moving to the next cadet.

Whatever his ultimate decision, there was little doubt as to what any of the other DIs would have done with me—and early on too.

As the weeks went by, things became more and more routine: workouts, running, academics, guest lecturers, quizzes, and tests. One of the DIs quietly encouraged me during our runs, helping me to feel a little more comfortable with my instructors.

Then there was the occasional field trip, such as our visit to the Los Angeles County Coroner's Office.

Our guide was none other than a fellow cadet who'd worked for the Coroner's Office prior to being hired by LASD. Carl Moseman escorted us through the corridors of his old workplace, describing the process by which bodies were brought into the location and handled.

In one room, we found naked bodies stacked on large metal trays from floor to ceiling. Despite the fact that the bodies were handled less ceremoniously than cattle, and that a pervasive odor would stay with us long after we left, Moseman was upbeat. Aware of my Latter Day Saints background, Moseman winked at me with Mormon conviction.

"We know they're in a better place."

I wasn't so sure.

Another room featured a gallery of gruesome pictures that included infamous crime scenes such as the Sharon Tate murder, and dead celebrities like Janis Joplin and the recently expired John Belushi. It was morbid stuff, and while I was surprised that they kept such pictures on site, I was more surprised that no one had seen fit to sell them to the *Enquirer* or *Hustler* magazine.

One fellow cadet collapsed after he saw a particularly tragic photo: a young girl, sodomized and dismembered by her father. The cadet later blamed the early February heat for making him feel a bit wobbly, but it was also common knowledge that his wife had recently given birth to a little girl.

Inside the autopsy room, a few two-person teams—a technician and an intern—wielded large scalpels as they went to work on cadavers. The technician started with a "Y" incision, beginning on the chest, then downward toward the pelvic region—then assisted the intern with removing the organs. After flaying the skin and much of the muscle tissue away from the sternum, the technician cut the ribcage and sternum and removed the breastplate, then systematically collected samples of blood and other fluids and placed them into various containers for whatever toxicological testing was to be conducted later. The lungs, liver, heart, gallbladder, etc., were removed and handed to the intern, who sliced samples from each of the organs with culinary finesse.

The body cavity excavated, the technician turned his attention to the head, cutting a swath from behind the left ear upward and across to the rear of the right ear. He then cut the skin away from the skull as one might peel an orange.

The technician wielded a small rotary saw with considerable skill and precision as he cut off the skull cap. This process got to me, as I was sitting only a few feet behind the flying bone chips. Soon the brain was visible and accessible, and sure enough, it joined the other duly departed organs. Weight: 1.3 pounds.

The technician—whose motto I imagined would be "I cut corpses, not corners"—then peeled tissue from the base of the skull to remove the pituitary gland. When they were finally done, the men dumped the bucket of collected organs into the body cavity.

It was this kind of appetite-suppressing stuff that would later drive *CSI* and its TV spin-offs to huge ratings.

Part of me realized that there'd been some collateral benefit to having watched so many horror films through the years: I was already less sensitive to gore than I might have been in the absence of auteur George Romero. Another part of me recognized that nothing could prepare anyone for this kind of display.

When Karen Carpenter died two days later, all I could think about was what awaited the body of the woman who sang "Close to You."

As winter wound down, so did our Academy class.

Already I was sufficiently steeped in actual police procedurals that I started to take exception to some of the crap I watched on television and in movies. A new release like Walter Hill's pyrotechnic-laden *48 Hours*, with Nick Nolte and Eddie Murphy, could have been watched six months before without objection. Now I was looking at them through a different prism and was increasingly disturbed by the amount of violence perpetrated against our on-screen counterparts.

Meanwhile, the attrition of my real-life peers continued. The class that started with 160 cadets had been whittled down to around 130. It was no record for the hill, but the DIs looked as if they could live with it.

With each passing week, my optimism grew. My performance in the Academy had not been attention-getting—at least as far as the DIs were concerned. But when it came to my classmates, well...

Graduation was just around the corner, and the cadets of Class 213 were given sheets of paper on which to evaluate their peers. Had I foreseen this, I might have in some manner tried to make a better impression.

Or not.

In any event, Wayne Lightner discussed the results with me and I learned that, for all my reservations about them, my platoon peers were nothing if not perceptive. To a man and woman, they had come to a consensus regarding me: "stress cadet."

Moreover, of the 21 cadets in our platoon, I was ranked 19th in desirability as a radio car partner. The only mystery for me was how the hell those other two could have possibly ranked lower. Obviously, my standoffish attitude had not endeared me to the group.

All this might have found me moping around like there was a portentous cloud hovering over my head. Instead, my attitude towards my peers was more like, *Fuck you if you can't see the beauty within!*

Nonetheless, I'd stuck it out. I graduated to the Los Angeles County Sheriff's Academy.

I was a goddamned deputy sheriff.

3

Working Custody

February 27, 1983, two days after attending a graduation party on the Sunset Strip and one day after a celebratory party at home, I returned to the Hall of Justice. This time, I bypassed the administrative offices and rode the elevator ten floors up to the Hall's custody facility.

After a quick introductory briefing and assignments to our custody training officers, my fellow graduates and I were escorted to our assigned deck modules. My training officer, Sam Shimano, introduced himself as a two-year veteran of the Hall and escorted me to the 1050 deck where I relieved a day shift deputy.

Three big, black inmates wearing lipstick and curlers eyed me over as Sam handed me a large set of keys and told me to rely on my row trustees—inmates who were assigned cleaning responsibilities and to whom a degree of peer supervision was conferred—and to call him if I got in over my head. I hurriedly wrote down his phone extension as I knew I was already in over my head.

With little in my middle-class upbringing having prepared me for these confines, I found myself wondering just how the hell I would be expected to keep control of my tie-dyed wards. Since there was no fooling anyone about my limited life experience, I followed Sam's advice and delegated as much responsibility as possible to the row trustees.

For the most part, this proved a safe practice, and I soon found there was little more for me to do than open gates, check wristbands, and generally keep what semblance of peace there was to be had. The capacity for things to quickly become routine once again surprised me.

Still, there was an undeniably surreal atmosphere to working the Hall. I found myself separating two highly agitated men, advising, "You leave her alone, and she'll leave you alone."

But then the Hall had long been a source of interest for me.

As a child, I'd passed under its shadow during treks to Hollywood with my Dad. Even then, its tall gray facade had a gothic appeal for me. About the only things it lacked were gargoyles sitting atop its upper terrace. (Not that some odd thing didn't attempt to gain a perch there from time to time. Unfortunately, it was usually an inmate whose ill-considered escape attempt with custodial blankets would find him short-sheeted and falling to his death.)

But for all the times I'd stared at the Hall's brick and mortar facade, not once had it crossed my mind that I might one day work there. Now that I was, part of me was sympathetic to those who advocated for its permanent closure. The facility had only been re-opened four years earlier. That previous concerns over its structural integrity had miraculously abated struck me as counter-intuitive and possibly irresponsible given the plate tectonics of the region and the Hall's 1920s construction.

And yet another part of me quickly grew comfortable with working the Hall and just as fond of its interior architecture and history.

Stepping through its brass-clad doors and ascending its marble foyer steps, one experienced a sense of time travel, a feeling amplified with each echoing step. Its floors and corridors were recognizable to anyone who has watched episodes of *Dragnet*, *Perry Mason*, or *The Fugitive*. The marble columns suggested Pantheon inspirations and I found it romantic to stare out the barred windows of the security stairwells to contemplate the pigeon droppings on the ledges as rush hour traffic wound its way down the southbound 101 Freeway.

The historical ambiance of the building was palpable. Until the opening of Men's Central Jail in 1963, the Hall had been the main custody facility for the County. I visited its isolation cells on the 13th floor and felt the remnants of the past that lingered. Charles Manson slept there. So did Sirhan Sirhan.

Its basement had also at one time housed the County morgue. Old vets reminisced about Marilyn Monroe's body being brought in and the long line of deputies who waited to get a gander at her body.

My interactions with the inmates largely consisted of letting them out of their cells for chow, showers, yard time, and the occasional visit. The rest of the time was spent perusing the stack of porn in the module desk or readings I brought from home. Paperwork was largely confined to inmate incident reports ("Inmate Jones was found in possession of..."), inmate injury reports ("Inmate Smith said his left arm was injured when the bars to his cell closed on it as he slept"), or both ("Inmate Turner attempted to punch Deputy Kline at which time..."). At least once per shift, deputies got to eat to their hearts' content in the officers' dining room on the 13th floor.

If having to work custody was something I'd dreaded after hiring on with the sheriff's department, it was also something to which I quickly adapted. My conscientious work as a module deputy found me quickly promoted to floor prowler.

Not only did floor prowlers enjoy considerably more freedom than module officers, but we were expected to snoop around as well. Among my responsibilities were making chow reliefs, escorting prisoners, and writing inmate incident reports ("Inmate Simpkins said that at the indicated date and time he was sodomized by..."). Downtime was spent spelunking the Hall's darkened corridors and reverberant stairwells, as well as policing those areas accessible to the public.

Occasionally, inmate visitors would secrete drugs and weapons around the 1st floor to be picked up by trustees, who, in turn, would sneak them into the facility. Occasionally, I beat the trustees to this contraband, but was never able to find a body to go along with the drugs. I was generally pleased with my vigilance, which by any measure paled considerably when compared to Tom Womack, whose omnipresent green LASD jacket had earned him the nickname "The Green Hornet" and could be spotted in the cat-chases behind the cells as Womack snooped for contraband and monitored inmates' conversations. Early on, he displayed every indication of being the outstanding street cop he was destined to be.

That I developed a reputation for being dependable and getting along with peers and supervisors alike did not blind me to a few of the less savory aspects of the Hall.

I realized early on that badge-heavy deputies did exist. Nowhere was their abuse of power more manifest than the processing of "fresh fish"—newly arrived prisoners—in the downstairs corridor. It wasn't so much that they were physically abusive. Oh, they would pull on their gloves in a menacing manner and threaten the occasional ass beating, but for the most part it was all show, a means of keeping the catenated population intimidated.

But their verbal abusiveness could be merciless. It wasn't just good-natured jibes that were encouraged by confused compliance ("Put your left shoulder on the wall. Your other left"), but the routine demeaning of the wards' lack of hygiene, compliance, and intelligence.

"Jeez-sus Christ o'mighty! When was the last time you wiped that asshole?"

"That thing between your legs looks like a penis. Only smaller."

"My God, but you are one stupid and ugly fucker!"

I didn't like the spectacle, particularly when it escalated and some inmate did get his ass kicked.

But these were the deputies that *had* been given polygraphs and psych exams and who I would have to rely on if I ever found my ass in a fight. So I prudently kept my mouth shut.

All of the jail cells and rows in the Hall were either to the front of the administration offices or upstairs.

Except one.

Located to the rear of the watch commander's office was the 1010 row. Once it had housed hardcore adult offenders. Now it housed the County's up and comers.

If juvenile hall offered a look at early onset assholery, the Hall gave me a peek at its most ignoble graduates. Housed there were the worst of the worst, killers who had not yet seen their 18th birthday, many with multiple homicides under their belts.

These wards didn't give a shit about anyone, but oddly bonded with one another. Even then, the ties were tenuous at best. Housed in cells furnished with only a bunk, a shelf, a sink, a toilet, and an unbreakable mirror-like thing that reflected the subject's warped soul, the young wards sublimated for their lack of Atari video games by throwing feces at the deputies and cussing them out. Virtually all were black or Hispanic, and God help the occasional white kid who was momentarily housed with either faction. Frankly, the prospect of dealing with these little bastards bothered me more than anything else the Hall had to offer, and I was thankful that my contact with them was largely limited to when I was working prowler and the shit had already hit the fan.

Because when that happened, we could hit back.

But while the Hall offered its fair share of inmate-deputy hostility and weasel-on-weasel crime, it wasn't all life on the razor's edge. Indeed, most of my time was committed to more boring enterprises. Escorting inmates, backing up chow, and walking wristband counts. Down time was occupied with reading, hiding in the exterior stairwells, and playing Pac-Man in the briefing room.

Occasionally I escorted trustees down to the basement via the trash and freight elevators. The design of these elevators had not changed since the Hall was built. There were no protective screens or gates to separate the passengers from the walls and alcoves that scrolled by as the elevator rose and fell. As I sat on a chair inside the elevator and pushed the control level forward to send the elevator upward, I walked my feet up the wall, timing my steps to prevent my foot from getting trapped between the wall and the moving elevator. It was an act of idle stupidity that tempted fate. One day, fate struck. I watched as the toes on my right foot disappeared from view, wedged in the narrow gap between the elevator and the outer wall.

"Oh, fuck!" The words were those of a trustee to my left, but they pretty much summed up my frame of mind right then too.

As I pulled the control level backward, cautiously lowering the elevator, 18 inches of shoe polish demarcated the path where my foot had been dragged against the wall. As the whole of my shoe emerged, I realized that nothing had been severed, but as it came free of its wedged position, it began to throb violently. Removing my shoe and sock, I found my toes discolored, the big one swollen to Looney Tunes proportion. I prudently refrained from mentioning this episode on my Mensa application.

I got off lucky. Eight years later, one of the civilian operators apparently mishandled the conveyance mechanism while operating the elevator and was decapitated.

If my ego was as bruised as my toe, I took solace that the inmates were not much brighter. Their own limbs proved even more susceptible to injury due to a lack of vigilance at the opening and closing of cell bars and ill-considered escape attempts from upper floors. They were as likely to mix ammonia and bleach as not, and more than once our toxic cloud drills paid off.

There were other casualties of my time at the Hall, including much of my liberal posture.

The whites among us were repeatedly chastised by our charges, and deemed culpable for cruel and arbitrary treatment or favoritism.

Black deputies were called "Uncle Toms" for being on the right side of the bars. I wondered if our critics ever contemplated filling our shoes, and considered how they would treat, and be treated by, one another.

Catcalls labeling me a "white, mother-fuckin' honkey racist" became so routine that I concluded there must be some validity.

"Yeah. You're right. I'm Casper the not-so-friendly white dude and you can see right through me." Fat lot of good reading *The Autobiography of Malcolm X* and Eldridge Cleaver's *Soul on Ice* did me.

My exposure to the gay world through its writers—often literate, thoughtful, and entertaining—contrasted starkly with what I saw in jail. Many lived as women, their mannerisms a high parody of femininity— shrill cat calls, exaggerated poses, and pitched falsettos. In their own way, they were the most sexist men I've ever met.

Despite a screening process designed to protect the gay jail population, there were other demographics mixed in with this sashaying anarchy. There were "custodial gays," men whose heterosexual lifestyles would be resurrected upon the completion of their time; and there were predominantly straight males who simply wanted to make sure that jail time was passed as comfortably as possible.

Among the latter was a man who got booked into the system under an alias, David Fishman. Fingerprint databases had not yet evolved to accommodate the needs of law enforcement, and so it was that nobody knew Fishman's real name was Kenny Coolidge, a straight man wanted by Philadelphia PD for rape. While being booked into the LA County jail system under a lesser charge, and under the Fishman alias, Coolidge claimed to be homosexual and ended up on my deck where he shortly embroiled himself with a couple of the row "matrons" before punching one out.

Rolling him up for discipline, I was fixed by the most malevolent stare I'd yet encountered on the job. It was the first time an inmate's mere expression scared me, and the first time that I genuinely believed that given the opportunity and a weapon, the man would kill me on the spot. His manner was so disconcerting that I vividly recalled him while watching the news a few months later.

The news anchor reported that Coolidge was wanted for the slashing murders of a Chino family. Between the time of my contact with him and the murders, Coolidge had been transferred to the California Institute for Men, a minimum security prison in Chino. It was from

there that he'd escaped and killed four members of a family while seriously injuring a fifth.

Coolidge ended up successfully evading capture for several weeks,
largely by employing the makeup and mannerisms he'd learned during
his tenure at the Hall.

When captured off the coast in Northern California, Coolidge was
masquerading as an ugly woman.

It was while working the Hall that I became good friends with Mike
Siegermoor.

We'd first met in the Academy where our general reticence to
engage in the more conspicuous acts of testosterone rage found us
inevitably drifting toward one another and discovering a shared interest
in movies and books. That Siegermoor had the sharpest wit of any peer
I'd met was a most agreeable bonus. That he exercised it on my behalf
in putting a couple of our fellow cadets and would-be adversaries in
check was a downright blessing.

At the Hall, our friendship solidified and soon we were heading to
the movies, the gym, and the beach together. At work we had each other's
back.

If there was a liability to Siegermoor's imposing wit, it was that it was
invariably lost on the inmates. Whereas most deputies were content to ask
inmates if they were homo sapiens ("Hell, no!"), or if Mickey Mouse was
a cat or a dog (after due deliberation, "Mickey Mouse was a mutha-fuckin'
rat!"), Siegermoor's comments—laden with all manner of polysyllabic
embroidery—tended to leave inmates and deputies alike with blank stares.

That inmates had no clue that Siegermoor may have insulted them
was just as well—he wasn't the biggest guy in the world. Not that he was
afraid to mix it up. More than once he and I tangled with some inmate,
to the latter's detriment.

But Siegermoor's acerbic tongue was never sharper than when
describing what he perceived to be the inalienable attributes of the
female gender. His tirades in the "bath"—that area of the jail where
inmates were processed—could go on for hours.

As my own breakup with a girlfriend of two years was still fresh in
my mind, I wasn't wholly immune to some of his vitriol.

*Yeah, it does seem sometimes that too many women will bang some
good looking asshole and not give a nice guy the time of day.*

Still, I found myself wondering if Siegermoor was putting me on. Surely, nobody could spew as much virulent crap as he did and mean it. Part of me was convinced that he was only sublimating for some manner of emotional pain.

Whatever his misogynistic thoughts about women, Siegermoor didn't seem to have trouble interacting with them. At Six Flags Magic Mountain in Valencia, I'd watch as he would approach girls—total strangers—and throw his arm around one with an invitation for them to accompany us on the rides. And they would.

At movies, he'd strike up conversations with everyone: the ticket booth cashier, the gal behind the snack bar, a trio of girls two rows behind us—and not once did he exhibit so much as a second thought about the prospect of rejection. It was as though he thought himself as God's gift to women, his protuberant eyes and large nose notwithstanding. It was an opinion apparently shared by his on again/off again girlfriend, an absolutely beautiful brunette with a great sense of humor.

Sometimes while headed for the beach, we'd take a meandering path through Topanga Canyon. Siegermoor would find a turn out and park, then get out of his Jeep to scale an outcropping. Standing atop it as though defying the fates and the wind to push him over the edge and into the abyss below, he'd proclaim his love of the canyons.

"Ever bring any girls up here at night?" he once asked.

"No."

"You can bring a girl up here and do anything you want with her and nobody would know. It's fucking great! There's no one around and it's beautiful at night."

My lack of subtlety in matters of social inquiry had earned me a rep as a nosy bastard. But Siegermoor's third degree carried things to another level.

"Have you ever used handcuffs?" he asked. "Have you ever fucked a girl with cuffs on her?"

"No." The idea of restraining a woman like an inmate had little appeal for me. As though he'd read my mind, Siegermoor removed from his jacket pocket a small metal object with cylindrical openings at opposite ends.

"How about thumb cuffs? You know, these things work pretty good too."

I had to smile. Siegermoor's kinky bent was infamous around the

Hall and it would figure that he'd have a pair. It was his willingness to try just about anything that gave me a sense of relief when I'd wake up after an uneventful night's sleep on his sofa to nothing more than the blaring of "Major Tom" on MTV.

But summer ended, and in September I found a note in my mailbox from Sgt. Sylvia Abbott congratulating deputies who'd made the pencil list to patrol, myself among them. Siegermoor congratulated me on my transfer to Temple Station.

Siegermoor was destined to stay at the Hall breaking up fights, while I'd finally be doing the job I hired on to do. Even if we didn't live in two different valleys, there simply was no way in hell that we'd be spending much more time together.

All the same, I was thankful that he'd helped make my stay at the Hall less of a challenge than it otherwise might have been.

4

The Happiness
of Pursuit

In October, we started patrol school, a two-week curriculum wherein station-bound deputies were expected to learn the basics all over again. My feelings of being ill-prepared proved well warranted.

As far as the phonetics and the more common radio codes went, it was game on. But role-playing betrayed just how much I'd lost when it came to gathering pertinent information for crime reports and making radio broadcasts. Being paired with deputies I didn't know didn't help, as we were apt to duplicate many of the same actions at the expense of one of us dropping the ball on some other front. Our officer safety was all over the place.

At one point during role-playing, I was called over to some tables that had been set up at the back of the Burbank Studios lot where we'd been playing out our scenarios. By now I'd been on the Department long enough to know that getting called to the back of anything, anywhere was never a good thing, and it occurred to me that I might be sent back to custody. In the moment, that was something I might not have objected to. The news I received, however, was definitely something I sure as hell objected to.

"You're going to Firestone," said a patrol school monitoring deputy I'd never seen before.

Firestone Station.

If any one station had helped establish the Department's reputation for bad-assery, it was Firestone.

Opened on South Compton Avenue in 1955, the station's jurisdiction covered Watts and Willowbrook—predominantly black neighborhoods with high crimes rates—and was responsible for many of the

43

Department's most memorable war stories, including the 1976 George Arthur-Mike Waters shooting, in which two deputies were attacked by three armed men on Christmas Eve. The duo came out on top in a vicious hand-to-hand combat that left two of their assailants dead and the third wounded, on a night when still another Firestone deputy had been shot and wounded and a third suspect killed in a separate incident. Such were holidays in the hood.

When I'd first transferred to custody, I'd intended to get out as soon as possible and saw Firestone, the fastest station on the Department, as my ticket. Custody deputies wanting to get out of custody as quickly as possible would commonly transfer to the Stone before transferring to some slower, more commuter-friendly assignment.

But within 24 hours of filling out my transfer request, I'd experienced buyer's remorse. Custody wasn't nearly as bad as I feared, and I figured that I could finish up my college degree pending my transfer to a slower station. This would save me from lengthy commutes to both the Stone and its courthouse. Finally, most of the Firestone deputies I'd met had proven to be over-the-top macho assholes, which was the last thing I wanted to see in myself or my co-workers. I let the patrol school monitor know as much.

"No, I'm not," I said. "I deleted Firestone my second day in custody and have a copy of the drop form to prove it. I'll go back to custody before I go to Firestone."

"Yeah, well, we'll see about that," he grumbled. "Go back to your scenario."

As though simply getting through patrol school wasn't enough to keep my mind occupied, now I had to sweat being transferred to a station that I absolutely dreaded.

But I never heard anything more about it.

A fellow Academy classmate ended up going to Firestone instead.

Patrol school wrapped up and on my first Temple Station ride-along I was paired with Deputy Stan Fitzpatrick, whose first order was to fill out the vehicle inspection sheet and the daily worksheet.

After a staccato rapping of the pen on the inspection sheet to represent existing dents on the vehicle—as well as any that might be added through the course of the shift—I was ready. Fitzpatrick bullshitted with a couple of other deputies while I got into the passenger seat to start filling out the deputy's daily worksheet. I tried to affect an air of professional decorum.

The beads of sweat pooling in my armpits on the late October afternoon didn't help much, betraying my nerves and leaving me looking less than squared away.

Not half an hour after leaving the station, Fitzpatrick told me to stop some kid on the sidewalk. But as I got out of the patrol unit, the kid took off on me. My beagle-like instinct kicked in and we were off to the races.

Fitzpatrick never exited our car. He just let me tire myself out as the kid disappeared over a fence.

"Why'd you chase him?"

"Well, he ran..." I puffed.

"Yeah ... so...?"

He didn't have to beat me over the head to make his point: If I didn't know what the hell I was chasing a guy for, I probably had no business chasing him.

After a couple of ride-alongs with other deputies, I was finally paired with my official training officer, Don Scott, who'd been on his regular days off.

To my relief, Scott was not caught up in all the macho posturing. At 6'5", the dark haired and good-looking Scott had something of a squeaky voice that only added to his clean-cut Jimmy Stewart persona. I found his laid back demeanor agreeably unintimidating.

Scott's rules were simple: Have the patrol unit prepped and ready to roll prior to the start of each shift, check with the desk to see if we had any calls before going in the field, and generally do as told. I was allowed to call him "Don" when it was just the two of us inside the car and "Deputy Scott" whenever we were in the presence of others.

Most nights we were assigned the 57/58 p.m. relief car, which meant working the City of Duarte and the Monrovia unincorporated County areas on the nights when the regular cars were off. When both of the regular units were on duty, we were either put in another city or County car, or delegated the role of a "bomber unit"—rolling wherever we were needed in Temple's patrol area. This meant that during a given shift we could roll from Bradbury to South El Monte; from Rosemead to East Pasadena, and from Temple City to the unincorporated County area of South San Gabriel.

Having grown up in the San Gabriel Valley, I was familiar with many of its cities. I knew West Covina and its Plaza like the back of my hand, could name every movie theater within a 15-mile radius of my home, and recognized that the only real difference between La Puente and Valinda was that one was an incorporated city and the other not. But the Temple Station area in the foothills of the San Gabriel Mountains proved largely foreign to me.

Cutting a swath right through Duarte, the 210 Freeway also formed part of the northern edge of an unincorporated County area adjacent to the City of Monrovia. Both were largely bedroom communities although Duarte had its fair share of commercial properties and was perhaps most famous for being home to the City of Hope cancer research and treatment center.

Nestled within the Monrovia County area was a small area that was like a section of Compton that had been uprooted and transplanted there. Roughly bracketed by Duarte Road to the north, Buena Vista Avenue to the east, Myrtle to the west, and Live Oak to the south, this small residential area would through the years have more deputy-involved shootings in its jurisdiction than anywhere else within Temple's area—including Robert Armstrong's the year before. (Years later, Deputy David March was shot and killed on a traffic stop just outside this area while working Unit 57, the Monrovia/Arcadia County car.)

The faces encountered while working Temple's northeast area—insincere smiles and sincere sneers—were disconcerting enough that I tried to depersonalize them as residual fall-out from the Armstrong shooting.

In 1981, Robert Armstrong, a former Firestone deputy who'd transferred to Temple, met with other deputies at a local Winchell's Donut Store. Armstrong was preoccupied with a house on Goodall Avenue where he was convinced the occupants were slinging dope. He wanted to "stiff in" or fake a call for service to the location so that the ensuing call—which doubtless would be assigned to him—would avail him a pretext to get inside the house.

One training deputy agreed to go along with the plan. The other did not.

Armstrong called the station later that night, affecting a black dialect associated with the locals and complaining about noise coming from the Goodall residence. The call went out shortly thereafter and the deputies responded as planned. Frightened by Armstrong's afterhours knock, a female opened the door holding a rifle. Fearing for his life, Armstrong fired three rounds into Dolores Young, killing her fetus.

In another time and place, the shooting would have been justified. And to investigators, it initially looked like an appropriate use of deadly force. That is, until the third training deputy and his trainee who declined to participate in the ruse related the conversation they'd had with Armstrong earlier that night. It was quickly realized that Armstrong had no business in being at the location and had precipitated the tragedy.

Four deputies lost their jobs. The *Los Angeles Times'* Paul Conrad rendered an editorial cartoon of two babies—one white, one black—floating towards heaven with the caption, "What's the difference between abortion and being shot and killed by a Los Angeles County deputy sheriff?" Armstrong did jail time.

It didn't matter that it was another Temple deputy that had come forth with the information. It didn't matter that the Department had fired, then prosecuted those involved. Suddenly all Temple Station deputies were "baby killers." By the time I got to the station, resentment over the Armstrong incident remained sufficiently strong that many of the area residents openly made disparaging comments about our service-oriented policing—at least those who weren't dirty at that specific moment.

Those currently in possession, carrying, or otherwise wanted by the "po-po" tended to be more deferential, blending into the background as well as possible and avoiding eye contact altogether. When forced to engage with us, they'd insincerely inquire, "How's it going, deputies?" Sometimes they'd dispense with any pretense of fear or hatred or stall-for-time civilities and just haul ass at the sight of a patrol car.

Stay or run, all were subject to our detention and it didn't matter if they were on foot, on a bike, or behind the wheel. If ever a forum existed for "where there's a will, there's a way" thinking, it was in patrol detention.

Even then, cops were expected to have some reason for detaining a person. Contacting someone was universally fair game; saying hello was not restricted. But when it came to actually causing someone to momentarily stop and be engaged in conversation with a law enforcement official, some probable cause was expected.

Not that cops were ever lacking for an excuse. Between generic suspect descriptions in crime broadcasts and violations of the California Vehicle Code (a.k.a., the "probable cause bible"), we had ample reasons to detain someone. The fact was that damn few cars were completely street legal. A cracked windshield, expired registration, tinted windows—any of a long list of violations could be used as a pretext to jam a motorist.

The irony was that when it came to "fix-it" tickets, law-abiding citizens were more likely to get cited than dirtbags. The rationale was simple: We didn't want to pull over John Q. Citizen repeatedly if we were not apt to find anything for which to arrest him, and making the dirtbag fix his car would kill our future probable cause. And so it was that we'd get cussed out by the working man and get all manner of gratitude from amnestied losers.

At least until the day we caught them dirty.

Whatever down time we had was occupied with catching up on paperwork or bullshitting about our own pressing family issues, like Scott's befuddlement over his daughter's affinity for Boy George.

Scott otherwise proved to be a by-the-book training officer, intent on communicating his knowledge to me in a leisurely manner during our three months together. He made traffic stops, handled calls to their conclusion, and familiarized me with the processes that accrued in all capacities. But he was plainly not the hook-and-book fanatic that some other trainees had been saddled with and I considered myself blessed.

Occasionally, the street proved less accommodating. Fridays and Saturdays were a parade of party and fight calls, and many an early morning hour on Saturday or Sunday were spent beyond the end of our shift finishing up paperwork.

It was while working the Monrovia County area that I was formally introduced to Phencyclidine (PCP).

I'd first heard of PCP in high school when I read of an incident in the *Los Angeles Times*. A black guy high on PCP had smashed a baby's head against the side of a pool. Since then, I'd heard stories about people on PCP exhibiting superhuman strength and a seemingly infinite capacity to administer harm upon others and themselves (even if they weren't cognizant of their actions or their effects at the time). Stories of dusters tearing their eyes out and slicing their penises off made the rounds— "I found his dick. It's over here where he vomited"—and yet the drug was incongruously known in local circles as "Angel Dust," its users dubbed "dusters."

One day we encountered a duster outside a liquor store on Live Oak Avenue in the unincorporated Arcadia County area. He was on the short side, but the chemical booster within him had him feeling like King Kong. I ended up taking several commensurately sized whacks at his appendages with my baton before arresting him for being under the influence and resisting arrest.

As we transported him in the backseat of our patrol car, the ether and nail polish–like odor of the PCP oozing from the suspect's pores became so overpowering that we had to roll down all four windows to avoid a contact headache.

The suspect was booked on a misdemeanor and was released the following day on a citation. By nightfall, when we encountered him again, he was dusted. However altered his state of mind was, something in his cortex seemed to remember how he felt after the drug wore off in the hours following the last beating, and this time he executed a robotic 180 and put his hands behind his back for me to cuff him.

It was that kind of Pavlovian conditioning, combined with the reputation of deputy sheriffs among Angelenos, that for many obviated the need for use of force.

It wasn't just inmates that generally abstained from messing with deputies. Pretty much any resident within LASD's jurisdiction knew better, although opportunists such as Goodall's residents could be counted on to hold the Department's fuck-ups over its head when convenient.

I'd grown up within its jurisdiction myself, and that reputation had helped keep my own ass relatively in line as a teen.

Throughout the seventies, I'd heard variations of the same admonishment: "Don't fuck with deputies." "You don't want to end up in County [jail]—they'll fuck you up!"

Personal encounters, while few and far between, stuck with me.

At the age of 12, an Industry Station deputy stopped me.

"Were you lighting firecrackers off your bike?"

"Yeah," I answered with a clear conscience and a "What are you gonna do about it?" attitude.

"Where do you live?"

"Down the street," I confidently replied.

"Ride there."

I pedaled my bike home with the deputy paralleling my progress. As the deputy got out of the car to advise my father of his observations, I was in as anxiety-free state as could be.

Yes, I knew that firecrackers were illegal despite their ready availability at a quarter a pack on the juvenile black market.

But I was also aware that Dad's only articulated prohibitions had been against blowing my "goddamned stupid head off" and burning the house down.

And so it was that I watched as Dad listened to the deputy's story, with so grave an expression that I gave him a mental thumb's up for convincing the deputy that there'd be hell to pay. Placated, the deputy walked out the front door as I smiled and thought: *Sucker.*

Only it wasn't the deputy who was the sucker.

Dad accompanied me to my bedroom where he took off his belt, sat down on my dresser bench, and told me to drape myself across his knee. I couldn't believe it. Was I going to be spanked?

"But you knew that I had firecrackers!" This seemed a reasonable and mitigating protest.

"Yeah," Dad conceded. "But I didn't think you'd be so shit-stupid to get yourself caught lighting 'em off in the middle of the goddamned street like that!"

And so I got another of Dad's ass-whippings and wondered if I couldn't call that goddamned deputy back to take Dad in for child abuse.

Whatever else, I learned that in the hierarchy of bad moves honesty wasn't always the best policy and getting caught was the worst.

Outside of a tour of the Industry Sheriff's Station during my short time as a cub scout, I didn't have any further contact with Sheriff's personnel until I was 16 and walking along with a couple of girls on Halloween night.

I'd met Cindy Jackman shortly after entering Workman High School, and we had a habit of showing up at the same places away from campus and hanging out together. That I felt comfortable around her was largely because she was even quieter around the opposite sex than I was (that she favored short skirts and had nice legs didn't hurt either). Yvette Donoghue was a friend of hers who I'd recently met and the three of us decided to stroll the streets and check out the trick-or-treaters.

I had a bit of a crush on Cindy, but no clue how she might feel towards me and so I never acted on it. Yvette, on the other hand, had given pretty broad hints of liking me and was therefore someone worthy of merit.

But on this night, Yvette did me no favors. The three of us were approaching the intersection of Aileron and Amar roads when she said, "Look out, there's a pig," well within earshot of a Sheriff's patrol unit.

No sooner were the ill-considered words out of her mouth than the car whipped a turn, stopped abreast of us, and two of Industry's finest bailed out.

Before I knew it, my cowboy hat was sailing off into the night and hands were shoving me up against the side of the patrol car.

"'Pigs,' huh?" one asked, focusing his contempt on the only male present. "That's what you think of us? Well, why don't you say that to our face, you pussy?"

There were a million and one perfectly good reasons for my not saying such a thing, every one of which involved someone's ass getting kicked (mine). Still, I kept my hands atop the car's too-warm hood and my mouth shut—although the possibility of diming off Yvette had growing appeal.

As the deputies proceeded with their "riddle-me-this" Q and A, I tried to tailor my responses so that I wouldn't look totally chicken shit in front of the girls, but also wouldn't piss off Reed and Malloy further.

Keeping my voice as even as possible was difficult, but my personal info came out as demanded, my only evasion being an inability to explain away this chance encounter that everyone seemed to resent.

Once given my name, age, and the certifiable truth that I'd meant no disrespect, the deputies half-heartedly jacked me up a bit more before growing bored and taking off, no doubt in search of some cholo who'd prove more accommodating of their desire for a fight.

Retrieving my hat was easier than my pride, but Cindy offered a smile that let me know that my company was still appreciated, and by the time we'd finished "mother-fucking" the long-gone and went our separate ways, all was back to normal.

A year later, I crossed paths with another Industry deputy when my friend's 1974 Nova failed to start after a football game at Nogales High School. We were in the process of trying to jump-start his car when a deputy lit us up with his spot lamp, at which time I'd lowered the mirrored visor to comb my illuminated hair.

"That's a nice way to get your ass blown away," I heard the unseen deputy say as he ordered me to put my hands up and remain still.

What a paranoid ass, I thought, not knowing how often I'd be making similar admonitions in the years to come.

Outside of a couple of deserved traffic citations, these were pretty much the sum total of my personal experiences with deputies. Not bad, given some of the crap I'd been party to, including Halloween and Christmas raids wherein we liberated houses of their decorations to have pumpkin fights or render a friend's house the most decorated in the area.

Still, if a dedicated bystander like me could be counted on to have this degree of contact with LA County's finest, then it stood to reason the kind of contact genuine badasses got and how that information was disseminated thereafter—growing larger with each retelling—created the mythos surrounding the Los Angeles County Sheriff's Department.

That I'd profited from that reputation had been apparent from my first day working as an "off-the-streeter" in custody, telling inmates when to eat, when to shower, and when to sleep. That they complied with a tall, skinny 21-year-old white male's commands had shocked the hell out of me. I'd expected resistance at every step.

That was how much cachet the uniform had given young deputies such as myself.

But I would soon experience some of the liabilities that came with the uniform.

One night while Scott and I were patrolling in the unincorporated area of Monrovia, we jammed two black males in an Oldsmobile. Scott began a search of the car's interior as I stood curbside with the detainees. I noticed that one displayed a shark-like grin—a look he probably intended as ingratiating—and seemed unusually fixated on my every word.

This, coupled with his habit of stepping to my right as I was getting his personal information, only heightened my fresh-out-of-patrol-school vigilance. Trained to be wary of detainees trying to seize my sidearm, I did not let his sidestepping go unnoticed. I swiveled to compensate for his every movement in an effort to keep my gun hip rotated away from him. Finally, I had enough.

"Look, just stand still. Don't move," I said. The man complied, then surrendered the only form of ID he had on him. I read the name on the military card aloud.

"Lionel Greene, huh?"

No sooner were the words out of my mouth than Scott was out of the Olds and telling the two men to get in the wind...

Back in the patrol car, Scott told me that he was familiar with the ex-military detainee, but only by name.

"Lionel Greene hates deputies," he said. "He teaches the local kids here at Pamela Park how to perform gun takeaways against deputies."

And Greene practiced what he preached.

Though his hatred for Temple's finest pre-dated the Armstrong shooting, it was around the time of that incident that he'd ended up fighting with two Temple deputies and succeeded in wresting one of the deputy's guns away from him. Greene was just about to fire when he felt the pressure of a revolver against his ear and heard the words of the second deputy filtering in around its bore: "Drop it."

"Greene dropped the gun," Scott concluded. "And so he lives to fight another day."

I'm thankful that this wasn't that day, at least not with me.

That someone would want to seize my firearm and execute me with it was a possibility I'd filed away early on. It was the reason I conscientiously kept my gun hip away from people, why my eyes always watched theirs, and their hands. The eyes pretty much let you know ahead of time what was on their mind. Whether they were fixated on your sidearm or scanning the horizon, you pretty much could tell which way someone was leaning on the whole fight or flight spectrum.

More difficult was determining the motives for either. Even if I didn't know exactly why a person might run—warrants? drugs? weapons? stupidity?—it was at least explicable: He didn't want to go to jail.

Killing a cop that hadn't done a damned thing to you? That was a new one on me. I didn't get it.

It wasn't like I was naive on that score either. Growing up in the sixties and seventies, I'd heard about the Black Panthers and the Weather Men, who'd taken the fight to cops. I found it cold-blooded, but at some

level understood that their actions were part of some larger scheme—
however asinine that scheme might be.

But Greene was a loner who seemingly wanted to kill a cop just so
he could say he had.

WTF?

Sadly, just because Greene was a lone wolf didn't mean he was
alone.

In the Academy, we'd heard of a black man in the Bay Area who
would bait pairs of cops to approach him so he could strip one officer's
firearm and shoot both. His technique was well practiced and effective,
but depended upon the first officer being right-handed and approaching
from the suspect's right. When he tried the maneuver on a left-handed
cop—his hand sweeping down the officer's hip and finding nothing—
they beat the crap out of him and ended that shit once and for all.

Whether Mr. Greene's hostility was congenital in nature or a
byproduct of less favorable contacts with deputies was of no matter to
me. I only cared to the extent that I wouldn't give cause for others to so
hate the uniform. It was enough to know that there was a constituency
of like-minded people throughout the country.

And Lionel Greene would not be the only one whose path I would
cross.

As the first few weeks of patrol passed, I received a form letter
telling me that one of our patrol school peers had succumbed to spinal
meningitis and I might have been exposed. I didn't recall the deputy,
but felt bad for him, especially as I'd heard how painful such a death
could be.

Still, I wondered if I wasn't experiencing a death by a thousand
cuts myself. It was nothing of Don Scott's doing—it was just the way I
was hard-wired and hell-bent on retaining my stress cadet status.

At some level, I felt like an imposter and was scared shitless I'd be
found out. That at any moment one of my badged brethren would point
at me like Donald Sutherland at the end of *Invasion of the Body Snatchers*
and yell, "You!"

Only unlike the freeze-frame ending that followed in the movie,
this would be followed by lengthy soliloquies enumerating the many
reasons why I wasn't one of them. I didn't live and breathe policing. I
wore makeup. Given the choice between beating the shit out of someone

or talking them down, I tended to go with the latter. I believed that some LASD shootings could have been prevented and the deputies involved were shit-stupid. Other shootings were more than justified and the involved deputies had no business getting fired save for self-serving agendas of their higher ups.

I didn't fit in. And I knew it.

But then the holidays arrived and Scott departed to take some time off with his family. That's when I found myself working a 10-day stretch with Deputy Bob Handleman.

Physically, there was something about Handleman that recalled Teddy Roosevelt. Thick mustache. Barrel chested. Funky glasses.

Mentally, I'd never met anyone like him, although politics and time would offer a reference point: Anthony Weiner.

From our first day together, it was apparent that the last thing on Handleman's mind was law enforcement. Any free minute was an opportunity for him to angle for some tail.

And so it was that I found my ass sitting in the passenger seat of a black and white, parked in any number of trailer parks while Handleman visited their occupants.

In these pre-handheld radio days, I was told to catch up on my reports and to monitor the car radio as I waited. If we received any calls, I was to "ack" the radio by depressing the transmission button once to notify dispatch that we received the call, then to honk the horn (daylight) or flash the headlights (nighttime) to alert Handleman. When I did, he would emerge shortly thereafter, flying out of some screen door as he re-secured his Sam Browne around his waist.

We didn't make a single traffic stop and when we weren't on a call or stopped outside some mobile home, he seemed intent on adopting me as his wingman, taking me inside various local eateries and introducing me to the waitresses and cashiers.

Even when we'd sit in the car together, he'd look at one of the porno magazines he kept stashed in the trunk of our car. On one occasion, he started yelling, "Cunt!" at the top of his lungs while driving. It wasn't an angry proclamation either, but a joyful proclamation of what was on his mind. To this day, I have never met a man more afflicted with satyriasis.

Given that we were assigned to the City of Rosemead at the height of the holiday season, Handleman's lack of proactive policing was appreciated, at least by me—the radio kept us more than active enough. Later, I would find it most ironic that I never worked harder more consistently than during my 10-day stretch with Handleman.

This was not as counter-intuitive as it may sound. Often, we were out the gate with calls in tow, arriving and compiling information which I would then transcribe into report narratives while Handleman indulged his proclivities.

In this short period, I found that while the streets teemed with thieves and vandals, residents seethed with domestic anger. People hit their spouses with canned ham. Clerks beaned would-be thieves with Butterball turkeys. Family get-togethers would dissolve into football versus Scientology, or some other religious war.

If it wasn't the happiest time of the year, it sure as hell was the most interesting.

There was an ancillary benefit to working with Handleman. I found myself feeling less stressed.

Hell, I figured, *if this guy can keep his job this long, then I have a shot too.*

That I didn't say something to someone about Handleman—or others not yet mentioned—is a matter to be addressed here and now.

On occasion, it was less a matter of cowardice than common sense. One thing the Department teaches its employees early on is the importance of picking and choosing one's battles. This necessarily factors in things like potential allies, the willingness of others to step up and do the right thing, and knowing what the hell you are talking about—that is, having the same kind of indictable facts at your disposal as you would with any other defendant.

Did I see Handleman doing the horizontal bop? Nope. Not once. Nor would I have wanted to (training was traumatic enough).

First, if I was going out on a limb, I didn't want some asshole like *A Separate Peace*'s Gene Forrester jostling it just so that he could make rank on my badge.

I'd already seen what happened to other trainees who'd done the right thing. One was Robert Underwood, the trainee who'd corroborated his training officer's story regarding Robert Armstrong's orchestration of events the night of his shooting. Underwood was subsequently deemed a snitch and nobody wanted to work with him. He ended up working as the jailer. His ostracism was so acute that he would lose everything near and dear to him—his wife, property, and pride—before eventually blowing his brains out in the Temple Station parking lot.

Nonetheless, it was inevitable that such men got the better of themselves. Handleman ended up getting caught while being orally serviced on duty—not once, not twice, but three times.

And by two different sergeants, at that (caught by, not serviced by).

Handleman's service with the Department would end before the decade was out.

When I was ten, Jasmine—a girl I knew through my cousins—had been attacked by her father with a claw hammer, leaving her severely injured. The man had used that same weapon to kill Jasmine's mother, brother, and grandmother before setting their house afire and turning the weapon on himself (he later successfully hung himself in custody).

A year later, I'd listened as a friend, Matt Grunewald, described the abuse he'd suffered at the hands of his mother and how he intended to kill her. Five years later, at the age of 16, Matt made good on his threat, stabbing her 50 times in their kitchen.

These were the only instances in which homicide had in any way affected me personally. It was while working with Handleman that I got the handle on one professionally.

The night had been a busy one, with the usual seasonal yuletide rob 'n' hides. Then it got one better: an assault with a deadly weapon call.

We arrived at the location in time to see the victim—a young man whose tattooed torso had been stripped bare, his torn and bloodied shirt on the asphalt nearby—taking his last breaths.

The significance of the ink on his chest was not lost on me. He was a *veterano* who'd fought the good fight, one borne of desperation, if not to save himself, then to at least wreak as much damage as he could in his dying. Even money said that his assailants did not go away unscathed. Bathed in the glow of flickering Christmas lights, the irony of such bloodletting at a time ostensibly filled with human compassion was not lost on me. When I checked his driver's license to find he was only a year older than me, a feeling of depression fell over me.

What is it that makes men so readily kill one another, I wondered. On this night, knives had been the weapons of choice. Motive? Well, his assailants not only took his life, but his car too.

His chest rose and fell ballast-like once more and then it was lights out.

There was the usual taping off of the crime scene, followed by the writing of homicide reports chronicling man's latest travesty against man, towards a prosecution that would not be forthcoming. Six o'clock the following morning found me with a blow dryer, trying to rid the victim's bloody t-shirt of its dampness before booking it into evidence. DNA was not yet a concern.

What did concern me was the fact this was my first murder, the first of many I would roll on throughout my career.

Back at home, only exhaustion let me get some sleep before reporting back to work later that day. The conscious moments that bracketed my slumber were occupied with thoughts of the man who had died before my eyes, and I was surprised at how much the loss of life affected me. Why him, and not me?

Hours later, I was back to work and the first call out the gate was to an address that I recognized: the victim's. We were to contact his family and advise them that the victim's car had been recovered.

I knocked on the front door, consciously ignoring the wreath adorning it. A woman opened the door. It was the victim's mother.

"What do you fuckers want?"

I advised her of the car's recovery. From behind her, the victim's brother chimed in.

"You assholes probably didn't even find it, did you? Somebody found it for you, right?"

Soon, I was surrounded by a cacophony of profanities and banalities from what appeared to be three generations of the victim's relatives. The legitimacy of my birth was questioned and I was alternately accused of having succumbed to Oedipal urges and having orally serviced my fellow man.

Though I was a rookie, I knew it wasn't supposed to be this way. Indeed, at no point during my succeeding 24 years did I encounter such hostility from a "bereaved" family.

Having met his tribe and been bid adieu in so many words ("Get the fuck outta here!"), I made my way back to my patrol car. As I did, I thought of the victim and, armed with new insight, no longer asked, "Why him, and not me?"

I wondered: *How did the S.O.B. live this long?*

It proved to be the first of many such juxtapositions of homeboys and homilies, homicides and holidays, and people treating us like we were the ghosts of Christmas Past who'd once taken away daddy for allowing some yuletide cheer to get the better of him.

And with each passing holiday season, I found myself becoming more and more accustomed to reserving my compassion for those deserving of it.

It took me many years to meet a man whose mercurial nature could rival my Dad's. When I did, it was my second training officer, Lynn Helbing.

A big man, Helbing had a mustache and a fringe of hair that wrapped around the back of his head and gave him the air of an intimidating friar.

In the time it took him to secure his firearm in a gun locker, Helbing's mood could change from cheerful to baleful and pissed off. Occasionally, this mood swing was precipitated by some act of stupidity on my part, but just as often it wasn't. I felt like I was walking on eggshells all the damned time.

Still, part of me was relieved to find myself finally working with a new training officer. I wasn't worrying any longer that some woman might come forward and I'd be put in the position of confirming or denying whether or not Handleman had promised her a job at Denny's. And during our last month together, I got the impression that Scott seemed to simply be biding his time with me, in anticipation of Helbing taking over.

But while I appreciated getting some distance from Handleman, between Helbing's willingness to buy calls—taking control on incidents initially assigned to other units—and his making me stay hours beyond the end of my shift, I began to miss Scott.

Helbing was not the touchy-feely type. There was no chitchat over the morning Casey Kasem countdown, no idle comparisons of new movie releases. Helbing pretty much confined conversation to work-related matters. He was a stickler for his own protocol too. I could call him Lynn— but only in the car. I could eat—but only in the car, unless invited to join him. I could write—but only in the car. But most of all, he wanted me to know what the hell I was doing—and not only in the car.

An ability to meet the expectations of one's training officers would seem to be enough for any deputy to navigate his or her way off of training. But sometimes it came down to other factors. One night, Helbing and I stopped at the Winchell's at Buena Vista and Huntington in Duarte, the same donut shop where Robert Armstrong coordinated his plans that resulted in the shooting death of Dolores Young's fetus and four deputies' careers being destroyed.

On this night, it hosted a windshield conference where several training officers convened about the hood of the patrol unit where I sat doing paperwork. A few parking spots away, Dave Oliver, a fellow Hall of Justice deputy who came to patrol the same time as me, sat writing his own reports. Through my cracked window, I heard his training officer's voice.

"See this guy?" he said, nodding in Oliver's direction. "He's not gonna make it. I'm gonna ship his ass back."

I looked at Oliver, the Honor Cadet of his class, dutifully filling out his paperwork, oblivious of the arbitrary decision his training deputy had made of him. Just like that, another cop's career had been decided at Winchell's.

Suddenly, Helbing didn't seem so bad.

In early 1984, Brad Pryor approached me in the report writing room of Temple Station.

"Dean, did you hear about Mike Siegermoor?"

I hadn't talked to our fellow Academy class graduate for a couple months. Training had been consuming my every conscious moment.

"No. Why?"

"He's dead!"

Pryor proceeded to lay out for me what had happened the night before.

For months, a serial handcuff rapist had been prowling Malibu and Topanga Canyon. Armed with descriptions of the suspect and his vehicle, LAPD officers and Malibu Station sheriff's deputies had been keeping hilltop vigils for the suspect when a Malibu sergeant spotted Siegermoor's Jeep—the same Jeep he showed up in every day at the Hall of Justice—as it sped around a curve.

That the Jeep matched the description of the suspect in the abductions was apparent. Less so was that Siegermoor had at that moment a 16-year-old male in the front passenger seat and a kidnapped girl handcuffed on the floorboard behind him. When the sergeant lit him up, Siegermoor hit the gas, setting off a pursuit that wound through the hills of Topanga Canyon until he lost control of his Jeep and crashed.

Siegermoor bailed out of the Jeep and fired several rounds at his fellow law enforcement officers before diving behind some bushes and yelling out, "I'm sorry about all this! Tell Mom I love her!"

The last bullet from Siegermoor's gun entered his temple.

Later, his body lay in the same morgue we'd toured only a year before while in the Academy.

Pryor's words hit me like a slow-motion punch to my gut.

I've often heard people say that they didn't think a person would kill—either himself or others—but they were not entirely surprised when they did. A similar feeling came over me and I found myself affected on multiple levels.

Part of me felt sorry for Siegermoor—more so for his family, including a brother I'd never met but who also worked for the Department. He might well have been a monster who deserved to die, but he had also been a friend.

But that bothered me too. Thinking back to the girls who'd gone on rides with us at Magic Mountain, I darkly wondered if they hadn't been persuaded to accompany by the prodding of Siegermoor's gun in their ribcage.

My mind's eye called up the image of a glass pane shattering in reverse, like a film played backwards, the pieces coalescing into a whole once again. In that moment, I felt like all the clues previously laid out before me had just fallen into place. A part of me immediately signed off on Siegermoor's guilt, as though some latent suspicion had been confirmed.

But if I'd really understood him at all, if I'd truly read what he was capable of, then why hadn't I been able to bring it to the forefront of my consciousness and do something about it? Might I have prevented at least one of his crimes? Could I have helped to save one of the eight women he'd kidnapped, dating back to our days in the Academy?

The personal recriminations never stopped.

They still haven't.

One night, we pulled over a car that blew a red light in front of us. Approaching the driver's window, I asked for his driver's license and if he knew why I stopped him.

"Yeah," he said. "Because I'm black."

It was the first of many such allegations, the majority of which were baseless. (The first time I saw a black man driving through South El Monte, I did make a U-turn to stop him. It turned out the car he was driving was stolen.)

But the vehicle he was driving had dark tinted windows. I wouldn't have known if it had been a black man or Shirley Temple driving. I told him as much in very assertive terms.

For all the talk people gave us about cops only seeing color, the fact was that most people didn't see us either. All they saw was the tan and green uniform.

And they knew there were always more of us just waiting to be called. Thus it was that I'd already grown accustomed to receiving some degree of compliance by the time I hit the streets. What I was less accustomed to were the overtures by which many arrestees attempted to ingratiate themselves. A favorite tactic was to criticize the cops of adjacent agencies as either unfair, or pussies.

"Man, deputies always been fair with me, man. You fuck up, you get yo' ass kicked. Not like LAPD—those fuckers will fuck you just for free."

"El Monte PD—they ain't shit! Not like you guys…"

No doubt this speech was somewhat modified in the back seat of an LAPD or El Monte PD unit.

"Those sheriffs—what a bunch of pussies! Now you guys…"

Rarely does someone call a cop a pussy to his face. It's not much of a conversation starter and is generally deemed offensive in polite circles. It does happen, however, with cops occasionally getting called that and more, usually by those who didn't know any better. But they learned.

One night, Helbing and I pulled over a motorcyclist. Helbing began scratching out a docket on the bike's owner while I was given the responsibility of watching the cooperative biker and his uncooperative passenger.

The biker was sweating bullets and for good reason: He'd been riding on a suspended license and it was his Harley that was about to be impounded. It was also his ass that would be going to traffic court for however many violations Helbing decided to lay on him.

The motorcyclist's passenger wasn't helping his cause. From the moment we'd stopped them, he'd been jaw-jacking about how "chicken shit" we were, first as it connoted anal retentive authority, then as it related to a perceived cowardice on our part.

For five minutes, he kept up the tirade. Five minutes became ten. Soon the tow truck driver was on scene and getting cussed out too.

Throughout his invective, I would occasionally step off to the side—keeping a vigilant eye on the rider and passenger—and whisper to Helbing, "Let me take him!"

Each time Helbing waved me off without comment and continued to methodically fill out his paperwork.

I couldn't believe it.

Why were we taking this crap? It didn't make any sense to me. I knew that Helbing could be undeniably chicken shit in writing up people who had it coming to them, but he was no coward. Nor was he the kind of guy to put up with any smart-assed crap—he let me know as much every night I was in the car with him.

Yet here he was, denying me the opportunity to arrest this belligerent loud mouth. Not only that, but Helbing wasn't saying a damned thing to him, not even so much as telling him to pipe down. Helbing was as close to serene as I'd ever seen him.

The passenger's tirade became more and more offensive. He said our mothers were of the species *Canis* and suggested that we perform anatomically improbable acts upon ourselves and one another. Hearing the commotion, some patrons exited a nearby bar to better take in the proceedings.

The growing numbers of potential hostiles concerned me at first. But then Mr. Loudmouth turned to the onlookers and yelled, "What the fuck are you assholes staring at?" thereby putting them squarely on our side. Nonetheless, the passenger knew he now had an audience to play to and became even more emboldened.

Then it happened.

"I'll tell you what!" he said, pointing at the star adorning my chest. "You take that badge off and I'll kick your ass right now!"

That was when I heard Helbing's voice from behind me.

"Take him."

Straight-arming the guy's shoulder, I spun him around then hand-cuffed him without incident. He proved to be all mouth. But it was that mouth that sealed the deal. The moment he threatened to kick my ass, he'd violated the law: challenging to fight.

Until then, he hadn't done anything illegal. Sure, he'd been loud, obnoxious, and a pain in the ass, but he hadn't committed a crime.

I like to think he learned a lesson that night. I know I did. Among them was to try not to allow my emotions to dictate my actions when it came to enforcing the law. For until he threatened me, there was nothing in the California Penal Code that I could have arrested him for. He wasn't interfering with our ability to do our job—he was just being an ass. As I would have been if I'd indulged my first inclination to arrest him.

Helbing taught me quite a bit in my time with him, but this was one of the lessons that really registered with me. It also made me think twice on a variety of other fronts, such as deciding to search something when I really had no legal standing to, or committing myself to some other precipitous action I shouldn't take.

But most of all, it taught me that people can and will talk themselves into jail.

All you have to do is be patient enough to let them do it.

That the patience Helbing generously extended to others was parsimoniously withheld from me was something I deeply personalized. It contributed greatly to my resentment of him, resentment that in time would only dissipate through later chats with fellow Helbing trainees who revealed that things had been no different with them. Still, even outsiders recognized what I was up against. For years afterward, the first thing Scott Walker would say whenever our paths crossed was how bad he felt for me having Helbing as a training officer. It was a pity exceeded only by my own.

One night, we received a call of a robbery alarm near Walnut Grove and Valley Boulevard in Rosemead. I stared at my map and had just keyed the mic when Helbing yelled.

"Come on, goddammit!! Your assisting units are waiting for you!! Start coordinating your goddamned call!!"

I snapped.

"I would if you'd quit fucking yelling at me all the damned time!"

"It's my goddamned car and I'll yell in it all I want. If you don't like it, I'll drop your ass off back at the station!"

Somehow I managed to coordinate the units then spent the rest of the shift sulking.

Things could have been worse. Temple Station had the highest trainee attrition rate in the County—a reality which, had I known about it earlier, might have seen me going to Firestone after all. It occurred to me that this whittling away at trainees was at least partly attributable to the Armstrong shooting, as one of the two deputies who came forward had been a trainee.

Whatever the cause, Don Edison and Jack Schuck were the top hatchet men among training deputies. Rarely a night went by that they did not leave their trainees buried with multiple arrests and loads of paperwork—all observation-based activity, not those fluky nightmare calls that somehow involved tons of witnesses or hours of booking evidence.

Of the latter, one booking stood out: A robbery/kidnap caper at a Montgomery Wards that tied up poor sleep-deprived Tom Womack for 20 straight hours. Any lesser trainee—and I considered every other guy on training of said caliber—would have been tied up for easily twice that. Whatever else, fate occasionally accommodated the right person for the task at hand.

By our fifth month at the station some of my fellow trainees—including Womack—were getting signed off and starting to work in one-man cars. My envy was palpable and I prayed that Helbing would sign me off soon as well.

To hedge my bet, I kept my mouth shut and tried to be as inoffensive as possible without kissing his ass. No more arguments in the car, I reminded myself each day I showed up for another shift of abuse.

But the following month, Helbing lowered the boom: He was keeping me another month.

Extended training.

The only thing more stigmatizing was being sent back to custody, which was my only alternative. So I accepted my fate, resigning myself to more nights of beating the shit out of my steering wheel and cussing all the way home.

At one point, Helbing told me that he wanted to send me back. I went into the training sergeant's office on the edge of tears and pleaded my case. For all his gruff manner, Mark Wiener proved at least sympathetic enough to give me another shot at humbling myself.

And so I did. As much as I resented Helbing's slave-driving attitude, I knew that he wouldn't ask anything of me that he wouldn't do himself. That he actually did independent work above and beyond what he saddled me with made me resent him all the more. Such a formidable work ethic precluded any claims of unreasonableness on my part. The sole legitimate gripe I had was how he articulated those expectations to me, but there wasn't a damned thing I could do about it. Even then, I objectively couldn't blame him—had I been the training officer, I would get tired of explaining things more than once too.

Whether or not Helbing respected me remained up in the air.

"Do you think I can do this job?"

"Of course, I do," he said. "But then, any damned fool can."

Well, this damned fool was determined to, so I committed myself to biting my tongue more than any natural inclination would lend itself to. In the back of my mind, I kept telling myself that there would come a time when I wouldn't have to couch sentiments for fear of pissing the wrong somebody off. I just didn't know when that time would come.

Helbing played his cards close to the cuff the entire last month. Often, he seemed preoccupied with something other than the job, but he never let on what it might be. All I got was the ensuing fallout of his deteriorated mood.

Later, during one of my note comparison meets with fellow Helbing trainees who'd come before and after me, I found that this was just his standard M.O. Shawn Malloy reported that Helbing had once stomped on the brakes while driving and, with the car stopped in the middle of the street, turned to her and asked, "Don't you want this goddamned job?"

"Of course I do," she replied.

"Then why the hell don't you ever argue with me?"

Somehow, I got a warm and fuzzy feeling hearing that.

In June 1984, Helbing signed me off training. I asked him if he had any parting words of wisdom.

"Yeah," he said. "Don't be a slapdick."

Freed from my training officers' refining influences and determined to make a good impression on my own, I set out on patrol in a one-man car.

I observed two young men standing near a bus stop. The two conversed briefly, then one attempted to hand the other a bulky paper sack. But the man on the receiving end shied away and walked off, leaving the first literally holding the bag. As they were completely unaware of my presence, his hesitance to accept the package made me even more curious.

It was my fourth day off training, twenty minutes before the end of my shift, and my probable cause was light at best. But in a world of nothing ventured, nothing gained, I approached. As I pulled in behind the bus bench where the bag-man had taken a seat, he glanced back at me and did a double take. I decided to strike up a conversation with the man.

Bracing a detainee with some Shakespeare—"Thou hast within thee undisclosed crimes"—is something I had always aspired to, but I went with my usual opener.

"Sure is hot."

"Yeah," the man replied, staring off anxiously for a bus that wasn't coming.

"That heavy bag doesn't help matters."

"Yeah, I can hardly wait to get rid of it."

"Why? What's in it?" Seemed like a reasonable question to me.

"Well, they're my radios."

I casually asked him where he got them. He said he pulled them out of wrecked cars he'd owned. I asked him for the license plate number to one of his cars. I didn't expect him to know; I just wanted to see what he said.

Rather than saying that he didn't know what any of the license plates were—like most of the population knows their plate number?—he quickly rattled off a seven digit license plate number. No phonetics. A red flag, at least in California.

The man's overly anxious desire to placate me was punctuated when he finally said, "Look, my dad lives right around the corner. We can go over there right now."

Taking him up on his offer, I had him get into the backseat of my patrol unit and tell me the address.

As I turned down the street of his dad's alleged residence, it quickly became apparent that the road was going to end long before we got to any such hundred block. The man suddenly pointed at a house on the numerically wrong side of the street.

"That's it," he said. "But it doesn't look like anyone's home, so I guess we can forget it."

I parked the car and knocked on the door. He was right. No one was home.

But the neighbors were.

In speaking with them, I found that the residents of the house were an Asian man and his wife … and their daughter.

Confronted with this information, the man fessed up.

"I lied. I don't have a dad. I just wish I did. Now, more than ever."

The conversation went on, with him painstakingly piling one lie atop the other, so that my curiosity became suspicion, and my suspicion probable cause.

I ended up arresting him for reasonable cause burglary. He, in turn, ended up clearing up some 500 residential and vehicle burglaries from Temple City to Santa Clarita—where he'd been shot by a victim, the bullet still in his ass causing him to squirm uncomfortably in my patrol car.

It turned out that he was the Chapman Woods burglar our station detectives had been searching for over the previous two years.

I'd just saved myself and my ungrateful peers a shitload of car burglary reports.

While I liked working day shift, the Chapman Woods caper only reminded me of how much of dayshift work was oriented around doing post mortems on what had happened over the previous night. Also, I regarded the alarm clock as one of mankind's most suspect achievements.

My decision to work nights was abetted by my lack of station seniority, and so in late 1984, I began working the early morning shift with Scott Radcliffe, who later became president of our union, the Association of Los Angeles Deputy Sheriffs.

On a cold Friday night, straight out the gate Radcliffe and I got a call of a "shooting just occurred" in South El Monte. Upon arrival, we obtained the backstory from a group of security guards.

An Asian motorist had struck a curb while attempting to park his vehicle outside a nightclub. Directly across the street, a group of young men—many of whom were security guards at the location—started laughing at his frustrated attempt to park. Laughter gave way to derision, with at least one bystander loudly attributing the man's inability to park to his ethnicity.

For the better part of five minutes this went on, the lack of any protest from the motorist apparently emboldening the observers in their roadside commentary. What they did not know was that the man had driven from San Francisco that day to do a hit on someone inside the club. For five minutes the driver sat brooding, a loaded .45 lay beside him on the passenger seat. Finally, he decided he'd had enough.

Abandoning the mission that he'd driven hundreds of miles to execute, he jumped out of the car and began firing.

"Oh, fuck!"

Those were the last words of a 19-year-old who was dead before he hit the ground.

The assassin jumped into his car, then made a U-turn before darting down a side street. A security guard pursued him in another vehicle, flying around the corner unaware that the suspect had stopped and was waiting for him. By the time the security guard reacted and hit the brakes, he'd slid half a car length past the suspect. The suspect fired one round from his open driver's window that passed through the right rear panel of the guard's car and struck him in the back of the head, leaving him with permanent brain damage. A third security guard who had detained the suspect at gunpoint turned him over to our custody.

Homicide detectives responded and assumed control of the investigation, noting that if the man had been half as proficient with his car as he was with his gun, his mission would have been carried out without incident.

I was still handling crime scene integrity when a distraught man showed up just beyond the yellow tape, begging one of the detectives to let him know if it was his son beneath the sheet. The detective looked around until he saw me.

"See that deputy over there?" the detective asked, pointing in my direction. "Go ask him."

The detective's response pissed me off. Not only was he acting like he didn't give a shit about the distraught man, but he knew as well as I that it was the man's child that lay beneath the sheet—yet here he was trying to pass the buck of breaking the bad news to me.

I proved no better than the detective in cowardly deferring the obligation.

"Where is your wife?"

"I'm waiting for her to get here."

"It's probably best to wait until she does," I said. "Whatever the news is, it's probably best if you get it together."

The man sat down on a nearby bus bench as Radcliffe and I committed our attentions elsewhere.

I hated the prospect of making a death notification, and I'd be damned if I was to do Homicide's work for them.

But no matter how hard one works to avoid dealing with the job's less pleasant aspects, fate eventually forces his hand.

Radcliffe and I were Batcaving it—parked in a dark parking lot trying to catch some shut eye—when over the radio came a courtesy advisory of a fatality on the 605 Freeway just south of Huntington Drive. Bored, we decided to check it out.

We found CHP officers bathed in the phosphorous glow of flares that cut off a sizable portion of the northbound lanes near the center divider. Occupying the number one lane was a body lying face-up.

The body was that of a Hispanic male whose truck had become disabled. He'd been changing the right front tire when a drunken motorist rear-ended the truck and propelled it into him. He was killed instantly.

The four of us stood there regarding a body that looked like a broken mannequin, a bloodless fissure running the length of his face, from the crown of his head to his chin. None of us were above commenting on it.

"What a crack-up."

"Yeah, a real split personality."

Radcliffe and I eventually left the scene and drove back to our Batcave. A couple hours had passed when a fellow Academy classmate, Jim Callahan, dispatched a call to us and had us switch over to frequency Henry.

"It's a death notification," Callahan said. "Homicide wants us to tell Consuela that Julio went to the Big Taco Bell in the sky."

Radcliffe pulled abreast of the curb as I turned off the spot lamp. "Want me to come?"

"No, I'll do it. Just wait here."

I skirted the lawn, walking along the curb in front of the house. As I did, Radcliffe called through my open passenger window.

"Hey! Ask her if she wants to sell that motorcycle!"

Next to a pair of men's boots on the front porch lay a pair of well-used work gloves. Like the house, the dirt on the shoes was two-toned, moist, and darker at the soles. Just hours before, the owner of those shoes had been turning the soil. Soon, I thought, he'd be beneath it. Such mordancy reflected no better on me than the gallows humor we shared on the freeway earlier, but I couldn't help it.

Or so I thought. The sight of two boys standing out front, each a portrait of brave and resigned bearing, had a sobering effect on me.

"Have you been told?" I asked the elder of the two.

"No..." the boy paused. "Our neighbor came home. He recognized our father's truck and saw a body covered by a sheet."

I placed my hand on the boy's shoulder. The overture felt phony. "Where's your mother?"

The boy turned and I followed him inside.

I found myself denying my peripheral vision as I passed the Kodak moments that adorned the hallway: the family unit, intact and happy. Turning right through a doorway, I found myself in a spotlessly clean living room.

Seated on the family sofa was the mother. Flanking her were two young girls, their bodies forming emotional bookends pressed up against her. Their inquiring eyes were as intent on hers as hers were upon me. Hope and dread shimmered in all of them.

Be Somebody's Hero, I told myself.

How often is an individual's decision to enter a profession truly an edified one? Just how much handicapping of a prospective career does the average person perform before making his bet?

In my case—not much.

Writing papers and making arrests were well-anticipated obligations; the prospect of physical altercations was the reason I jogged the streets at night for years after the Academy.

But one thing I never really anticipated, or appreciated, was the difficulty of making a death notification. And as much as I dreaded making my first, subsequent experiences only rendered me more phobic of the enterprise.

Scant attention was given to the matter in the Academy. Perhaps the prospect of deputies getting early morning erections was a more pressing concern to the drill instructors, and while we still came away knowing how to break an arm or leg, we hadn't been trained at all when it came to the prospect of breaking some stranger's heart.

Unable to anticipate how people would react upon hearing such news, all I could do was think about how I might deal with it on the receiving end (poorly) and expect as much from others.

Reality offered a wide variety of reactions that covered the gamut from dumbstruck horror to denial, anger, and finally, apathy.

In the best of situations, the bereaved had some comfort available to them—a friend or family member, at the very least some obligation to distract them. Widowed spouses could sometimes be counted on to put up a brave front, deferring their anguish in deference to their children. And even the atheist in me came to appreciate the comfort that could be found in another's faith.

The worst notification I handled was only because I'd made it so.

I'd been assigned the call of a man who'd suffered a fatal heart attack at his home and arranged transport of the body when a neighbor advised me that the decedent had a daughter living in Northern California.

As the daughter needed to be notified, I searched the house and eventually found a phone book with the daughter's name and number inside. I dialed.

A woman answered and told me to hold on while she got the woman I'd asked for.

"Hello?"

The voice on the other end was unbelievably chipper and bright. Things suddenly became that much harder.

I identified myself and advised her that I had some difficult news to give her. She indicated she was ready to hear it.

"Your father has passed away."

"What?"

"Your father has passed away?"

"What?"

"Your father has died."

The blood-curdling scream that followed was immediately followed by racking sobs. I could hear the woman who'd initially answered asking what was wrong. She got back on the phone just long enough to say that she needed to hang up and I heard a click.

I'd blown it. I could have contacted her local police agency and asked them to make the notification. Failing that, I should have asked who the person was answering the phone and, if circumstances permitted, advised her of the situation and asked that she tell the daughter.

As it was, the only thing I could do was to make damned sure that I never made the same mistake again.

I belatedly did some homework on the making of death notifications and discovered that I could often find others who could do it— like the Homicide detective had tried to do with me—thereby insulating myself from having to deal with the bereaved. I also found out things that no cop should do, but apparently had: calling and asking people to come down to the station without saying why; leaving voice messages; referring to the deceased as "the body" and not by name. Finally, it was not out of the question to have a chaplain or mental health professional on hand. Consideration should also be given to ensure that the grieving party wasn't left alone.

I had joked that I would sooner kill someone than make such notifications. Admittedly, that was a stretch, as already the job had made me appreciate the fragility of life. I wondered if I would have been so happy at seeing the idiot with the knife on Hollywood Boulevard charge at me now.

But no cop goes through his or her career without incurring an inordinate exposure to such eventualities. I took pride that onlookers would be hard-pressed to recognize whether or not I was affected, particularly if I was multi-tasking at that moment with crime broadcasts, detaining persons of interest, identifying witnesses, coordinating EMS resources (you still make the effort, even if you know they're probably gone), etc. The need to prioritize and compartmentalize things in order to do what needs to be done is something a cop learns early on.

But often it did bother me. Compartmentalizing the more difficult aspects of the job may have permitted me the ability to act, but the reality was still there. Even the sight of some deceased dirtbag would lead me to wonder what he'd been like as a child and what had put him on such a dead end.

I often came away from the proceedings profoundly depressed. Even news stories surrounding the long-term implications of a person's death, such as a father who committed suicide on his murdered daughter's gravestone, stuck with me.

Then there was dealing with those in mourning. Once the immediacy of anguish has been expressed, people start to process their new reality. They could be philosophical; they could grow numb; they could turn nasty. It may be less grievous than making a death notification, but that didn't mean it was all fun and games either.

The poignancy of one woman's off-handed observation registered with me.

She'd returned to her Temple City home to find her husband's body in the den. An elderly man, he had been battling stomach cancer. He left a suicide note before placing a shotgun against his abdomen and pulling the trigger. On the page in shaky scrawl were the words, "Dear God, forgive me. I just can't stand the pain."

I'd responded to the call and tried to help her as best I could. The woman sat on a living room sofa, by turns taciturn, angry, and resigned.

"What will I do?" she asked of no one. "He handled everything."

There was a pause, then she threw up her hands with a mirthful laugh.

"My God, I've never even pumped gas in my life!"

What I would have given had my Dad possessed the decedent's chivalrous nature.

Instead, life with a manic-depressive had found my stepmother and me living under the shadow of an incipient suicide and in a state of anticipatory mourning for dear old Dad. Having endured many lectures on the virtues of suicide, I'd acquired a general resentment of it and of those who would take such an out.

Nonetheless, I understood the circumstances that could lead to such a desperate act. I wouldn't want to suffer either, and only lamented that the options available to the elderly man had proven so limited.

If patrol was nothing but death, depression, and the opportunity to have one's nose rubbed in a profound sense of existential impotence, it would make for a short career.

Fortunately, there was more to the job than death and dismemberment, and if the prospect of someone's dying had a dampening effect on my enthusiasm, the corresponding and omnipresent chance to save a life was enough to keep me interested.

Already, I figured I might have unwittingly saved a life here and there—on two occasions I had grabbed an assailant from behind as he reared back to punch someone, only to find a knife clenched in his hand. But it would be while working with Eric Shepherd that I solidified my case for rescuing people from death's door.

Shepherd and I paired up once my stint with Radcliffe ended. While Radcliffe and I had gotten along fine, we had little in common. With Shepherd, there was an expectation from the outset that we'd have a great time working together.

This optimism was largely due to the vicarious exposure we'd gotten to one another's work. Neither of us had been off training very long, so we both perused the report board, which afforded wisdom from the experiences of others. Reading about each other's exploits had left us with mutually favorable impressions.

Shepherd was a portrait short-cropped guilelessness, a modern-day Huck Finn. Yet his easy-going bearing belied a sharp mind, and his well-detailed reports led me to believe that he wanted to go out and take lots of dirtbags to jail. Through my offerings, Shepherd thought me smart enough to go places in the Department.

Each of us was onto something, at least in part. Shepherd would end up with more suspects in custody than he knew what to do with, and I would go on to serve in several of the Department's gulags.

But the reality was that our agendas, at first, were the obverse. Shepherd wanted to get his patrol ticket punched as soon as possible before moving onward and upward. And my priority was to arrest deserving dirtbags.

All of this became apparent soon enough and accounted for why we lasted only two months as partners.

But what a two months it was.

Few colloquialisms are as universal within the parlance of law enforcement as "shit magnet," a term that refers to those cops who seemingly attract all manner of activity, be it arrests, force incidents, foot and vehicle pursuits. In other words, all the exciting things associated with law enforcement.

Individually, neither Shepherd nor I were worthy of the appellation. But the synergy we experienced together damn near made us so, and we seemingly could not drive down the streets of South El Monte without ending up with a body or two in the back seat.

Part of it was to be expected—we were working a target-rich environment and early morning was the shift of vampires, douchebags, and drunks. But we were clearly getting more than our fair share of action.

Some of it came from calls. Disturbance calls, in particular, resulted in all manner of felony arrests. One motel disturbance call put us in contact with a paranoid couple whose blown pupils suggested an apathetic take on Nancy Reagan's "Just Say No" campaign. A search of their room confirmed it with five ounces of recovered cocaine. Another late-night call in response to a burglar alarm turned out to be an actual burglary in progress (a rarity … ask any cop) with three in custody (one with injuries sustained post-pursuit).

But much more of it was just stuff we'd stumble upon.

If we came across a guy pushing a motorcycle down the street at 3:00 a.m., it wasn't because he'd run out of gas but because he'd just stolen it from a driveway up the street. Pedestrians encountered after midnight were apt to be whacked on PCP. For once we were actually throwing smaller fish back in the water. If someone was under the influence (a misdemeanor), we knew we could find one in possession (a felony). If we could find one in possession, we might just get one for sales.

But sometimes our hands were tied, and we couldn't just put up the blinders. Driving down a residential block, we found a trio of dusters passed out on a local's lawn.

"When did they get rid of the pink flamingos?" asked Shepherd as we hooked them up.

Driving through nearby Whittier Narrows Park, we came across four dusters in a parked car. Their robotic asses were out of the car and getting patted down for weapons when the fourth one started getting froggy. Shepherd attempted an assertive grip on the guy, who shrugged it off then threw a punch.

The fight was on, with Shepherd throwing his would-be prisoner against the passenger side of our patrol car in an effort to gain control of him. With Shepherd directly behind him, the suspect started kicking his heel up between Shepherd's legs so hard that it made me wince. Pain-enraged, Shepherd proceeded to smash the bastard's head up and down the length of the car, busting our side spot lamp in the process, while I kept the other three assholes at bay until the cavalry arrived.

Outside a used car lot at the intersection of Garvey Avenue and

Rosemead Boulevard, we noticed a cholo acting suspiciously. Shepherd made a U-turn and pulled up to the curb about 25 feet away from the man, putting me smack dab in the kill zone. As he did, the guy suddenly levitated like some martial arts master in a kung-fu flick and landed behind a bus stop bench as I bailed out of the car and took cover behind the trunk.

From his glassy-eyed stare, I could see the man was dusted, with just enough presence of mind to try and dump his bottle of PCP, but not the coordination to pull off the act. Worse still, he was multitasking, his other hand grabbing at something shiny and metallic stuffed in his waistband.

"Shoot him!" Shepherd yelled between our commands for the idiot to put his hands up. "He's got a gun! Shoot him, Dean!"

From my perspective, it looked like Shepherd was right. The guy had a .25 caliber automatic in his pants.

But something was bothering me. From his vantage point—leveling out across the hood of our unit and using the engine block for cover—Shepherd had a better view and therefore a better shot. Moreover, between the two of us, Shepherd *was* the better shot. Why wasn't *he* taking it?

At the time, less-lethal weaponry options were limited. Not all patrol cars carried Tasers and pepper spray was generally recognized to be ineffective against sensory-impaired dusters.

Unlike the time on Hollywood Boulevard, I didn't want to shoot someone—particularly one who didn't need shooting. But I sure as hell didn't want to get shot either, and the more we fucked around yelling at this guy, the greater the likelihood he would embolden himself to do the very thing we were seeking to prevent.

Seeing that his attention was increasingly focused on Shepherd, I shut up. There was a telephone pole between the bus bench and the rear bumper of the car where I was crouched. Darting for its cover, I halved the distance between myself and this dipshit while acquiring better concealment. From behind the pole, I made eye contact with Shepherd, who grasped my intentions and began yelling even louder at the suspect, who continued to fumble with the object at his waist.

A couple seconds passed. When it looked like the suspect had forgotten about me, I bum-rushed him, pinning his body against the back of the bench. Shepherd immediately assisted me in getting him to the ground and handcuffed at which time we retrieved the object from his waistband.

It turned out to be a hubcap he'd stolen from a car in the dealership's lot. The idiot was trying to dispose of it and nearly paid the ultimate price for it.

"I could have sworn it was a gun…" said Shepherd.

Refraining from taking a shot was one thing. Actually doing something to resurrect the dead was another.

Shepherd and I were at the end of our shift when we got a "person down, not breathing" call on a secluded cul-de-sac in Duarte.

We arrived to find a man in full cardiac arrest on his kitchen floor. Owing to the confines of the kitchen and how we'd entered, Shepherd was pretty well obligated to handle the breath of life thing while I did the chest compressions.

At first I was relieved. More than once I'd done mouth-to-mouth in those pre-filter days and been rewarded with regurgitated last meals. Give me chest compressions any day.

One-two-three-four-five-six-seven-eight-nine-
BREATH
One-two-three…

But as the minutes ticked by, I began to wonder where LA County Fire was. We knew they'd been en route because we'd passed them on the way.

One-two-three-four-five-six-seven-eight-nine-
BREATH
One-two-three…

Perspiration first dampened my brow, then my armpits, then my back as my ballistic vest slickered itself to my torso.

My class A uniform was soon saturated with sweat and I was getting tired and sore—suspecting that I was about to have a heart attack myself.

One-two-three-four-five-six-seven-eight-nine-
BREATH
One-two-three…

Fifteen minutes passed and then they arrived, firemen dropping their gear on the floor and relieving us. Their captain apologized and said they'd gotten lost trying to find the location (did I mention it was secluded?). Later, at the fire station, the captain told us that the man had survived thanks to our efforts and that he'd called the Temple Station watch sergeant and said we should be given a commendation.

Shepherd and I kept busy, arresting our fair share of dope dealers, thieves and still more burglars. What little down time we had was spent cruising around South El Monte singing "King of the Road."

All of this came at a cost. Despite my help, Shepherd suffered a bad case of writer's cramp (over a two-day period, he ended up documenting 50 handwritten pages among four complicated criminal reports). Well before the end of our second month together, he was showing signs of burnout. When we began arguing in the car, he asked the scheduling sergeant to move to another car.

I was disappointed, but got it. Even without the workload, I was not an easy person to get along with. My mercurial disposition and hypersensitivity precluded my being an easy-wear partner. At least Shepherd and I parted on reasonably good terms.

Twenty years later, our paths would cross again when Shepherd made captain and was in charge of the Department's new downtown crime lab.

I attended its ribbon-cutting ceremonies and listened to a parade of dignitaries make the obligatory remarks to congratulate one another, including blow-hard-destined-for-prison Sheriff Michael Carmona's usual stomach-turning, self-aggrandizing crap.

I got up to leave when I heard a voice call my name. Turning, I saw it was Shepherd.

The last time we'd talked was when I called Shepherd over a dispute I'd had with his brother over some comic books he was selling. Shepherd had proven categorically disinterested and seemingly resentful that I'd called him (not that I could blame him). But the incident had left a bad taste in my mouth, and I'd given him a wide berth ever since.

On this day, he proved more than cordial, shaking my hand warmly.

"You know, I was telling someone the other day about you," he said. "Of all the people I've ever worked with on the Department, I never argued with anyone the way I did you. But I also have to say I never had more fun working patrol. We were like brothers."

It was good to hear. I told Shepherd that my freelance writing for *POLICE* magazine virtually assured that I would have reason to call him sometime in the future and wished him well.

But I never did call him. I liked knowing that the last conversation we'd had ended on a good note.

That most of the two years following my stint with Shepherd were spent working alone didn't stop me from making double the norm of arrests—no small feat at a station where deputies prided themselves on making hooks. I began to think that maybe Helbing was right ("Any damned fool can do this job…"), that I was up to his implicit challenge ("The question is, can they do it well?"), and that I might yet acquit myself within the profession. At some level, I'd embraced Helbing as a father figure and wanted to make him proud. Or at least invalidate his having extended my training.

Though still not a team player and remaining envious of those who were, I was at least feeling more and more secure in my position. That I had compensatory skillsets was increasingly apparent. My natural resistance to learning anything that I was categorically disinterested in did not preclude my retaining it far longer than the average guy. I had inherited enough of my Dad's artistic talent to study the facial structures of my fellow man and immediately recognized wanted suspects. Had I also inherited his thespian bent, I might have better concealed my recognition of suspects driving towards me, and not tipped them off, giving them a chance to flee before I could execute a U-turn.

Still, the fact that I was looking for criminal activity and recognizing them was paying off.

I received a "defrauding an innkeeper" call at a motel on Colorado Boulevard. I contacted the clerk in the lobby who laid out all the fraudulent paperwork, as well as the story of what had happened and descriptions of the perpetrators.

As I headed back to my patrol car to put out a crime broadcast, a female matching the description of one of the suspects approached on the sidewalk. Just as I pointed at her for the benefit of the clerk and said, "Is that one of them?" the girl took off running before the guy even started to nod his head.

I chased her on foot while pedestrians made like toreadors and ignored my request for assistance in stopping her. Fortunately, she was about the size of a water buffalo and so it wasn't too difficult for me to catch up with her.

But as I threw my arms around her back, I belatedly realized that some of my evidence was still clenched in my left hand. She grabbed the papers and stuck them in her mouth. Reflexively my hand followed the evidence at which time she bit my thumb like a shark. The pain was such that I experienced an immediate surge in adrenaline and punched her once in the back with my right hand. The blow broke one of her vertebra and caused her to release my thumb.

We both ended up getting treated at the hospital for our respective injuries. I had to wait a couple of weeks to make sure that I hadn't acquired some ethyl methyl bad shit when her saliva had commingled with the blood oozing out of my lacerated thumb.

Sometimes, I didn't even need to see suspects' faces to take their ass to jail.

I was driving northbound on Goodall Avenue when I noticed a black male leaning against a front yard mailbox. The serpentine bend of the roadway was such that I could only see him from the neck down through the windows of parked cars. At the sight of my light bar approaching, he tossed something into the mailbox and slammed its lid shut. As I rounded the bend and came into full view of him, I grabbed a random piece of paper as a prop, then stepped out.

"Do you know the Greens?" I asked, scrutinizing the notification that my *Playboy* subscription had lapsed.

It was the Greens' front yard in which the man stood—I'd had sufficient contact with the Greens to know he wasn't one of them. That, coupled with his having been messing with their mailbox, gave me more than enough probable cause to detain him. But I didn't want him to know that.

"Yeah," the man replied, flinging his thumb in the direction of the house behind him. "They live here."

"Oh, yeah? Cool," I said in appreciation. "Hey, you don't mind if I pat you down, do you?"

"Oh, no, you go right ahead," the man encouraged me. "I got nothing to hide."

I was glad the man felt that way, as it allowed me to slip a cuff on him as soon as he turned his back to me. He started to pull away.

"Hey, this is for your protection and mine," I said asserting my grip. "Besides, you have nothing to hide, right?"

"Yeah…"

I threw open the mailbox lid and retrieved a prescription bottle filled with crack cocaine.

"...except this," I noted.

I was always up for the street's version of hide and seek. I didn't always win at it and sometimes had to settle for a booby prize ("You got warrants, Bubba"). But if practice didn't make perfect, it at least taught me where things tended to be hidden and how. The game could be dangerous, such as when a patdown search revealed the presence of a firearm on a detainee's body. What might be perfectly fine in Texas would make the asshole of any cop in antigun California pucker.

Then there was the threat of the discovery itself.

One day, Deputy Joe Sanford and I pulled over a driver that I recognized to be a hype as soon as he exited his car to walk back to us.

"Where's your kit?" were the first words out of my mouth.

"In the car," he answered.

I had him turn around and began a patdown search of his body. I wasn't yet in the habit of wearing protective gloves—but soon would be—and as my hand came down the left cheek of his ass, I felt a prick on the wrong side of the pants.

Withdrawing my hand, I saw blood beginning to bead at the tip of my middle finger.

A hypodermic needle hidden in his back pants pocket had poked me.

"What the fuck?" I yelled. "I thought you said your kit was in the car!"

The man shrugged.

"I guess I forgot about that one."

Normally, I was compassionate towards hypodermic drug users. Outside of heavy-duty speedballers—users of both heroin and cocaine, like River Phoenix and John Belushi—most heroin addicts impressed me as simply low-brow hedonists and depressives striving for some chemical relief from the emotional and physical pains afflicting them: There but for the grace of circumstance and a few more mean spirited sons-a-bitches go I, I thought.

But this fucking asshole had nothing coming to him and Joe Bob and I let him know as much, telling him that he was going to give a blood sample for screening if we had to draw the goddamned thing ourselves.

The hospital gave us a more hygienic sample and once again I worried whether or not some son-of-a-bitch had Hepatitis C, AIDS, or some other blood-borne damnation. A week later I received notice that all should be fine.

Not that I was ever hurting for things to sweat. Years of Dad's constructive/destructive input had left me with vacillating self-esteem.

"Jesus Christ," he'd mutter at the sight of my untucked shirt and torn jeans. "You dress like a slob. You sure as hell didn't get your fashion sense from me. You need to stand up straight and learn how to walk with some class. Study how John Wayne walks. Or Robert Mitchum. Those guys know how to walk."

Years later, Nathan Lane's pathetic attempt at replicating the Duke's strut in *The Birdcage* recalled my own. The thing was, I didn't want to walk like John Wayne or anyone else. I wanted to follow my own path in my own way. Curiously, this was also a source of pride in the old man.

"You do your own thing," he'd say. "I respect that."

Yet he never saw that many of the things he both liked and hated about me were born of that same impetus. I wished I could discount his criticisms as easily as I could his praise. ("You're the smartest kid I know." "I'm the only kid you know.")

But I couldn't.

And for all my romantic belief that I did think and act for myself, my actions were often externally predicated. A compliment would fire me up to do more of the same; criticism would provoke an "I'll show you…" response.

At work, the fact that I was doing a more than adequate job was formally communicated to me via commendations and evaluations. For some reason, supervisors from other LASD assignments were more apt to give me a thumbs-up. An off-duty Homicide lieutenant happened to stop where I'd detained three suspects through creative use of two pairs of cuffs and the doorframes of their old Ford Courier. Another took the time to make sure I was commended for my off-duty chase and capture of a felony hit-and-run suspect who'd crippled a man in Rosemead.

Informally, validation was communicated through the comments of others both within and outside the Department. Lawyers from both sides of the legal fence would corner me in the hallways of Rio Hondo Court.

"I've never heard anyone testify like you before," they'd say. "Why didn't you become a lawyer?"

There were any number of ready excuses—affirmative action, lack of academic pedigree, a categorical contempt of lawyers—but none got to the heart of the matter so much as I was just lazy. That, coupled with the obligatory prospects of advocating for or against some asshole who didn't deserve the effort, was enough to keep me in the witness chair.

I knew that was where I belonged, testifying about how I'd contacted some victim, detained some suspect, booked some evidence, written some paper, and appeared in response to some ensuing subpoena.

Those appearances often found me feeling as though I was on trial. This was fine with me, as I knew the lawyers had their hands full in making a case against me. Just how difficult was it to find some excuse to strike up a conversation with someone ("Sure is hot..."), or justify a detention ("I observed the vehicle's registration tag to be expired...")?

Simply put: It wasn't.

What was difficult was feeling more and more like an actor, obliged to recite lines from the witness chair. The truth, the whole truth, and nothing but the truth was subordinated to some version of the truth that conformed to judicial expectations.

It was understandable that I didn't necessarily want to say that I had been sneaking up on a blacked-out car in hopes of catching lovers in flagrante, and instead found a car thief in flagrante. But instead of simply being allowed to articulate the confluence of factors that predicated an arrest, I was obliged to spit out some alternative reality. Suddenly, everything germinated from a cracked windshield or an expired registration tag, the underlying precept being that there was no way in hell I'd simply performed a split-second profile of the defendant and decided to stop and snoop.

But more often than not I had done just that.

Nor was I repentant about it. One of the profession's most widely accepted maxims is "If it walks like a duck, quacks like a duck, and looks like a duck, it's probably a duck." Its beauty is in its simplicity. Everyone gets it.

But were a cop to make such an assertion from the witness stand, in an age wherein anything could be—and often was—misconstrued along racial lines, the backlash would be considerable.

That someone could be judged for something as seemingly arbitrary as their appearance?

No fucking way was that acceptable.

And yet people did as much with cops all the time.

The mere sight of a uniform tempted all manner of regressive interpretations of the person wearing it. It was emblematic of being an agent and practitioner of discrimination. The uniform had manned the battle lines at Birmingham, Orangeburg, Harlem, and Watts; its epaulets, leather, and cut recalled Buchenwald and Auschwitz. Nobody—least of all the news media—thought twice of broad-stroking the whole of the profession.

That our most vocal critics would begrudge us a similar visual shorthand seemed a curious judgment. At least we were relying on actual experience and going through the formalities of confirming some nascent suspicion before passing verdict. Fucking hypocrites.

More curious was the judicial system's insistence that we articulate every written and verbal detail when it came to documenting the defendant's violation of the law.

The same system that recognized a "reasonable cop" standard—that is, what course of action would be deemed reasonable when evaluated by a veteran officer—when it came to evaluating uses of force and other actions did not acknowledge a seasoned narcotic officer's ability to spot a dope user or dealer. It was as though the courts were terrified of creating a frightening precedent.

It was all so much judicial foreplay to making sure the defendant was fucked for having violated societal prohibitions.

Thankfully, most of my field endeavors never obligated a court appearance. If one learned to bite one's tongue at every act of on-duty idiocy, broker peace accords between bar room dipshits, and encourage some split-second sobriety, life went on without any intervening cell bars.

Those situations that did generate paper were, to my mind, to be well documented so as to mitigate the prospects of some lawyer making a viable defense. Just because I felt comfortable testifying in court didn't mean I looked forward to it (nor did my not looking forward to it translate to my not occasionally enjoying it).

Some deputies didn't hew to such philosophy. The greedy bastards were alleged to have written crappy reports so as to allow for an affirmative defense that would guarantee them court overtime.

5

The Pursuit of Meaning

When it comes to Judeo-Christian tenets, neither a moralist nor an ethicist am I. What passed for my moral compass was but a mishmash of Aesop's fables, pulpit parables, and having my ass spanked at impressionable moments.

My inchoate value system was still under construction at the time of my hiring. Things I'd intuited from an early age about what constituted right and wrong were somewhat clarified in college, and I totally got the whole "mala en se" and "mala prohibita" thing.

But immersion into my newfound calling found me dwelling on the laws I was enforcing and how they came to be. Questions of which laws were enforced, as well as how and whether or not they should be, started to weigh on me. After all, some statutes on the books didn't make any sense. Less than a decade before, it'd been legal to kill a Mormon in Missouri. Some thought it still should be.

When it came to professional ethics, I'd come to realize that people on both sides of the legal fence were exploiting the wiggle room the system generously afforded. Back in the Academy, I'd been encouraged to exhibit some flexibility in ethical matters. Lectures on the subject emphasized the need to use some common sense while on patrol. ("If your training officer is offered a free meal, don't make a federal case of it. By the third time you've tossed a meal you just paid for to roll Code 3 on a call, you'll be thankful for them.") We were reminded that there was the letter of the law and the spirit of the law, and sometimes it wasn't always necessary, or even desirable, to take someone to jail. Finally, sometimes you had to pick and choose your battles. ("Yes, you can arrest the mayor for littering," an instructor observed. "But is it worth losing your job?")

If I wondered why we should occasionally be obliged to turn a blind eye to certain offenses, I soon realized that there were few in the Department who wanted to make waves. I brought up the matter with a sergeant.

"I don't understand why men who wouldn't hesitate to take on an armed suspect would back down from supervisors."

"Simple," he said, looking at me like I was an idiot. "No gang member ever tried to take my stripes."

Sooner or later, everyone could be counted upon to hedge their bet.

There were many open secrets on the Department, sordid stories that everyone had heard but nobody had ever done anything about. Long after his departure, a former sheriff remained the subject of rumors about his keeping dirt on his political rivals and blackmailing them to get whatever he wanted, from news coverage to deputy pay raises. We heard that he'd mandated his secretaries not wear panties at work, that he would routinely fire anyone above the rank of sergeant on sight (in fact, those "terminated" would merely end up transferred to another Department assignment).

That parties to such transgressions didn't always have the balls to do something about their plight was something I'd been quite pious about.

That is, until I wasn't.

"Well, hello, Deputy Scoville!" he'd say, before reaching out to pinch my ass.

Just what I'd done to encourage Sergeant Gustafsson's overtures remains a subject of speculation. The best I could come up with was my wearing of eyebrow liner—both a nod to Gibran's axiom that personal adornment was the acknowledgment of one's ugliness, and a concession to Dad's exhortations to do something about my lack of these defining features. ("If eyes are the windows to the soul," he'd noted, "then your eyebrows are the frames. The thing is, you don't have any.")

I'd sweated the discovery from day one, despite the fact that only one person had ever actually brought it up to me. ("Are you wearing eye makeup?" "Are you kidding?")

But the sergeant had apparently been emboldened by my habit. In those pre-metrosexual days, he took it as evidence that I might be gay.

"Knock it off!" I'd protest, before dropping my voice to a loud whisper. "I'm not gay."

"Right!" And with that he'd make another lunge.

With every trip to the sergeant's office to retrieve my car keys, I ran the risk of encountering his free-range hands. The situation got so bad that I had to ask other deputies to get the keys for me.

If it wasn't cowardice that kept me from doing something about Gustafsson, it might well have been a simple matter of wanting to limit my hypocrisies. I'd always been sympathetic to gays, and viewed the Neanderthals who bashed them as suspiciously defensive on the matter.

Having made it clear that I wasn't interested in men, I hoped that my ass would be covered by something other than the sergeant's hands. But the situation continued to stress me out until a shift change took me away from Gustafsson and his middle-aged sexual identity crisis.

If there was a silver lining to my experience with Gustafsson, it was in getting some understanding for what women go through in keeping some horny bastard's hands off them. It'd also given a laugh to those who knew of the situation, i.e., the key-getters.

In time, I even laughed about it too.

But then humor was the non-drinking cop's coping mechanism, something to keep the blue steel from pursed lips.

Deputy-made flyers hung around the station featured photos with wholly inappropriate smart-ass comments appended beneath, in the style of Shel Silverstein's Teevee Jeebies. Humorous videos featuring Arizona cop Darren Jones' clueless alter ego, J.D. Buck Savage, were staples of our officer survival training seminars. Briefings were dissections of the previous shift's fuck-ups, conducted with the knowledge that our own would be recounted by the next shift as well.

Some deputies' exploits were good enough to make the rounds of all three shifts. Tony Stockdale—always good for a laugh and a prospective lawsuit—gave his peers a morale boost when it came to the matter of relative competencies.

Once, Stockdale had pulled abreast of a parked vehicle to investigate a suspicious person. That he'd done so with his gun out and just below the visual plane of the adjacent driver's door was an acknowledged officer safety tactic. That he then accidentally discharged his weapon so that a round entered the civilian's car was not. Thankfully, while literally scared shitless, the man in the driver's seat was not hit. And whenever we were bored, we could always reminisce about the time Stockdale had faced off against a hoe-wielding Japanese gardener with his PR 24 baton. At least the gardener had some business being on the property.

Practical jokes could be merciless, and a less than vigilant deputy might find a snake coiled in his trunk or sliding out the air vent of his patrol car.

When one deputy lost his helmet, ransom notes began popping up around the station with instructions as to how and where money was to be dropped to ensure its return. Addendums were added to the ransom note, with one deputy demanding the owner's street wife in exchange for the helmet, and another writing, "I've seen her! Keep the helmet!"

When the ransom didn't come through, the helmet was found hanging from the ceiling in the report writing room. Someone had peppered it with shotgun pellets.

Then there was the stuff we encountered away from the station.

Drunks frustrate the street cop on multiple fronts—from their unpredictable aggressiveness to their hygienic nightmares. They are full-time underminers of law enforcement's mission. Yet many of us found humor in their behavior out of desperation.

They could be great debaters.

"You shit your pants."

"I did not!"

"Yes, you did. You shit your pants!"

"No, I didn't."

"Oh, yeah? Drop your pants."

(Does as told.)

"See? I told you."

"Oh, I thought you were talking about today."

Within Temple's jurisdiction, no drunk was a bigger pain-in-the-ass than Ricardo Costa. With well over a hundred bookings into our jail facility, Costa was known to have been in and out and back in within a day. Any deputy who'd been signed off training had probably booked the man at least once. We even took up a collection to put him on a bus to Las Vegas. The unwashed curly-haired man with the reeking mustache was back in three days.

For the cop who didn't want to deal with a hygienic nightmare—particularly if that walking petri dish was abusive—dumping him in an adjacent jurisdiction was an option.

Now some will take exception with this initiative, but it was hardly anything new, and positively innocuous when compared with other interagency kiss-offs. Supposedly, there was a Compton shooting wherein deputies could see where the PD had dragged the victims' bodies from the city's jurisdiction into the County's. Later, Compton PD folded and LASD absorbed their jurisdiction, so I guess it all worked out in the end.

When it came to drunks, I like to believe that we generally got the better of this prisoner exchange program. But one night, as we rolled eastbound on Lower Azusa Road, our latest drunk in tow, we passed an El Monte PD unit headed into our jurisdiction, doing their part for interagency shuttling.

Through the rear passenger window, Ricardo Costa beamed back at us.

Some incidents weren't so funny at the time of their occurrence.

One day we got a call of a shoplifter at K-Mart. When first detained, the Vietnamese suspect fell to his knees and begged security not to call the cops—and fully collapsed when they did. He didn't say a word thereafter.

Upon our arrival, we tried smelling salts on the man. His tear ducts opened while his eyelids stayed shut; his mouth opened to breathe (we closed it).

Despite all manner of prodding, tickling, and name-calling, the man wouldn't budge.

We requested paramedics, who plied the tools of their trade to similar effect before acknowledging a temptation to strangle the guy themselves (they did not, however, want to generate any more paperwork for us).

A joint-EMS search of the store commenced to find a translator. Security escorted another Asian gentleman back to the office where we had the suspect detained.

"Do you speak another language?" we asked.

"I'm enrolled in Spanish 101."

Eventually, we found someone who spoke the detainee's lingo. As soon as the detainee heard the translator say that we'd intended to release him on a citation, the guy jumped up and experienced a full recovery.

On another occasion, a partner deputy and I had to transport a runaway to a SODA bed in Covina. These temporary detention homes were mandated by the courts for runaways, truants, and generally incorrigible children who, for whatever reason, couldn't stay at home with their parents and couldn't be sent to juvenile hall. The entire way the kid was talking about "nigger" this and "nigger" that, and pointing at various black motorists she saw on the freeway and telling us to stop them.

We tried to explain the nature of probable cause, but she wasn't having it.

"You guys are chicken shit!"

We finally reached our destination and opened up the back door to let the girl out.

As we escorted her to the front door, it opened and an elderly black woman stepped out to greet us.

"Oooooh, is this the poor child?" She smiled warmly at the girl. "Well, you just c'mon in, sweetheart…"

As she ushered our fair damsel into her home, our runaway turned and shyly smiled, "Bye."

It was easily the best "I feel real shit-stupid right now" grin I've ever seen.

I was on a traffic stop with a partner deputy on Lower Azusa Road when a car pulled over ahead of the car that we had detained. The passenger exited and approached my partner. I heard him ask if he could speak with "Dean."

The familiarity with which my name was used, combined with the unfamiliarity of the voice using it, aroused my curiosity.

The petitioner bent down, but it wasn't for a couple of seconds that I recognized him. It was Steve Jungeschock.

Jungeschock had been a teen when I'd first detained him near where a series of car burglaries had taken place. Given the tools on his person, the time frame, and the M.O. with which the crimes had been committed, I was sure in my heart that he'd committed them.

That I didn't have a witness didn't stop me from telling him I did, and so I extorted some cooperation from him with a promise: My priority was getting the properties back to the victims. If he helped me do that, I'd cut him loose. But if my "witness" identified him incident to a field lineup, I'd have to take him in. He ended up giving back the stolen property.

I kept my end of the deal, but told him that he was going down a bad path. He'd been conducting himself like he was the biggest badass in Temple City, which for all I knew he was. But I warned him that if he kept fucking up he'd end up in juvenile hall with some genuine badasses and regret it.

A month later I got a call of a residential burglary. As we rolled to the location, I recognized the address and told my partner that this was not going to be any burglary—at least in the whodunit sense.

Sure enough, we pulled up to what I recognized to be Jungeschock's front yard, mainly because he was standing in it with his visibly agitated mother. Seeing me in the passenger seat of the patrol car, he did an "Oh, fuck" eye roll.

As he was quiet and avoiding eye contact, I let his mother explain to me how $4,000 worth of jewelry had been stolen from their house. Accompanying the two inside, I was led to where the "suspect" had supposedly removed a screen and climbed inside a bedroom window before going through a few dresser drawers and removing the stolen items.

It was a poorly orchestrated crime scene, and the dust on the window sill was visibly undisturbed, a feat that could have only been otherwise accomplished via an Olympic high hurdler.

I told the mom as much. Then I told her my suspicions.

"I think your son has taken your jewelry."

Jungeschock immediately protested.

"Mom! You know me better than that! I would never do that!"

But the sideways glance his mother gave him was devoid of any maternal affection, and suggested she'd had her own intuitions. I handcuffed Jungeschock and sat him in the backseat of the patrol car in preparation for looking around the property for the items. As I walked to the house, he called through the window at me.

"I have to go to the bathroom!" he yelled.

"Tough," I said. "You can wait till we get back to the station."

I turned back towards the front door.

"If you let me use it now, I'll show you where they're at!"

A couple minutes later we retrieved the jewelry from where he'd stashed it under the house.

It was a strange coincidence that I would encounter him again after he served his time for stealing his mother's jewelry. He'd just been released from custody and said he wanted to thank me for arresting him.

He said that I'd been right about what would happen to him while on the inside: He had three of his ribs cracked. He also had done a lot of thinking and realized that what he was going through was child's play—literally—compared to what would happen when he turned 18.

He'd decided to clean up his act. He then showed me his 60-day Narcotics Anonymous chip—he was obviously proud and scared, and admitted that he was still tempted to go back to the dope, but so far he had been hanging tough.

I told him that I would help him in any way I could. I honestly wanted to. What he said meant a lot to me. It was one of the few times I felt that I had accomplished something while working patrol.

But I never heard another word from him.

Years later, I ran his name. Somewhere along the line he'd gotten out of NA, returned to his old habits, and become an adult felon.

By now, my eagerness to get out of the gate at the beginning of my shift and grab someone to haul back to jail was dissipating. Part of this was simply a case of the novelty of the job wearing off; part of it was a growing awareness that I could do the right thing and still get screwed; and part of it was a growing fear that it was all a farce.

I'd registered for college again, this time at California State University–Los Angeles. This gave me some desperately needed distraction from the task at hand, but I still had an eight-hour shift with which to occupy my time.

Up to now, much of that time had been occupied with self-initiated activities: citations, arrests, field interrogations, reports, etc. By the summer of 1985, something else was occupying the minds of just about every cop within the San Gabriel Valley.

I was working the desk one Sunday night when another deputy took a 911 call. The woman identified herself as Maria Hernandez and said that she'd been shot. Her unknown assailant had also shot her roommate, Dayle Okazaki, in the head before fleeing.

Within an hour of Okazaki's death, a woman was pulled out of her car in Monterey Park and shot twice in the head with a .22 by the same assailant (later, an investigator close to the investigation confided to me that this second victim was a spy for China).

Temple had its fair share of murders through the years, including the shooting death of a deputy in 1959 during the robbery of a local restaurant. But most of the murders were gang-related or had a discernable nexus between shooter and victim. These recent shootings were indicative of something different and inexplicable.

It wasn't that Temple Station had been wholly insulated from serial killers. Just the year before, our area had been hit by one who killed several people, including a pregnant woman in South El Monte and a woman waiting for a bus in the unincorporated area of South San Gabriel. The stabbings were brutal, but the killer—who turned out to be a newspaper deliverer—had been captured relatively quickly.

But what none of us could have known was that these latest murders were but the third and fourth in a series committed by a depraved man whose crime spree was just starting, a sexual sadist who would soon be dubbed by the news media as the Night Stalker.

Over the next several weeks more murders followed, the next attacks occurring in the nearby cities of Whittier, Monterey Park, Monrovia, and Burbank. Through it all, Temple's jurisdiction was at the epicenter of the violent attacks. As the killer's victims included the old and young, the healthy and the invalid, the panic of local residents grew over the succeeding weeks as they took to locking their doors and windows to literally sweat the nights away.

Many locals weren't able to sleep at all, and called us at all hours to investigate all manner of noises, both real and imagined. As temperatures surged, prowler calls and gun sales did too, with even anti-gun types suddenly stopping to ask us what firearms were the best for home protection.

Despite the fatigue, I chased one prowler call to the next. Since I wasn't sleeping all that well either, I couldn't blame them. More and more I hoped that I or one of my peers would be the one to take the son-of-a-bitch out or, failing that, that some citizen would get the drop on him.

At least my enthusiasm for the profession was re-invigorated. Like every other street cop, I wanted nothing more than to be the one to collar this hot-prowl burglar, and I entertained fantasies where I'd happen upon the blood-thirsty bastard as he dropped a window screen to the ground. As he spun towards me, I'd deposit six .38 rounds into his fucking chest with the calm and easy trigger-control of Dirty Harry.

Towards the end of summer, LASD Homicide had come up with a fingerprint that led to a name for this predatory asshole: Richard Ramirez. A mug shot from an arrest the previous year was disseminated through the news media and soon Ramirez was recognized inside an East LA store by elderly women. Panicked, Ramirez attempted a series of ill-executed car jackings before several citizens cornered the Night Stalker and gave him a taste of richly deserved justice—a beating that included deftly wielded metal pipe.

He was no doubt relieved when an East LA deputy—also named Ramirez—arrived and slapped the cuffs on.

Things soon got back to normal.

My developing patrol competencies found me streamlining things, creating shortcuts, and fashioning downtime for myself. And as I saw all arrests and no play made for one discontented cop, I opted for the occasional extracurricular activity. This came about as the result of my lack of maturity, new and long-held resentments, and a natural inclination to indulge one's pleasures—all abetted by the examples of my peers.

I wasn't aware of but one deputy who insisted on paying full price for anything. If a discount or gratuity was offered, it was accepted ("If it's for free, it's for me!"). I was no different, and I'd reconciled myself to readily accepting whatever I could get on the cheap the first time I'd tossed my just-purchased meal to roll Code 3 on a call (just as our Academy instructors had predicted).

And so it was that I'd periodically venture to neighboring San Gabriel and patronize Gary's Corner Book Store on duty. Except for groceries, I did most of my shopping on duty—with a blue line discount on the back end.

None of this was unique to Temple Station. The same year I was hired, the French film *My New Partner* prominently featured the protagonist making a daily circuit of his favorite establishments. The difference was that in real life most businesses welcomed the badged patronage as it dissuaded would-be thieves.

Often, I'd make a token bid for full price, only to get rebuffed.

"Oh, no, no, I insist," they'd say. "We like having you here."

Then there was the matter of the opposite sex.

One night, when I'd accompanied Scott into Vermie's, a bar in East Pasadena, I was greeted with catcalls and whistles, and women's voices saying things like, "Wow, they sure are sending them out young and handsome, aren't they?" The bar was dark, its demographic a cypher, the whistlers unknown. By the time our bar check was finished, I was fairly floating out the door with my inflated ego.

That Vermie's was a lesbian bar I found out only later.

That even a cop of average looks could have an inordinate amount of luck with women was a well known fact, and most—married or not— had their badge bunnies, street wives, and holster sniffers.

My own prospects were strengthened the first time I asked an informant for her firepower—contact information—which she gave me. Her crimson fingernail stabbed at her phone number.

"Call me."

I did—as I did with any number of women who made similar requests during traffic stops, fast food orders, or service calls. I was young, in the best shape of my life, and I looked good if your tastes ran to the tall Nordic type. And I was a late bloomer, determined to make up for lost time.

Still, there's a saying in law enforcement: The badge will get you tail, and tail will get your badge. Worse, it can get you killed and perhaps nothing has proven more fateful for cops than sexual indulgences.

When it came to force incidents and the like, cops were savants at learning from their peers' mistakes. But when it came to the prospect of getting their dicks wicked, they were moths to an all-consuming flame, cautionary examples be damned.

Most skated on their dalliances, such as the DI who'd zeroed in on one of the female cadets in our Academy class, despite such fraternizations being verboten. Glass ceilings didn't stop a number of women from sleeping their way up the Department's food chain (others slept their way to the bottom). LASD offered all manner of STD opportunities, irrespective of assignment. Hell, even a one-man outpost like the Gorman substation had visiting hours.

I wanted my fair share—STDs withstanding. As such, I had a few ground rules:

One: Never hit on a woman I pulled over on patrol. In a world where citizens could be counted upon to make up shit to file a complaint on a cop, it didn't make sense to hand them any ammunition.

On occasion, I'd stop a female for some vehicle code violation and approach the driver's window to find her cleavage in glory, her pouty lips sporting a fresh layer of red lipstick, complementing a skirt hiked up to the panty line. Her license and registration in hand, I'd walk back to my patrol unit to fill out the citation, then return to find a picture of matronly decorum, her blouse buttoned up to the neck line, skirt hem draping the knees.

Two: Less attractive female motorists sometimes got off with a warning (I figured if God wouldn't give them a break, I would).

Three: Generally, duty-incident contacts had to be incident to calls, but not always. When I told one errant motorist that she needed driving lessons, she campaigned for me to be her instructor, even dropping off a cake at the station desk. Thus I was not hitting on her. She was hitting on me.

Four: When there was nothing reasonable prohibiting me from letting members of the opposite sex know I was a cop while off duty, I did. Not so much in biker bars, but when it came to local eateries, school, or even on the Department, it was game on.

Five: Bat-shit crazy could be seductive, sometimes fun, and often exciting—but never worth it. I was content to let my peers tell me their horror stories later.

When it came to personality types, the atavistic groupies who liked macho males rarely fell on my radar, nor I on theirs. The few shy girls who had similar tastes I could easily live without.

Fortunately, there was a sizable constituency that gravitated to shyer types, such as myself. Often, these were women who'd tired of entertaining recycled pick-up lines from the alphas. My self-deprecating sense of humor, and my ability to keep my mouth otherwise shut, served me well. Off duty, I was mistaken for being everything from a teacher to a preacher.

As if.

Opportunities popped up all over. There were the girls at the McDonald's drive-thrus and other burger joints, donut dollies, and the waitresses at our freebie diners. Models, socialites, and actresses would have been interesting, but then this wasn't West Hollywood, and there was always Rule #5.

One big enabling factor was that I could do paperwork faster than

95 percent of the deputies in the field, and do a better job of it too. This was not a point of arrogance so much as an acknowledgment that report writing was a source of resentment for most deputies, whose prose often reflected all the grammatical lapses of a country song. Many cops could find a felon with greater ease than I, but few could write the attendant paperwork as quickly. This had the ancillary effect of my calls and observations being handled faster than the average bear's, generating less court overtime, and fewer citizen complaints. I could devote some of those newfound hours to things that were closer to my heart.

While my extracurricular activities never rose to the level of full-fledged satyriasis and priapic indiscretions, they were always a part of my itinerary. On duty and off, I'd meet women in parks, at their work afterhours, and in their homes. Younger women were more adventuresome and energetic, but as Franklin aptly noted, "Older women don't tell, don't swell, and they're grateful as hell." I would add that they tended to be more discriminating and had fewer expectations.

They could also be less tactful.

Basking in the post-coital bliss of a parking lot tryst at Rio Hondo Court House, I received the sweetest smile from my elder partner.

"You know what I like about you?"

"No," I smiled back. "What?"

"You don't have any hang-ups about your dick."

Ouch.

Despite my determination to make up for lost time and keep pace with my fellow deputies, I was deathly afraid of catching something, and not just through sex either. Long before books like *The Hot Zone* amplified my concerns, I was petrified of all manner of microbial threats and diseases through saliva, needles, and blood-to-blood contact.

Having reached adulthood just as AIDS was on the ascent and the sexual revolution on the decline, I felt screwed, but only in the negative sense. That I was still able to find willing partners in this age might have been comforting if I didn't have a bit of that Groucho Marx "I wouldn't belong to a club that would have me" thing going on. If they were willing to have sex with me, then God knows who else they'd had as partners. Thus it was that at a penultimate moment of penetration, I more than once backed out for fear of catching something—if not a disease, then some pissed-off husband's bullet.

Apparently, I didn't back out often enough. One day I found a cluster of bumps on my groin.

"Oh, yeah," mused my physician. "We can take care of that."

He cauterized the damned things without saying what the hell they were.

My campaign of debauchery relied on subtlety—relative to the competition—as I wanted the woman to have the impression that it was as much her idea as mine. But my tactics as "take it or leave it" guy were really nothing more than fear of rejection.

I was surprised at how easy it was. I was big, but non-threatening, and had a pretty good sense of humor. Thanks to Harold's patient mentoring on how to drive a stick shift, I was tooling around in a Porsche 924—the Volkswagen of Porsches, but the majority of women didn't know as much. And like one of my favorite essayists, Wilfrid Sheed, I'd found that rigorous intelligence was a great way to get girls in the sack.

Sometimes, wit didn't even enter the equation. That some women barely spoke English didn't mean I couldn't communicate with them sexually. A Columbian who didn't seem to speak more than ten words of English smiled encouragingly at me one night, and I ended up going to her apartment on duty and getting to know her in the biblical sense. Such rendezvous took place in pre-radio days and could only be exploited if I, like Bob Handleman, had a partner to let me know if we got a call.

But I didn't bat a thousand. On one ride-along, the niece of a sergeant let it be known that she was up for some playtime while we were patrolling together. She was no less candid in expressing her lack of interest after I got off work.

However *Penthouse Letters* my rendezvous were, I didn't make my excursions known but to a handful of associates. It was enough to know that I was the beneficiary of attentions from some woman that every other guy was salivating over. This was payback for my teenage years when most of my friends were sexually active, while I was relegated to playing counselor to their girlfriends as they cried on my shoulder about how shitty my friends were treating them.

One day a civilian volunteer at the station asked me to stop by her house. I had no idea what she wanted, but my partner and I pulled into her drive straight from the station.

Once inside the house she created some pretext to have me accompany her to the back of the house while my partner waited in the living room.

"I trust you," she whispered in the hallway. "I don't trust your partner."

I liked my partner enough to trust him with my life, so already I was curious what the hell she was talking about—particularly as we'd just left him with free rein of the front of her house.

Inside her bedroom, she led me to a dresser, pulled open a lower drawer, then removed a manila envelope which she handed to me.

"These were taken a few years ago."

I reached into the envelope and pulled out several 8 × 10 glossies.

They were black and white nude art shots taken in a forest setting. The model had struck various nymph-like poses, her breasts angling towards the sunlight that pierced the canopy of trees above. The lady was the model "a few years ago." It had been at least 20.

"Don't tell anyone," she winked.

I said thanks for sharing them, promised I wouldn't breathe a word of them to my partner, and returned to the field.

There was something sad about her wanting to share the artifacts. The photos left no doubt as to the natural attributes she'd once possessed.

Kind of like these anecdotes.

In a world where women used sex to get love and men used love to get sex, someone was destined to get screwed.

My every indiscretion was with a willing partner. So averse was I to the prospect of being perceived as forcing myself on someone that I would back off at the slightest hint of rejection.

To be sure, some who'd donned the uniform were sexual predators. Mike Siegermoor had been my first exposure to the type. But there were others.

Despite working with him for several years, I didn't even know Deputy Cordwain's first name. It was only after he'd been arrested that I read it in the *Los Angeles Times*—Nathaniel.

Nick—as I'd known him—was a decent looking guy, the Owen Wilson nose notwithstanding. He had a beautiful wife, took inordinate pride in being Christian, and seemed to have a few things going for him. That was why many deputies—myself included—couldn't imagine what might have induced him to extort sex from women.

It was the victims' familiarity with our judicial system that Nick was exploiting. Once he'd detained them and run their names to find they had outstanding arrest warrants, he'd give them a choice: blowjob or jail. The victims did not end up going to jail. But Nick eventually did.

There were plenty of other activities that brought attention to Nick. He had a habit of "accidentally" keeping the house keys of females on traffic stops and returning them at three o'clock in the morning. When the shit hit the fan, Nick spent his non-legal time convincing his wife that his arrest was a sign from God that he was to go into the priesthood.

The closer they were to the investigation, the greater the befuddlement of Nick's fellow deputies. As one told me, "I wouldn't have touched these broads with *your* dick."

Nick ended up sentenced to 14 years in prison for raping or sexually assaulting three women.

When it comes to officer indiscretion, there is one variable not endemic to other professions: a firearm.

Within and without LASD, I saw all manner of otherwise squared-away cops dying because of sexual relationships they had with their peers. One 14-year-veteran was killed by a fellow officer who'd hidden inside his van and shot him as he drove home from work, apparently in a bid to ingratiate himself to a female deputy, with whom both were involved. The murder went unsolved for years until DNA evidence implicated the shooter who, when he learned Homicide investigators were on to him, went into the forest near his home in Idaho and shot himself.

The longer I was on the Department, the more I felt my adrenaline dissipate. Outside of the sexual hijinks, it took more and more to get my blood pumping. But sooner or later something would happen, and I would once again find myself scared shitless.

On one occasion, Radcliffe and I received an "assault with a deadly weapon" call at a Mexican nightclub on Valley Boulevard. We contacted the victim, who told us that a Hispanic male in a cowboy hat had grabbed her in the parking lot, pointed a gun at her head, and threatened to kill her. She said that he'd gone back inside the club.

Armed with the suspect's description, I headed back for our patrol unit to put out a crime broadcast and get other units to assist. As I did, I glanced through the club's large plate glass windows and saw a man matching the suspect's description. He had a .45 semi-automatic shoved down the front of his pants and was plainly not happy to see me.

I drew my revolver and yelled at him in English and Spanish to put his hands up or I'd shoot. He stared at me and shook his head.

I felt a sudden surge of adrenaline, confronted with someone on the wrong end of a firearm who was calmly brushing off the threat of imminent death. The rush that came over me was crystallizing the moment in frame-by-frame progression. The man sidestepped towards a table, then sat down in a chair opposite me, his left hand lifting the tablecloth as his right hand went for his waist.

I couldn't believe it. Could he really be so *baracho* as to think I wouldn't recognize what he was doing, attempting to camouflage the retrieval of his firearm with the checked cloth like some half-assed magician?

He was bought and paid for. I could feel the familiar pressure of a 2.2 lb. trigger pull as I zeroed in on his chest.

And that was when it happened.

Behind the man was a doorway. Into this doorway a waitress stepped and froze directly behind him, transfixed at the sight of my firearm. Many urgent thoughts cascaded in my mind simultaneously: *Plate glass window ... bullet deflection ... shoot/don't shoot ... miss him, hit her ... don't fire ... get shot...*

I ducked out of the kill zone just as two other deputies rushed the man through a side door and took him down. With the man handcuffed, they lifted the tablecloth. The cocked and loaded .45 was there beneath it, its barrel pointed towards the window where I'd stood.

Part of me was pissed at the woman. Not because she'd deprived me of taking the shot, but because she'd come so close to getting herself or me killed. And yet it was just a fluke of timing. It simply wasn't the man's time to die. Nonetheless, I hoped that my split-second amnesty would not one day result in someone else paying the price for it.

On another occasion, I was rolling to assist Deputy James Wallace on a routine call in East Pasadena when I heard emergent radio traffic coming from our destination. Wallace was requesting assistance.

Activating my lights and siren, I arrived seconds later. As a transplant to California, Wallace's Lone Star accent came out in moments of stress, and at this moment he was sounding like he'd just stepped off a westbound Greyhound.

"I don't know what the hell this asshole's problem is!" Wallace said, his revolver trained on a black male in a t-shirt and jeans seated curbside. "I pull up and get out of my car, and he just attacks me and tries to take my gun!"

By unspoken accord we agreed to handcuff the guy.

But the moment Wallace re-holstered to reach for his handcuffs, the man was off the curb and going for it once again.

Withdrawing my PR24 baton from its ring, I struck the man seven times as Wallace backpedaled from his assailant. These were power strokes—one hand on the baton's pivoting peg, the other on its short end—that resulted in a compound fracture to the man's right forearm and the cessation of his attack.

We handcuffed the suspect then transported him to the station where Wallace and I found the watch commander, watch sergeant, and watch deputy on the rear patio awaiting us.

"What the hell are you two doing beating the hell out of a black man in the middle of Colorado Boulevard on a beautiful sunshine-filled morning?" the watch sergeant asked.

Wallace and I looked at one another with the same unspoken thought: What the hell difference did it make where, when, or who was involved? What the hell are *you* doing aggressively challenging us when you know there's a story forthcoming? Especially when you know we're not badge-heavy types?

After Wallace and I told our story, we became privy to another: our assailant's backstory.

It turned out that the suspect's brother had been shot and killed by LASD Lynwood deputies two years before; the suspect had himself pulled a knife on Pasadena PD officers only two weeks prior to his attacking Wallace.

While subsequent policy changes would dictate that only those deputies not involved in a use-of-force incident would transport injured suspects, Wallace and I retained our custody of the man and transported him to a local hospital.

"What happened to you?" the attending physician asked the suspect.

"I got in a fight with a couple of cops."

The man's gaze wandered from where his hand was cuffed to a gurney, to Wallace and me, then moved on. That he didn't recognize either of us was obvious, and I realized just then that he'd never even seen us at all.

All he'd seen was the uniform.

Like Lionel Greene, the suspect reminded me what it meant to be wearing a target.

"Well, why the hell didn't Pasadena shoot him when they had the chance?" I asked.

Wallace's reply was terse.

"Why the hell didn't we?"

In March of 1982, Jeff Fenn was a Sparkletts water truck driver out on a delivery when he spotted a knife-wielding man attacking actress Teresa Saldana on the street. Jeff came to Saldana's rescue and detained the man for police. He then went on to his own career in law enforcement and ended up being one of my co-workers at Temple. One night I had left my flashlight in its charger at home and had to borrow Fenn's backup.

Later that night, I had a deputy on training riding with me in the unincorporated area of South San Gabriel. We were driving down a residential street when I noticed a car parked curbside with the driver's door ajar and a pair of feet dangling beneath, as though the occupant was trying to work on something inside.

I told the trainee to stop and check it out. My directions probably should have been more specific because instead of stopping short of the car and approaching on foot, he pulled abreast of the driver's door and asked the man inside the vehicle, "What's up?"

Startled, the man replied, "Oh, I'm just..." and with that he was out of the car and sprinting.

I jumped out of the patrol car after him, chasing him through several residential properties and finally catching up with him in a backyard.

As I grabbed the man from behind, I felt his hand reach back and unsnap my holster. I did the only thing that immediately came to mind— dropping us both, so as to pin my sidearm between my hip and the ground.

Fortunately, I had Jeff Fenn's flashlight in hand, and I figured that if the son-of-a-bitch wanted to kill me, then all bets were off. I began hitting him in the head in the hopes of rendering him unconscious.

But the blows were having no effect, and he continued to angle for my gun while striking me with his left arm. I'd never seen the man before, but recognized that he must have been fresh on parole. He had that prison-acquired musculature unique to ex-cons—all upper body strength from push-ups, pull-ups, and bench presses.

What I did not know was that the crime he was on parole for had also been committed in Temple's area sometime before. He had been found in a stolen vehicle—just as the trainee and I had found him on this night—which had precipitated a vehicle pursuit, which resulted in a car crash and his getting run over by the pursuing vehicle, getting shot in the leg, and taking on four deputies and a canine. He might not have been the biggest bastard, but pound-for-pound he was one of the toughest I'd come across, and I had my hands full trying to beat the shit out of him with the borrowed flashlight.

Eventually, I was able to roll him face-down on the ground and hold him there. Just then, the trainee deputy arrived and kicked the man in the head. I happened to glance to my left and saw three generations of a Hispanic family staring at us through a chain-link fence.

Any other time, I might have chastised the deputy for the questionable use of force. On this night, I figured that the suspect was lucky enough just to be alive. Me, too. Afterwards, I ended up buying Fenn a new flashlight.

I'd broken his over the asshole's hard head.

My ability to talk arrestees into the back of my car was a source of pride for me. Yes, I could use force when I had to. But with my size, countenance, and wordplay, I was often able to lead detainees to do their own cost/benefit analysis when it came to resisting versus taking flight.

Prompting that analysis was a matter of tailoring my spiel for my audience. Some—the more lightweight offenders, like open container violations—could be dealt with straight up and with minimum debate. Others required just the right tone and words to get the point across.

While it was ideal to treat everyone with respect, I'd learned early on being deferential could be dangerous; some detainees interpreted civility as a sign of weakness and would become emboldened.

"Excuse me, sir, but would you mind adopting a sedentary position at the curbside?" might sound nice, but "Sit your fucking ass on the curb!" was more apt to get the job done.

In instances where there was no overt resistance, but the hamster wheels were in full revolution, I'd give them food for thought. For smaller guys, I'd try to remove the intimidated ego from the equation.

"True, you might be able to kick my ass up around my shoulders," I'd tell them if they weren't likely capable of doing so (I'm no idiot and knew better than to embolden *big* assholes). "But then you'd be facing a shitload of serious charges and have a dozen guys dressed like me waiting for you at the station."

This little speech could get even gang members to go along with the program.

But a couple years into patrol, I was getting a little tired of the program myself. Between station politics, an undiagnosed case of ADD, and the Department's ever morphing policies governing uses of force, I was experiencing premature burnout.

Although I'd hated Helbing while on training, I'd always respected him. He was a hard worker, fair, and knew his shit. With time, I even came to love him, as he'd taught me what I needed to know and helped me create the requisite work foundation upon which to build my career. I wanted to do as much for someone else.

When it came to the prospect of my becoming a training deputy, I might have had my captain's vote had I not butted heads with too many sergeants to help my cause.

The new training sergeant, Jerry Lansing, was among those who were less than wild about me. At least he was fair in sitting me down and laying out my predicament.

"Look here," he said, showing me the comments and ratings from my supervisors.

"Some sergeants rank you among the top three candidates," he said, not attempting to hide the surprise in his voice. "But others have you near the very bottom. It's kind of weird…"

He leaned back in his chair, steepled his fingers, then rotated the paired hands towards me to emphasize his final thought on the matter.

"The bottom line is that for whatever reason, some supervisors don't think much of your becoming a training deputy. And until you stop averaging out to the middle, you're not going to be."

Having asked for an explanation and been given one, there wasn't much for me to say other than, "Thanks." I left his office knowing that loved or hated, respected or not, I was not going to be a training deputy. Sergeant Lansing knew it too. He'd been at the station long enough to know that my disposition wasn't apt to change.

Part of it was that I didn't want to be accused of campaigning or kissing ass. I'd never understood why someone should have to campaign so arduously to make someone like them. I was increasingly determined to try and be myself in the hopes that others, if nothing else, would appreciate my forthrightness.

Another part of it was recognizing that when you throw your hat into the ring, and it comes whizzing back at you, it's probably better to forego a second attempt.

Not that there were many inducements to becoming a training deputy.

Ever evolving "use-of-force" policies were becoming more and more asinine, with commensurately more paperwork. What had once required only a verbal notification to the watch commander now required formal documentation; increasingly, *any* physical contact with an individual, be it to overcome resistance or not, could constitute force. It seemed to me that we were documenting ourselves into a corner where we would look positively barbaric next to those agencies whose policies didn't saddle their employees with such stringent policies.

A saving grace was that we at least had the latitude to use the carotid restraint or sleeper hold, which put us one up on LAPD.

Finally, there was the workload I'd imposed upon myself. I was still taking more than my fair share of bad guys to jail and between the attendant paperwork and a growing number of questions as to what constituted a bad guy, I was frankly getting tired of the charade.

I thought that teaming up with a partner might help. It would divide the workload and lend me a commiserating ear. Hell, it might even light a fire under me.

For three months, I worked with Derek Thomas, a stint that was followed by another quarter with Ricky Wise. In each case, and by mutual accord, our basic working arrangement was that I'd write all arrest reports and they'd handle the booking of suspects and evidence. It helped streamline things and up the odds of our finishing our shift on time.

I liked both men and, for the most part, got along with each. At least, that was my initial impression. But as each three-month period ended, both partners decided that our partnerships had too.

With all my partners, my mercurial disposition had something to do with our ultimately going our separate ways. With Thomas, that disposition got to its all-time worst.

The eighties was a time of big hair, big disasters (*Challenger*, Chernobyl), and big muscles. Of the mesomorphs, none were more dominant than Sly Stallone and Arnold Schwarzenegger. Their physiques were on everything from Joe Weider's muscle magazines to movie posters to the big screen itself. All around me it looked like more and more guys were getting bigger.

But despite working out myself, I was still being referred to as "Lean Dean" without any sense of irony. Wanting to kick things up a notch, I hit up a fellow deputy who I'd noticed had been making decent gains in the station gym. He turned me on to an Alhambra-based doctor who didn't have many qualms about prescribing steroids, and who counted some of the biggest stars in Hollywood and the sports world among his clients.

He started me out with Anavar, one of the milder performance-enhancing drugs available.

I rationalized my taking the drug, figuring that I was under a doctor's supervision, and even Dad had given his cautious blessing as it wasn't a "mind altering" substance.

The thing was: It was mind altering.

It did what it was supposed to do. In a matter of weeks, I saw my bench press improve by ten percent, with commensurate growth in my muscles. My uniform grew tight across the chest and arms, and I felt stronger too.

But the drug also did something else. It had the side effect of agitating me and making me even more of an asshole than normal. While it could have been the natural result of changes to my body's chemistry, it could have been something else as well.

I knew my steroid abuse was due to nothing more than insecurity, and that had put me on edge from day one of the experiment. I justified it as a means of getting a necessary edge on the street, but I knew that was just a bullshit excuse. There were women a lot smaller than me who were doing the same job, and they weren't resorting to modern chemistry to make up for any physical differences.

One day, I grabbed some mouthy teen in a particularly aggressive manner, using his torso as a chamois against the hood of our patrol car.

"Dean, I don't know what's going on with you, but you better get a handle on it," Thomas said quietly. "You can't be doing this shit. And I'm not going to let you get me in trouble out here, or back at the station."

He was right. I stopped the Anavar, which was just as well. Doctor Feelgood's eventual bust for unethical prescription practices would have dried up my supply.

For some time to follow, I ceased being an asshole.

But just because I wasn't fucking things up, didn't mean there wasn't somebody else willing to pick up the ball.

Frank D'Apuzzo was a gregarious guy, funny as hell, and great to be around … at least in social settings. We'd gone out drinking enough to know we had fun together. His generally rude, crude, and lewd nature appealed to my subversive side in a developing age of political correctness run amuck.

D'Apuzzo was a throwback, a goof who wasn't about to stop and do an ideological 180 simply because the rest of society had. As such, his personality appealed to those more subversive aspects of my own. (Jeez, if this guy is this much fun off duty, I bet he'd be a kick in the pants on patrol.)

With visions of Wambaughesque Choir Boy practices dancing in my head, I asked to work with D'Apuzzo. I got half my wish. Sure enough, I was assigned to share a car with him, but I soon found myself doing all the work.

The first arrest we made, he bitched and griped all throughout the booking process while I wrote the report. The next night, I ended up writing the arrest report and doing the booking.

When I pulled over a dirtbag parolee and his old lady on our third night out, the first words that came out of D'Apuzzo's mouth were, "Holy fuck! Don't tell me you're gonna try and make another chicken-shit go-nowhere fucking hook!"

I didn't get out of the patrol car. That is, not until we drove right back to the station where we got a mid-shift divorce. I couldn't stand the fact that all he wanted to do was be a slug. He hated me for making what he saw as pointless arrests.

D'Apuzzo was eventually fired because even the laziest of cops will find something to occupy their subsidized time. Sometimes, the distraction is not only out of the Department's purview, but against the law.

I had barely eked out a diploma from William Workman High School, but would graduate from California State University–Los Angeles with a 3.5 GPA—despite carrying a full load, working odd hours, having an active social life, and going to court in the morning.

My work at Temple Station impressed former LA County Undersheriff Herbert Shields, and I was awarded the Criminal Justice Department's Government Service Award, which was personally presented to me by Sheriff Sherman Block in 1987.

I was being productive on other fronts as well, writing Temple Station's contribution to the Department rag sheet, the *Star News*.

Featuring columns written by members of the Department's various units and stations, the *Star News* was a mix of historical profiles of various assignments, training aids, and anecdotally driven pieces highlighting what was taking place throughout the County. *Temple Times* was the title of our station's column and I inherited it when my predecessor moved on.

Typically, I proved selfish in my handling of the column. The pieces should have featured as many names and pictures of both sworn and non-sworn personnel as possible, but I saw it as an opportunity to indulge in a little creative writing and dove into the assignment. I was never hurting for material and I gained something of a favorable reputation both within the station and elsewhere. For years after, people would recall my columns upon hearing my name and comment favorably.

The column also helped foster a favorable impression of me in the mind of my station captain, Mike MacCloud, who embodied more than a few stereotypes I'd come to associate with Irish cops: big and gruff, but often good humored and fond of his drink. One day, he told me that I should consider working at the Sheriff's Information Bureau (SIB).

"You'd do well there," he said. "And there is no place better on the Department when it comes to networking and making rank."

At last, there was an alternative to patrol in sight, one that came with cautionary admonishments from others.

"Great place for job recognition. Definitely high profile. But if you think you've got assholes out here to deal with…"

"No place is better for learning the Department's inner workings. But you may not like them."

"Great place to network," said another. "Or burn bridges."

Under different circumstances, I would have taken such counsel to heart. But I didn't care. Surely it couldn't be any worse than having to toil for asshole supervisors. Once there, I wouldn't have to worry about whether or not Ernie Hoferschwein might resurrect his campaign against me should Captain MacCloud be promoted or transferred. Besides, I was tired of having to move my ass as quickly as possible in and out of the watch sergeant's office, lest Gustafsson try to pinch it.

Having taken the Bureau's written test and told that I'd come out number one, I began badgering its captain, Rick Wallis. The campaign was a short one.

"You tested number one, did you?" Wallis asked me on the telephone. "Well, that's news to me."

My impatience had gotten the better of me and I felt like a goddamned idiot. It looked like I was at Temple to stay. But a few weeks passed and I received a call at home in early June. I'd be going to SIB after the first of July.

An acute case of short-timer's syndrome followed. I was determined to do the bare minimum and try to avoid making any arrests that would saddle me with court appearances after my transfer.

This didn't mean fate wouldn't accommodate me with things I'd just as soon not roll to. One such call was an accidental shooting during my last few days working Temple.

Two unsupervised boys had found a rifle in a closet in South El Monte. The 14-year-old had taken it out of its case and was aiming to the left of his 11-year-old cousin's head when he jerked the trigger. The round struck the boy in the eye and killed him instantly.

The sight of the lifeless boy seated in a family chair was one of the sadder images I'd seen working patrol, right up there with the two women who were stabbed to death in a church by a transient who was later picked up at the border. If these weren't the main reasons for my wanting to get out of patrol, they were good enough.

6

"The Department is truly remorseful"

In April 1908, saloonkeeper Hootch Simpson in Skidoo, California, shot and killed Joe Arnold, the town banker. Simpson was hung and buried the next morning. A newspaper reporter showed up afterward. Simpson was dug up and re-hung for the journalist's benefit.

I had some idea what SIB was all about. It prepared press releases for newswire services like the Associated Press and United Press International, acted as a notification liaison between the Department's various units, and served as the afterhours hub for the Department.

What I didn't know was just how much activity revolved around the unit or that I would learn more about the Department and its operations in my one year there than my entire time elsewhere on the Department.

SIB operated from the lower floors of the Hall of Justice, far below the less seemly operations of the jail floors. From day one, it was evident that a different breed of cat prowled the gilded halls of the Hall. Some were warm and engaging; others taciturn and inclined to play their cards close to the cuff. But to a person their ambition was evident, as was their regard of SIB as a layover on the way to something better.

Some personnel were married, but many more were players. One deputy routinely hung his freshly scrubbed underwear out of the drivers' side window of his car as he zipped down the I-10 freeway so they'd be dry by the time he got home. Another dated local anchorwomen despite his widely known preference for males.

Irrespective of any personal agendas, SIB deputies were expected to handle whatever situations came their way. Any given shift could find a deputy preparing news releases, authoring operations log entries, making afterhours notifications to a variety of Department personnel, and taping local newscasts. We were the most visible faces in the Department, doing TV and radio sound bites on everything from homicides to residential doors the Department had erroneously kicked in. (For incidents like the latter, I was called upon to stare into the camera and mutter, "The Department is truly remorseful.")

The skillsets necessary for meeting these challenges included street and office smarts, political savvy, and a certain flexibility of character. These attributes the deputies had in spades. What they didn't have was the rootin', tootin', shootin', straight-from-Newton (of course not, that was LAPD) machismo that non-cops often associate with the profession.

If the Bureau was the face and voice of all the Department's units, then it had a responsibility to portray them in the best light possible. Unfortunately, our relative ignorance of the actions of each and every unit sometimes revealed itself to the detriment of all involved.

I fucked up royally early on.

In response to a reporter's question as to how intel for a particularly successful search warrant was developed, I said something to the effect of, "I don't know. It could have been through any number of possibilities, including an anonymous informant."

And that was what the reporter went with. A lead investigator called up and chewed me a new asshole.

"'Anonymous informant'?! We busted our asses working that case!" he snapped over the phone. "Thanks a lot for fucking us over!"

Part of me didn't blame the deputy for getting pissed. Right then I felt the same way towards the reporter.

Another part of me thought, *Get a fucking life.*

SIB's non–Department critics were largely members of the news media. No matter how much we busted our asses to accommodate them, they always saw us as too slow to release information, too unresponsive to their requests, and too tight-lipped in our responses to their questions (despite my foregoing evidence to the contrary). They were always quick to register their displeasure with the sheriff himself, who, in turn, would see to it that some lieutenant jumped on our shit.

But such vicious cycles were the baptisms by fire one endured working at SIB. It was on-the-job training, and accounted for the Bureau's choice of a shark with its mouth agape—like in the *Jaws* movie poster—as its avatar. The Bureau could chew you up and spit you out.

As so much revolved around the Bureau, it was inevitable that its staff interacted with just about every person of rank on the Department. If a custody deputy was assaulted, we authored an Ops log documenting the nature of the attack, the status of the involved deputy and suspect inmate, and who was handling the ensuing investigation. This information would then be forwarded to the appropriate commander and chief, and so on. Similar protocols were adhered to whenever a deputy fired his gun or was relieved of duty, or a Narco or Vice operation resulted in a large number of arrests, or a celebrity was detained. In short, just about everything and anything of import was funneled through the Bureau.

A collateral effect of all this was a continual exposure to members of the Department I never had cause to interact with during my six years working patrol. This contact could be as limited as a one-way memo, or a late-night telephone call following a particularly significant incident, or simply working out with them in the downstairs gym. It was easy to see why the Bureau was the choice of many looking to make rank.

And the Department's upper echelon was well represented with some of the nicest people you could hope to meet. These were the principled people whose upward ascents offered hope to others determined to attain things through personal merit.

But then there were those whose true natures became more and more manifest as they ascended the ladder. Increasingly insulated from those below and protected from peers by those above, these sons-a-bitches could make a deputy's life miserable.

Some Homicide lieutenant forgot his tickets to the theater and called to demand that I run up to the Homicide Bureau and get them for him. I told him that when I got the time I might do just that, but it was a lesser priority as I had other things to attend to. He mother-fucked me to no end and bitched about me to the powers that were on the back end. I didn't care. The way I saw it, I was supposed to be handling things in order of importance and, in any event, was not predisposed to tolerate some delusional asshole's bullshit.

I might have been on training at the Bureau, but I was no longer the wet-behind-the-ears, insecure rookie I'd been years before—just insecure. But one thing I'd never been was a sycophant.

This might have marked me as something of a maverick around the Bureau.

Early on, I saw things at the Bureau were destined to be considerably different than anything I had imagined.

For one, we were expected to be, if not people pleasers, then as inoffensive as possible. I saw this on the front end, and tried to be as accommodating as possible. But I'd never hewed to "the customer is always right" adages—sometimes, the customer was full of shit.

This, coupled with a holdover philosophy from patrol—not to put up with people's bullshit—didn't serve me well on the Bureau front. The way I saw it, if someone misinterpreted an extension of respect as a sign of weakness, it was incumbent upon me to set them straight.

The problem with acting upon this was that I was dealing with people who'd been conditioned to a different kind of response. If I didn't quiver in my boots every time some ass-wipe asked me, "Do you know who I am?" with a minatory air, they were apt to go running to one of my overseers and bitch.

But I couldn't help myself.

Still, life's lessons will inevitably register with even the most stubborn bastard, and whether or not I acted upon their wisdom there were plenty of them to be learned at the Bureau. Lessons such as:

Never think aloud within earshot of a reporter.

Some assignments within the Department require you perform "yes man" services for assholes who didn't have it coming to them.

There really are people who believe the best way for them to shine is to make others look bad.

Homicide lieutenants don't give a shit who you were talking to or how important the call might be. It is their God-given right to pop a video into the VHS player and play it at full blast whenever they want.

Finally, you really should be careful what you wish for.

I'd wanted nothing more than to get to the Bureau and already I was missing patrol. I felt like a shit-head and wondered if Captain Mac-Cloud—whose transfer to the Bureau coincided with mine—was already missing Temple too.

My head might have been in the job, but only because it had to be. My heart was elsewhere. I couldn't give a shit about promoting, which seemed to be the main driving mechanism for everyone else's presence at the Bureau, guys who were continually jockeying for position in a race I was only belatedly aware of being able to run. Any expectations that I might play a role in fostering a better image of the Department through reciprocal dialogues with the press were fast dissipating as (1) I'd only be deviating from the script; and (2) nobody in the press wanted to hear what we had to say as individuals, anyway.

With others, it appeared that promotion was the primary impetus for their being at SIB, and none wanted to say or do anything that might jeopardize those prospects. That they might say or do something to jeopardize one another's was another thing entirely and I came to a belated appreciation of the candid exchanges routinely encountered in patrol.

On the street, deputies mother-fucked one another to their face.

"Goddammit, Scoville! Will you clean your car when your shift's over? I'm tired of having to dump your trash from the backseat."

Or…

"Jesus Christ, Scoville! Aren't you done booking that prisoner already? We need your ass back in the field."

At SIB, it was largely a matter of oblique commentaries, catty asides, and the kind of innuendoes chauvinists normally associated with the fairer sex.

I wasn't wholly naïve. I knew that there were all manner of cliques on the Department, small cadres of deputies who rubbed elbows with one another and reassured themselves that their shit didn't stink. Such group-think could probably be found in most professions, and I'd hazard a guess that even the experimentalists and theorists at Caltech have the occasional pissing contest.

But this chicken-shit, behind-the-back scurrying to dime off another deputy at every given opportunity was something else. This was the first time I'd encountered it as an institutionalized practice. I couldn't even take it personally, as nobody was immune. If a deputy forgot to write an operations log or make an appropriate notification, the peer who recognized the problem was less apt to simply correct the deficiency than to beat feet to make its existence known to a supervisor. And all the while they'd be smiling good-naturedly and patting one another on the back.

When not stabbing co-workers between the shoulder blades, most of the Bureau's deputies were angling for camera time and a chance to rub elbows with Department bigwigs and others. I could get behind the five o'clock news appearance or radio sound bite. It was fun to have friends say, "Hey, I saw you on…"

But I didn't get the hobnobbing thing.

For one, the higher up you went in the Department, the greater the likelihood that you would run into some first-class ass-wipe.

Justice.

Someone once suggested a circular etymology of the word—from justice to just; from just to righteous; from righteous to equitable; from equitable to just; and back to justice.

It might have been a hard thing to define, but my childhood intuitions on the matter had never abandoned me. I recognized fair play, when someone was getting the short end of the stick, and when some prick was getting away with murder. Few things drove me as bat-shit crazy as the lack of parity in the world.

My constant exposure to news broadcasts at the Bureau helped solidify this view. Daily local news broadcasts were taped and reviewed for coverage of Department-related events, particularly any featuring Sheriff Block. All of this was noted, logged, and subsequently taped onto a separate video for the sheriff's review.

The cumulative effect of watching all this coverage—not only of our Department, but of LAPD and other police departments throughout the country—fostered an appreciation for just how much culpability the news media had in law enforcement's eroding credibility with the constituency it ostensibly served.

Television news segments would report that suspects were "alleged" to have done a crime, but that cops had "beat" a black man. Sound bites of the most ignorant of "concerned citizens" conveyed asinine speculations as to officers' motives in matters involving uses of force; self-proclaimed community activists controverted matters along racial lines and got more than their fair share of camera time for it. The pot-stirring was incessant and emblematic of what I could only determine was a most concerted effort to undermine law enforcement on every conceivable front. Seemingly every context was just a pretext for their subtext: Cops were racist, abusive, and corrupt.

The possibility that any arbitrary or excessive use-of-force event might truly have been an anomaly was ignored. As far as the news was concerned, it was business as usual. As far as I was concerned, their campaign was chickenshit. Seemingly every anchorperson or news producer was a Berkeley grad, and none of them had loved ones manning the thin blue front lines.

If anything helped to temper my piety over such matters, it was our own in-house cowardice at the Bureau.

A Carson Station deputy called in a news story involving an assault on a 16-year-old white male. The boy, visiting from Northern California as part of an inner-city fund-raising band, had been attempting to buy a soda at a local market when he was robbed and beaten.

I wrote it up and gave it to my sergeant. He read it and handed it back.

"Make it an 'inquiry only.'"

Code 20s were news releases; Inquiry Only Code 20s were those held in reserve until someone made an inquiry about them. Some of these incidents eventually did result in inquiries, such as that of *Die Hard* actor Reginald VelJohnson, who was arrested for cocaine possession during a surveillance operation, and Chaka Khan's bust on drug-related charges.

But most didn't garner any questions, either because nobody in the news media knew of them or because they didn't want to cover the matter. And so it was that in making the assault an "inquiry only," we effectively blacked out any media coverage on it. I was incredulous.

"You're kidding."

"No, I'm not."

"He's on life support with possible brain damage!"

"Look, it's not the kind of thing we normally put out, and we're not going to start now."

"Well, the Carson deputy thought it was important enough. And if the races of the parties involved were reversed, you'd be insisting that I write it up—then the story would receive international exposure and be fanning the flames of racial discontent."

The sergeant glared at me and spoke in a tone that left no doubt that pushing the matter further was ill-advised.

"Inquiry only."

Neither the Associated Press nor United Press International were notified, at least not through us.

Given the volatile nature of race matters, the irony of the boy's purpose and the attack, there was little doubt in my mind that the story would get the traction it deserved if it was made known. The roughly contemporaneous rape and murder of a white 19-year-old American girl on a humanitarian mission to Africa received international coverage.

Nowadays, I'm sure that no news outlet this side of Fox would have covered it anyway.

With each passing week, I was made increasingly aware that every decision within the Bureau was predicated upon potential political impact. We tailored our press releases not to offend, and kept editorial comments regarding others' Darwinian idiocies between ourselves. God forbid anyone should rock the boat. We were to keep our mouths shut unless a microphone was shoved in our face and then we'd better stick to script. But we would jump every time somebody from Associated Press or United Press International called.

If journalists thought they could run roughshod over SIB deputies, field personnel were even worse. Occasionally, they would push too far, like the night when a news crew showed up and stepped over the tape at a crime scene where a deputy had been injured in a shooting. One of the deputies responsible for containing the scene confronted the reporter and ripped the press pass off her neck.

"I've got a right to be here," she protested. "I'm a reporter."

"Wrong," the deputy advised her. "This ain't no natural disaster, asshole. It's a crime scene. Get the fuck out of here before I hook your asses up."

The next day, the deputy was chastised regarding the incident, and two days later a regional order was distributed to prohibit deputies from making field revocations of press passes.

Personally, I thought the deputy had a King Kong-sized pair of cajones and deserved a pat on the back for not having backed down once his hand was forced. As far as the journalists themselves were concerned, it appeared that those who didn't know history, or the law, were destined to report both.

It wasn't all bad.

At least that's what I kept reminding myself. My neck was constrained by a knot of my own fashioning, but it no longer chaffed under the collar of a ballistic vest, and lunches were eaten leisurely and never had to be dumped for a call.

Daily ethnocentric calls from Korean news outlets gave me a laugh.

"Is the suspect Korean?"

"No."

"Is the victim Korean?"

"No."

"Are any witnesses Korean?"

"No."

"Thanks."

Click.

But outside of these incidents and a few others, laughs around the Bureau were few and far between. The tight-assed, tight-lipped dynamics and the constant jockeying for position didn't mesh with my personality.

In patrol, there was competition. Deputies were always trying to one-up one another when it came to arrests, citations and dalliances. In a land of alphas, it was to be expected.

But all of that took place on different shifts, in different cars and in different patrol areas, with tallies to be compared later. The Bureau didn't offer so much as a cubicle partition to obscure the competition. We were like unwelcome mirrors, facing our rivals up close and impersonal, and reminding one another just how shallow our pursuits really were.

That I was once again getting caught up in a defensive mindset bothered me. If I wasn't angling for a promotion or trying to make anyone else look bad, then why was I was suddenly concerning myself with what the hell others were up to?

Because I had to.

One day I returned to work after a tonsillectomy to hear that one co-worker had told another that he had to completely rewrite a Code 20 of mine owing to factual discrepancies.

I found this most curious, as what I documented had been related to me by a Sergeant Viramontes of Homicide. Moreover, after writing the finished Code 20, I'd called the sergeant back for his distracted approval—although he later claimed otherwise, which pretty much shot the shit out of any credibility I had with one Homicide investigator thereafter. I confronted the deputy on the matter.

"Why didn't you talk with me about this?"

"Because you weren't here."

There was also a growing consensus among Bureau deputies that I was using too many big words. My initial thought was that if they'd quit treating English as a goddamned second language, and open any of a number of dictionaries that languished on the shelves at the Bureau, they might learn something. That is, until I was forced to read one of my Code 20s on the radio and found myself thinking, *What asshole wrote this wordy piece of shit?*

That said, I never understood the "one size fits all" mentality that was embraced Department-wide when it came to writing. Just describing the illegal physical contact of a simple battery narrative offered all manner of possibilities, including "hit," "struck," "pummeled," "beat," "thumped," "slapped," "smacked," "punched," "jabbed," etc. A suspect's actions could be made to seem absolutely horrible ("He pummeled her face"), or relatively benign ("He cuffed her cheek").

That "one size" thing was entrenched in the Bureau and deputies wrote bone-dry narratives that hardly addressed the concerns of the audience. As there wasn't much in the way of serviceable templates around the Bureau, I decided to meet my critics half way. I'd leave out the polysyllabic crap.

But that didn't mean there wasn't a hell of a lot room for improvement when it came to our communication with media.

I began to feel disassociated from what was going on around me and experienced anxiety attacks and bouts of ever-escalating paranoia. Every slight—real or imagined—generated more of the same. Soon, I was second-guessing the actions of myself and those around me and not enjoying the moment.

A December return to Temple Station to pick up some Narco evidence for a court case only amplified my woes. It was good seeing old co-workers and being exposed to genuinely good-natured ribbing. But later while driving home from the courthouse, it occurred to me that another advantage to working patrol was that when a superior or peer made me feel bad, I could go park somewhere and suck my thumb. At SIB, I was obliged to just stew in my cubicle and wonder why battery wasn't legal.

Hank Goodall made a beeline to read press releases anytime a radio or TV spot came up, but was defensive enough about his written product that he would duck writing them as often as possible. The rest of us never complained as we'd have been the ones having to read his offerings otherwise. But when Sergeant Bert Ross made some innocuous comment over a spelling error Goodall had made, Goodall lost it.

"Just because you've got three stripes sewed on your arm sleeves doesn't make you a goddamned know-it-all!"

Ross didn't respond. He just smiled that inscrutable smile that probably served him well during his time with Vice and would, in time, prove a concern for me, as well.

Then there was Ted Court, a sergeant whose physical and mental attributes to this day recall a pit bull that'd once latched onto my uniform pants leg. Court loved nothing more than to argue points that had very little import, just to assert his presence. His alpha male personality and intimidation at my vocabulary made me all the more determined to exercise it in his argumentative presence.

I'd arrived at the Bureau feeling like the insecurities that had plagued me my whole life had abated. But environmental circumstances at the Bureau had resurrected their full bloom.

At the time of my transfer to the Bureau, my Academy classmate, Carl Moseman, had been tasked with mentoring me and getting me signed off on things. But it seemed that he was always dragging his heels to show me this or teach me that and he acted like it was all no big deal. But with nothing getting signed off, the perpetual state of being on training ate at me. I should have been signed off after three months. But four months went by, then five, then six…

At some point, I stopped bugging Moseman about getting signed off. If he didn't give a shit, why should I? But if I couldn't trust Moseman—who I'd at least always considered to be something of a friend—to be acting in my best interests, then who around the Bureau did have my back?

Ross didn't. He'd taken to documenting minor mistakes I'd made, such as second-hand errors like my having failed to compensate for another employee's not videotaping a sheriff's TV appearance. Individually, these black book entries were not particularly worrisome, but their aggregate effect on me was undeniable.

Winter's onset brought with it a recurrent cold and general foggy-headedness that plagued me for weeks; a coincident melancholia only begged the "chicken or the egg" question as to the etiology of my twin maladies. The high hopes I'd had of my tonsillectomy sparing me from such episodes only compounded the depression, and I was convinced that if I could just improve myself physically that I would be able to get my depressed frame of mind turned around too.

But it seemed that I was destined to be on a cyclical tailspin, with one thing setting me back on one front, then the other front following in tow. And there was no shortage of things to bring me down. Sleep-deprived and unfocused, I began fucking up on duty and off. In January, the loss of my Department ID card and badge necessitated an embarrassing memo to my superiors.

On January 23, 1990, a deputy-involved shooting resulted in the death of one Muslim and the wounding of a second. Three days later, Assistant Sheriff Jerry Harper and Captain Ken Smith had a 13-minute-long videotape on the shooting produced as a counter-point to ever-escalating controversy surrounding the incident by Muslims and the local news media (though not working hand-in-hand, as sympathetic cameramen were chased and beaten by Muslims at the funeral).

The whole thing had been orchestrated by Muslims who had suckered the deputies into pulling over a black male in front of an Athens apartment complex. The driver's friends then came out of the complex and attacked the deputies from behind, stripping the trainee deputy of his firearm before the trainee pulled out a backup gun and killed one attacker and wounded another. The suspects, adherents of the best defense being a good offense, then claimed that it was a racist police shooting.

"So, what are we going to do? Send these to the news media?" I asked hopefully.

"No," I was told. "This is strictly for in-house purposes so that our deputies know what really happened and there's nothing to worry about."

While I thought it was great that the tapes were disseminated to all LASD stations, I was disappointed that no similar outreach was being made to the news media. This, coupled with the Department's soft-sell on the realities of the incident, pissed me off to no end. Already, rumors were circulating that the Department didn't want to bestow its highest honor—the Medal of Valor—to the trainee as it might possibly inflame the passions of locals.

As far as I was concerned, we should not only give that deputy every damned medal the Department had available, but whatever embellishments LAPD had too.

By February, I got a bit of a bounceback, thanks in part to some of the occasional perks that came with working the Bureau.

In a bid to foster mutual empathy, some of the local news media and the Bureau would allow their employees to visit one another's camp for the day. This vocational exchange was how I got to spend one day with ABC News.

I met with an executive with ABC News who assigned a couple of news editors the responsibility of keeping me amused for the day. To that end, I ended up spending the morning with reporter Susan Campos and her cameraman, Russ.

We had a so-so morning, arriving late for one news conference, and early for another.

Around noon, we ended up attending an "intimate" news conference attended by Ed Asner, Robert Foxworth, Jackson Browne, Daryl Hannah, Hector Elizondo, and a couple of Nicaraguan artists. I was amused and embarrassed when someone interpreted my presence as a "bodyguard" for the news crew and passed this info onto Robert Foxworth, who seemed genuinely surprised and interested. I downplayed my value as a celebrity centurion.

We eventually made our way back to the station where Campos and I made an implicit and mutual agreement to split company and I was set up to ride with the Channel 7 "Air 7" helicopter thereafter.

The pilot and I were idling on the helipad when the news director got him on the radio.

"Where are you?"

"On the pad," replied the pilot.

"Well, get up in the air!" the director said. "We just had an earthquake!"

The pilot and I looked at one another in confusion. We hadn't felt a thing.

It turned out to be a 5.5 shaker centered in the Upland area, and rumors of the Disneyland sign having collapsed found us flying by the Happiest Place on Earth, living up to its still upright name. We then flew towards the epicenter, but didn't find much more than a few downed chimneys.

Later in the month, Lt. Mark Quincy gave me a badly needed shot in the arm.

"We like you here," he said. "You belong here. We'd like to see you in Media."

The Media arm of SIB was something I could see myself doing and enjoying. They coordinated celebrity ride-alongs for actors like Charlie Sheen, who was researching for his role in *The Rookie,* and did liaison work between the Department and film studios on everything from filming permits in LA County to authorizing and coordinating usage of the Department's name and image in films like *Tequila Sunrise, 8 Million Ways to Die,* and *No Man's Land.* I was flattered to think that there were those in the Bureau who were already thinking of my next bump up.

But if others had forgotten that I was still on training, training sergeant Bert Ross sure hadn't.

One Saturday, he sat me down to tell me that I would be on training for no less than two additional months—and possibly more. He tried to make it sound like it was no big deal and joked about my uncanny ability to piss off the likes of Associated Press' Donnette Wilder, certain administrators, and others that held sway with the Bureau.

"It's not because of incompetence," he assured me. "It's just some interpersonal issues. We want to smooth out some of the edges."

But the news only put me more on edge.

Paul Burlanger was a Temple lieutenant whom I'd given cause for some legitimate past grievance that gave him a hard-on for me thereafter. One day he called and requested that I do an OPS log entry on some minor event. Once he'd detailed the incident to me, I made the mistake of asking him if he felt the OPS log was really warranted. He got pissed and told me to do it. *No sweat off my balls,* I thought. *You just look like a dumbass for initiating it...*

But later, forcibly reflective on the matter after he'd bitched to those above me that I'd "tried to talk him out of the log" and too late for it to do me any good, I realized that there was a reason why certain assholes were calling in needless OPS log entries: The logs were a great way of getting their names beneath the eyes of the various commanders and chiefs reviewing them. The prevailing wisdom seemed to be: So what if you looked like an idiot to those above you—at least they knew your name.

But as previously noted, the Department did occasionally promote its deserving members and at the end of March, Lt. Quincy was promoted to captain. I was happy for him and told him as much at his farewell party. Had I known just how much a supporter's departure could portend, I might not have been so enthusiastic.

One April morning, I was called into the captain's office and introduced to Lt. Ron Phillips, a recent transfer from the Special Enforcement Bureau who'd replaced Quincy. Phillips' reputation for being a straight shooter proved warranted.

"I don't know you, Dean, so please don't take this personal," he said. "But we'd like to ask you to leave."

Wow. My own captain—the man who encouraged my transfer to SIB in the first place—wanted me gone. That he had Phillips ask me on his behalf hurt almost as much as the request itself. What could I possibly say to this stranger? There wasn't much to say.

"We can't make you leave," Phillips made a point of saying, which was nice and might have been a lie; any environment can be rendered unlivable. But I could take the hint.

Part of me had been anticipating all of this. Ross's initiative in documenting every little mistake I'd made had not been without purpose. The only question in my mind was whether or not the poker-faced ass was doing so because he'd simply wanted to (I'd never kept my contempt for Vice Bureau or its agents a secret), or if he was carrying out someone else's marching orders.

But in my shattered and vindictive heart, I knew that even in their aggregate these mistakes did not warrant my dismissal, particularly when weighed against more bone-headed ones made by others.

I knew that I'd tried to do a good job, often without support and frequently against adversity. And here I felt sucker-punched on the back end.

Most curious was the ill-defined sense of betrayal that I experienced. How can you feel betrayed if you haven't any cause to expect anything otherwise?

I left Phillips' office in stunned silence and returned to the Bureau's operations center where I sulked, making no pretense of my displeasure or that I suspected my co-workers of knowing my days were numbered before I did.

I could forgive myself this. What I could not forgive was something I did thereafter, more because I have to admit to it here than because it smacked of desperation and was ethically and legally questionable: I began secretly taping my conversations with others at the Bureau, specifically supervisors and those peers who I deemed to be least trustworthy.

One was the Ted Court. We'd given each other a wide berth while working Temple Station where he'd transferred as a newly-promoted sergeant. But the confines of SIB precluded any elliptical orbiting. I decided I might as well exploit those confines and expressed my displeasure at having to work with him.

If I thought I was baiting Court, I was fooling myself. He was no less game for laying cards on the table, as well as laying out the case for my being a lousy fit for the Bureau.

"You're moody. Your Code 20s are too wordy—you're not here to write a book—and you piss people off. You've got no one to blame but yourself."

His complete lack of warmth or couching of sentiments so surprised me that I found it oddly endearing. It was the first time I felt like I could trust him.

I even shared the presence of my recorder with him before shutting the goddamned thing off.

My final days at the Bureau were occupied with a fair amount of soul searching.

That I'd proven myself capable of doing the fundamental project work was, I felt, mostly inarguable. True, I could be needlessly flowery in my written product, but had reined in the practice in recent months.

More inarguable was that I had failed at those things that were informally expected of an SIB deputy. The cauliflower ears from being on the phone all day I could tolerate, but never would I get callouses on my tongue from biting it. Not when people expected me to jump just because they'd barked and occupied some upper rank, worked for the news media, or had some political clout. To my mind, that was part of the problem with the Department and the profession: Too much ass-kissing and an anxious desire to placate the implacable. Sometimes you had to exhibit some backbone, even if you felt uncomfortable doing so.

As my time at the Bureau waned, I worked at taking a more objective view of things and even wondered how long some, such as my captain, might have advocated on my behalf before unseen forces had the axe fall. It was a reasonable consideration as no matter the assignment, I'd always had some support, if not the numbers. In any event, I was surprised to have lasted as long as I did, given that I'd proven no more adaptive to its ways than adoptive of its rules.

Nor was the experience without its benefits.

I learned more about the Department's true operations during my year there than the aggregate amount of time I spent elsewhere on the Department.

Finally, I came to truly appreciate why SIB's avatar was a shark.

But on that April day I felt more alone in the world than I could remember, despite knowing that I had plenty of company when it came to the cadre of those asked to leave.

When both Phillips and MacCloud were eventually asked to leave the Bureau too, I only felt sorry for them.

They, at least, had some business being there.

7

Recidivist Behavior

By June, I was on my way back to Biscailuz Center where I'd started a decade before.

Fuck!

That the administrators at SIB had at least tried to make my departure as comfortable as possible provided a much-needed balm to my battered self-esteem. They'd arranged for me to interview for a Bonus One spot at the jail, a position that would allow me to get my first shot at supervising and a bump in pay too. Shortly after the interview, I was told that the position was mine and would be formalized shortly after my transfer to the facility. As gratifying as the news was, my state of mind would have just as soon had it in writing.

Out of a suit and back in a Class B uniform, I was eating by myself in the Officers' Dining Room of Biscailuz Center my first night back when a deputy called me over and invited me to sit with him and several others.

"My name's Abel Gonzalez," he said, warmly shaking my hand.

Deputy Gonzalez's initiative in introducing himself and several others at the table was an overture that went a long way towards dissipating much of my self-consciousness at the circumstances surrounding my transfer.

Up to that moment, I'd regarded every new face with the question of "Does he know…?" at the back of my mind. I realized that most of my new co-workers probably not only didn't know the circumstances surrounding my transfer, but really didn't give a shit. It was all good.

Unfortunately, I would never be able to let Gonzalez know how much I appreciated his kindness. That very morning at the end of his shift, he drove to San Bernardino to go off-roading near Forest Falls with another deputy, Rob Bakshi. In traversing the undulant terrain, the two lost control on a curve and plunged 200 feet over a cliff. Bakshi was critically injured. Gonzalez was killed.

The news hit me surprisingly hard. Gonzalez had been little more than a stranger to me. And yet he'd left such a big and immediate impression. Suddenly, I felt enormously stupid for worrying about my status on the Department.

The fact was that I was still alive, despite all the haphazard realities of an existence that could end at any moment. Carpe diem.

And so, while I harbored few illusions about promoting, I began studying for the sergeant's exam and spending the early morning shift listening to Pirate radio as the inmates slumbered in their bunks. There were no escapes on my watch this time, and pretty much the only problems entertaining me were non-inmate related.

For the most part, there remained a wonderful consistency about the deputies assigned to Biscailuz. They were young, enthusiastic, and personable.

Exceptions were thankfully few, but they included a trio of deputies who'd tossed my dorm while I was eating in the dining hall.

I was all for searching inmates' belongings, as I didn't like the idea of getting shanked any more than the next guy. But such searches could be done without destroying property, demeaning its owners, and leaving the dorm in a mess and its wards borderline mutinous.

The following day when the watch commander finished his business at briefing, he asked if anybody had anything else to say. I said, "Yes."

The SIB imbroglio had left me shaken and feeling less secure of my standing on the Department than I had a year before. But I also recognized that I was not the deputy I'd been a decade prior and had developed some backbone. I had enough self-assurance to know that I sure as hell wasn't going to tolerate any peer-initiated abuses.

"I recognize the need to search inmates' properties as it relates to officer safety and inmate welfare," I said, staring directly at the deputies who'd visited my dorm in my absence the day before. "But you can conduct these searches without destroying their property or pissing them off. And if you think that you can come into my dorm and pull that shit and leave me to deal with the aftermath, then you're as wrong on that as you are playing the whole avenging angels thing."

I might not have used their names, but there was little doubt as to whom I was talking about and their sullen expressions communicated as much too.

Shortly after I got back to my dorm, the phone calls started.

Most were complimentary, with deputies thanking me for having put the disrupters on notice. Apparently, this had been standard operating procedure with the trio.

But interspersed with these calls were a few others of the "watch your back" variety. As the callers quickly hung up without identifying themselves, I figured I didn't have much to worry about.

I was wrong.

At the conclusion of a briefing, Lt. Benjamin Welk made a point of walking by where I was seated and whispered that he needed to talk to me after briefing.

"It's important."

I had no idea what the problem could be. I'd been keeping my nose clean and getting along well with the other deputies assigned to the facility, a particular trio withstanding.

I caught up with Welk in his office. Normally, he was easygoing with me and sociable. On this day, he retained an uncharacteristic formal posture and his speech was consciously modulated. I asked him if there was any trouble. He said there might be.

"That's why I need to talk to you."

Lt. Welk then plopped a stack of papers atop his desk and started asking about my marital status and its stability. At some point, I saw the name Doug Roman on a document and realized what the inquiry was about.

Roman was an ex-boyfriend of my wife, Stacey. He'd been visiting her parents' house and dropping off flowers in a bid to re-insinuate himself into her life.

Whether or not the spousal unit ever wanted an affair or not was her business. But as she'd made the guy's overtures known to me and expressed concerns about his behavior, I decided to call the number he'd thoughtfully included on a card with the flowers.

"Hi."

"Hello. Is this Doug?"

"Yes."

"My name is Dean Scoville. You've been leaving flowers for my wife at her parents' home."

"Yes."

"Well, I just wanted you to know that I'm a deputy sheriff and…"

"Yeah? So?"

"So you're a rude asshole and I'd like to kick your fucking teeth out!"

Those were the words accurately attributed to me by said asshole in the ensuing complaint he filed with the Department. The onus on Lt. Welk was to determine whether or not I'd made a threat while in an official capacity.

In speaking with Welk, I explained my frame of mind at the time of the call, how I'd been concerned over the man's stalking behavior and what it might portend; how my initial identification of myself as a deputy had been in anticipation of explaining my familiarity with the law and how he was running the risk of being subject to stalking charges; how once the man had interrupted me with a dismissive attitude I'd reverted to my spousal frame of mind and expressed a heartfelt desire I was feeling at that moment; how that desire was sincere, but like my no less heartfelt desire to live in the 90210 area code, was not apt to be realized anytime soon and did not rise to the level of an actual threat.

Lt. Welk was sympathetic to my predicament and, dare I say, supportive of my posture and actions. The idiot's allegations were unfounded and the investigation closed, meaning that the dumb bastard had done little more than enhance my standing around Biscailuz.

Oh, and the asshole was told by the good lieutenant to back off.

We never heard another word from Roman.

When not dealing with avenging angels, would-be Lotharios, and nursing my ego as Biscailuz's prodigal son, I continued my exam studies.

I was well aware that I had a snowball's chance in hell of promoting. Having failed to exhibit some silly-assed obeisance or be some diligent propagandist, I knew that any forthcoming appraisal of promotability by SIB would be middling at best—and that component had historically provided a third of a candidate's final exam score. But taking the exam meant I had nothing to lose and much to occupy my time and addled mind by doing so.

There was another exam on my mind as well.

Having left SIB with my already questionable self-esteem in shambles, I needed some sense of validation.

Growing up I knew that I was at least a little different, and despite some academic evidence to the contrary, smarter than the average bear. It accounted for some of the nicknames bestowed upon me by my peers: "Bomar brain," "Einstein," and "Helen Keller," the last one a nod to my supposedly being able to "see" things that others couldn't.

But after all these years of people telling me how smart I was, it seemed that life was presenting me all manner of evidence to the contrary. Why was my life so damned difficult? Did the desire to live in concert with my own principles and beliefs doom me to forever butt heads with others?

I decided to take the test for Mensa. Despite all manner of encouragement and exhortations to get some sleep, I nervously tossed and turned most of the night. I arrived at the test site with two hours' rest and scared as hell that I'd merely identified one more thing to fail at.

Those with similarly fragile self-esteem will understand how much emphasis I placed on passing this fucking exam. And how good I felt upon finding out that I had passed.

I was surprised, but not impatient, at how long it was taking for my promotion to line senior to take place. But I didn't mind waiting. Working the dorms remained largely uneventful. On Halloween, I brought a bag of Snickers bars into the dorm and was surprised how much the inmates really appreciated their treats. They reminded me how childlike they could be—admittedly, sociopathic children, but all the same...

Many inmates took up drawing to pass the time. Inevitably, they ended up bringing their work to my booth to solicit my opinion.

Having been raised by a commercial artist and spoiled by the likes of Alex Ross, Hal Foster, and Neal Adams, I tended to view their work with a more critical eye. But I was reticent to fess up any honest evaluation, and tended to gloss over their works with, "That's nice. Keep it up."

It struck me as odd that most of my wards tended to be heartless and unsympathetic towards their fellow man—and yet I avoided hurting their fragile egos.

But then, part of me couldn't help but wonder if someone with a writing background wouldn't look at some of my scribblings and say, "That's nice. Keep it up."

For a time, I worked Biscailuz operations, filling in for a deputy who, as a military reserve, had been deployed for the first Gulf War. It was an easier way to bide my time ending my senior stripes than working the dorms, and I appreciated the vote of confidence.

One Monday morning, I sat down at my desk and read a story in the back pages of the *Los Angeles Times* about a videotape that had captured the beating of a motorist named Rodney King.

Wow. Why I haven't I heard more about this?

Lunches were spent in the officers' dining room among the newly promoted and old deputies who were riding it out till their retirement—guys like Jack Marshall, who while working patrol was known to arm-wrestle detainees to see if they'd go to jail (hardly a sporting proposition; he was a perennial favorite in the Police Olympics).

One of the newly promoted was a lieutenant who took a liking to me and began coaching me on the promotional process after I'd passed the written exam.

"Look, it's not enough to just hit the usual bullet-point highlights," he counseled regarding the oral exam. "Whatever problem scenario gets tossed to you, let them know that you are capable of handling it, not only at the supervisor's level, but at a managerial one too. Let them know that you aren't so far removed from patrol that you've forgotten the resources available to you as a deputy and that you'd ensure they are put into play too."

Holding his hands so that their palms faced one another, he slowly retracted them from one another so that an initial gap of perhaps three inches became four feet, his slow expansion emphasizing the words he spoke.

"You need to take it wall-to-wall, A to Z. Don't leave anything out. Touch on the things that the Department finds most important these days—things like lawsuits and things turning to shit. What will you do as a supervisor to make sure that nobody gets their tit in a wringer?"

The lieutenant was Gabe Juarez, and he'd never spent more than 18 months at a given assignment; most he'd been at barely a year. This was of his choosing. He wanted to be exposed to as much of the Department as possible, and go as far up the ladder as he could.

I had absolute faith in his ability to do so. He may have had Cheech Marin's mustache and the residue of his East LA upbringing sometimes asserted itself even when unintended, but he was diamond-sharp and had a fantastic sense of humor.

It occurred to me that he might be grooming me as one of his chosen ones, someone to accompany him on his upward trajectory. Wishful thinking or not, I appreciated what he was doing for me and came to regard him as a friend.

"Be Somebody's Hero."

I had plenty of heroes.

But this period forced a different kind of introspection upon me. I'd always recognized that I was out of sync with the majority of people, but genuinely believed that I'd at least tried to do right by the Bureau—*as I saw it.*

My idealism be damned. I'd recognized the Machiavellian maneuvers for what they were and refused to play the game. But that posture also left me without allies and therefore vulnerable.

Throughout my time with the sheriff's department and since, my choices of role models and heroes have been at play. It wasn't that the men and women I adopted as spiritual guideposts weren't worthy of the respect others and myself accorded them. They were.

One was a legend, working in a merciless capacity as a traffic deputy at Temple Station where the consensus opinion was that the man would even cite his own grandmother. God knows he had enough multi-generational dockets among many of the local families.

Tall and lean and prone to addressing everyone as "Bubba," the cigar-chomping Chuck Thorpe cut a memorable image. Having been voted "most likely to succeed" in high school, a Vietnam war veteran, and the honor cadet of his Academy class, Thorpe possessed the type of pedigree that suggested a person destined to go places.

But Thorpe was not one to suffer fools gladly, irrespective of where they were encountered, or what rank they occupied. If someone made the mistake of soliciting his opinion, he was apt to share it with a candor that inspired much respect and little appreciation by its intended audience.

Still, I believe that if he'd wanted to that Thorpe could have promoted and gravitated as high as he desired on the Department. But he retired as a deputy.

The inability of certain deputies to co-sign someone else's B.S., accommodate the insincere, or bite one's tongue had left big impressions on me.

I always wondered how far such men and women might have

ascended within the Department's ranks had they exhibited as much political tact as they had political savvy (just because they didn't play the reindeer games didn't mean they didn't know how to or were incapable of recognizing who was). Had they been burdened with the kind of Type A personality that caused a fellow Industry sergeant to retire because of a heart attack, they might well have. But the fact that they didn't endeared them to me all the more.

My romantic take on their attitudes had a lot to do with my own. I probably internalized more than I should have each time I saw Clint or the Duke take some martinet down a peg or two.

Despite my having ended up at one of the Department's gulags, a fellow malcontent and I still ended up making sergeant before everyone else we'd left at the Bureau, and I would be a damned liar if I said that outcome didn't warm the cockles of my spiteful heart. It'd be similarly wrong of me not to acknowledge my having been the beneficiary of a timely and singular change in promotional protocol. Whereas the "appraisal of promotability" portion of previous and succeeding promotional exams were factored in arbitrarily apportioned numbers, this particular exam obligated evaluators to simply conclude "yes" or "no" as to whether or not the candidate was capable of performing as a sergeant and deserving of it. Even SIB couldn't deny me that.

Subsequent appraisal portions of promotional exams would revert back to a numbers-weighted one, thereby ensuring many more years of intra-Departmental ass-kissing. But I'd lucked out.

That the transfer out of SIB and its attendant bump in pay ensured a commensurate increase in my starting sergeant pay was just icing on the cake. It looked like the SIB fiasco had, in the long run, actually worked out for my benefit. There would have been no way in hell I could have studied as much or as well at SIB.

Whatever my assignment, I wanted to be accepted for who I really was and what I really believed in.

That this bid for candor proved costly at my prior assignments was as evident as the fact that I hadn't learned a damned thing by it. And at Biscailuz, I screwed up a good thing with Juarez.

My straight-shooter act was abutted with the sincere conviction that I not only could be honest with my friends and co-workers, but that I should be—particularly if they were one and the same.

And so it was that when the cultural sensitivity training commenced, I vented to one of its most adamant supporters: Juarez.

"It's bullshit," I said. "All it did was give me another way to say 'fuck you' to an Eskimo."

"No," Juarez asserted. "You're missing the point. It's to remind you that people who've been raised differently than you have different viewpoints too. That you should be sensitive to them."

"Why? Why do I have to familiarize myself with them? Hell, there's some 300 different languages spoken in the County. How many am I supposed to take up? Whatever happened to people just moving here and assimilating? It's all B.S."

Juarez glowered at me, but didn't speak any further. He didn't have to. His expression communicated all I had to know. I'd blown it.

We barely spoke another word to one another again.

8

What Did You Do During the Riots, Daddy?

In the spring of 1992, I was promoted to sergeant and, after a supervisory course, transferred back to the division of status and olfactory offenders.

This time my custody stint was to be spent at Men's Central Jail—known as MCJ throughout the Department, and as CJ among local criminals.

I'd been aware that MCJ deputies tended to have a more aggressive reputation than custody deputies elsewhere and were on the cliquish side. Faced with the prospect of walking into a lion's den, I was perhaps more sensitive to the prospect than I should have been.

In any event, I braced a deputy who'd situated his ass in front of me and was jaw-jacking while I was giving briefing in the jail chapel. In fairly assertive terms, I told him to be quiet and that shit wasn't going to fly on my watch. The deputy sat up and stared at me in aggressive silence and I realized that I'd not only pissed him off, but many of his friends sitting in the pews behind him. My first day and already I was on the verge of all hell breaking loose in this custodial house of God.

Cutting the briefing short, I let the deputies go about their duties, monitoring inmates, addressing their needs, escorting them to chow and yard time, and conducting their cell searches. While I tried to be more diplomatic thereafter, I knew that I'd left a bad initial impression by trying to assert my authority from the get go. It was a lesson I'd have to learn all over again and for the same reason: my insecurity in a new environment.

That said, I felt more comfortable in my new position otherwise. I had good senior deputies—deputies who worked in the same capacity

I had at Biscailuz the month before—who acted as insulating buffers between the line deputies and myself. It was through them that I gave many of my marching orders for a shift, and from whom I acquired intel on what was going on out of my view. I came to appreciate most of them, although a couple gave me pause.

One with a thousand-mile stare downright creeped me out: Trevor Church. This was the same Trevor Church who before the decade was out would kill himself after having been identified through DNA evidence as the man who'd shot and killed LASD Sergeant George Arthur in 1985.

I wasn't naïve, and suspected that there was some selective exposition to some of the narratives describing what had happened between a deputy and an inmate. But I was also reasonably sure that whatever I wasn't made privy to was not of earthshaking importance. So long as a deputy didn't give me cause to second-guess his actions, I wasn't going to. The Department had enough of that shit going on already. I hoped to generate a reciprocal expectation that just as I would trust their actions and have their backs when it came to force incidents, they would likewise have mine in not needlessly generating force incidents or going overboard in handling them.

For all the import the Department gave to developing operations plans for well-anticipated problems, I was surprised and disappointed at the lack of the Department's prior planning when it came to the pending Rodney King verdicts.

Perhaps it was following LAPD's lead. After all, if LAPD Chief Daryl Gates had backpedaled after the black community accused him of helping to fan the pending flames, then Sheriff Block sure as hell wasn't going to put his political ass out on a limb by implementing his own politically incorrect drills and procedures.

Still, every cop in Los Angeles County knew things were going to kick off. It was that thought that accompanied me as I made my way down to the watch commander's office shortly after my arrival at MCJ.

Likewise, newly promoted Lt. Mitchell Jones was the watch commander that day. As watch sergeant, I suggested that it'd be prudent to lock down all of the inmates until the fervor settled down outside the jail.

"We can feed them in their cells," I said. "Otherwise, these fuckers will go off as soon as they get the news and we'll have our hands full. We need to cancel visits, turn off the TVs, and lock down the rows. Just keep them isolated from what's happening."

Doing so would be a violation of California's Code of Regulations Title 15. It would also run the risk of our asses getting sued if someone caught on. I could see the wheels turning in Jones' mind as he digested the suggestion and factored in these and other concerns.

But given the atmosphere of the jail and the grumbling of the inmates, it not only seemed like the lesser of two evils, but pretty goddamned necessary. That I should have to be saying this at all surprised me. I would have thought someone would have had the foresight to develop an operations plan for the riot that everyone was anticipating and nobody wanted to talk about.

Finally, Jones said, "Do it."

I contacted the floor sergeants and passed on the word. There was more grumbling from the inmates, then the jail became early morning quiet.

A couple hours later, I was back in the watch commander's office watching Reginald Denny taking bricks to the head and thankful that Jones had acted on my suggestion as, by nightfall, riots were breaking out at the County's other custody facilities.

Indeed, all hell was breaking loose throughout the County.

But at MCJ things were surprisingly quiet, despite the fact that the jail's population more than doubled over the next four days to the point that we even had inmates sleeping in the chapel.

Much has been said regarding the riots, particularly about what fomented them and how they were handled. Or not handled.

That the leaders of both LAPD and LASD had fucked up was a given. It may be apocryphal that Nero fiddled while Rome burned, but Gates had certainly gone to dinner, leaving his friend Sherman Block effectively immobilized for fear of stepping on Gates' toes by taking any action without his input.

By the time Gates did show up, it was too late. At night, the newscast started off with, "They came demanding justice, but settled for stolen tennis shoes…" and followed with images of stores being gutted by looters and fires.

That the news media was largely calling it civil unrest struck me as an oxymoronic euphemism. There was nothing civil about it; and as far as unrest was concerned—give me a fucking break: It was a full-fledged riot.

The idiots who attacked motorists and pedestrians were wholly and solely responsible for their actions—that was a given. But the failure to stop the riot in its nascent state was a systemic one, with the confluence of factors including self-proclaimed community activists, cowardly city council people and one vindictive police chief.

That Gates continues to enjoy a fairly favorable reputation in local circles continues to astound me. True, his successors have in some ways made him look better by comparison; certainly, he was for a time more supportive of his troops.

But I'd read Gates' autobiography and, to my mind, any man who'd tested number one on every promotional exam he took and was a veteran of the Watts Riots knew very well what he was doing when he elected to do nothing the night of April 29, 1992. Gates, already on his way out, was giving a big ol' *digitus impudicus* to the city.

Emotionally, I couldn't blame him. He'd been vilified seemingly every time he'd opened his mouth, sometimes with good reason. He'd even implemented riot contingency training, only to cancel it incident to protests by community leaders.

Still, he was wrong. Over 50 people would die in Los Angeles over the five days following the verdict, and next to the murderers themselves, I held Gates and his kind responsible. They could have taken control of the situation early on, but failed to do so. It was derelict in my book and that of many other cops. Hell, guys at the jail were chomping at the bit to jump into a hoopty and roll Code 3 to Florence and Normandie to get that truck driver the hell out of Dodge.

Instead, we monitored the inmates as they were fed on their cell rows.

As our shifts switched to 12-on/12-off, smoke hung over downtown and the freeways were empty. The only commuters were EMS workers hauling ass to and from work. Some were attacked—one deputy shot and killed an attacker while off duty. I found the drive to and from work surreal, keeping my gun unholstered and by my side the entire time.

When the riots officially ended five days later, 53 people would be dead and over a billion dollars lost in property damage.

Every custody facility in the County would have a riot-related disturbance, except one. Men's Central Jail, the largest custody facility in the otherwise free world.

I didn't end up pulling my weapon during the riots, but did a couple of months later.

I was driving home after my shift at MCJ when I saw a bloodied Hispanic man stagger off the curb and into the lanes of traffic on the Macy Street Bridge. As he came into view of my headlights, I could see the man's upper torso saturated with blood and his face, a portrait of abject terror. He glanced back to where a second man was stepping off the east curb 100 feet behind him.

In marked contrast to the first, the second male's expression was one of resolve, a determination to finish whatever it was that he'd started. With cars behind me and still more oncoming traffic, I was forced to drive past the two men to a point where I could safely activate my hazard lights and effect a U-turn.

Concurrent with my turn, the bloodied man crossed to the south-bound lanes I'd just vacated in a bid to put northbound commuters between himself and the man trailing him. With traffic between himself and his assailant, he began to run back across the bridge towards me.

But nighttime traffic was fast thinning out, and the second man rapidly crossed the street behind the first. Hitting my high beams, I parked in the number one lane just as the red-shirted stranger ran up to my car. I stepped out of my car, my .38 revolver in hand. The man immediately lifted his shirt. Blood streamed from two large holes in his torso.

"Is that the man that did this to you?" I pointed at the man in the coat behind him.

A terrified nod yes and I realized my victim was Spanish speaking. Damn.

The second man stopped momentarily and studied me, then did an about-face, doubling back double-time for the opposite sidewalk. I called out, "Stop!"

And with that the man suddenly spun towards me, something long and metallic in his right-hand momentarily coming into view.

Gun or knife?

Had he shot or stabbed the victim?

What immediate threat does he pose for me?

The thoughts were spinning in my head like a slot machine. Intuition, more than anything else, locked each wheel into place as my trigger finger began to constrict.

But then the suspect reversed rotation, turning fully away from me and taking off in a full sprint. I gave chase, but he jumped over the side of the Macy Street Bridge and disappeared into darkness.

Cautiously skirting past his point of descent, I rounded the end of the bridge. The sight of numerous street denizens, living in the darkness beneath the overpass, greeted me. My suspect could be hidden anywhere among or beyond them.

I paralleled the bridge for a time, trying to determine just which of the portals the assailant might have entered. But without my flashlight, and with my safety compromised by the LAPD helicopter that backlit me, I gave up. Retreating to my vehicle, I held my flat badge over my head in the hopes that the pilot would spot it.

As I neared the car, I found my victim resting against it and pantomimed a skyward request for an ambulance that was soon accommodated.

Several LAPD black-and-whites arrived shortly thereafter and effected a containment. But an hour later, it became clear that the suspect had evaded detection. Later, I was advised that my victim had a 40 percent chance of survival.

My inability to discern the nature of the suspect's weapon had allowed him to escape, and that bothered me. I'd been on the Department long enough that I should have formulated a better game plan in the seconds available to me. My frustration was doubled as for all my desire to give the handling officers as accurate a description of the man as I could, the image that kept flashing to mind was that of the man who'd charged me with the knife on Hollywood Boulevard a decade before.

The feelings I felt on the drive home that night were markedly different than those felt a decade before. Whereas I'd once brooded about having been prevented from shooting someone wielding a knife, I now agonized about my own decision not to fire.

Had my hesitancy to fire my weapon resulted in the suspect's hurting or killing another person?

Had I the presence of mind to ask the victim *cuchillo* or *pistola*, would it have made a difference?

I will never know.

Working the sheriff's department sometimes left me feeling like a goddamned platypus. There were custody deputies, patrol deputies, and all manner of specialized deputies working all kinds of assignments.

That I was now part of the jail supervisor phylum was evident by the lack of a gun on my hip, the absence of a ballistic vest on my torso, and a cloth badge on my chest where a metal one had once been. The color scheme of the uniform adhered within the color prism of the basic eight Crayolas, but was cut of a different, more comfortable, cloth. I carried pepper spray, but never had cause to use it thanks to one of God's greatest creations, delegated force.

If I hadn't quite come to terms with what I was destined to be on the Department, I at least had some sense of what I wanted to be; figuring that if I couldn't be one of its defining agents, I might be a redefining one.

But even here I was frustrated. More and more I saw that things I'd suggested at SIB or patrol were often destined to be dismissed out of hand.

In patrol, there were times when I'd been immobilized by optimism, that any number of the myriad options available to me were viable and no single one more desirable than the other. I'd acquired faith in my ability to justify my every action and inaction, and justified in offering dissent to opinions that threatened what I perceived was our mission.

But my return to custody, and the circumstances preceding it, had left a more monochromatic take on my mood and energies. I felt that I was destined to follow a middling path to some inconclusive end and continually pursue agreeable distractions with which to entertain myself.

Sure, I was determined to keep putting shit in the pipeline, if not with the frequency or enthusiasm I once did, then whenever it was convenient. Nor did I care about getting acknowledged for my ideas (so long as nobody else received credit for them. That would piss me off). The important thing was that I knew I'd at least tried to do something and that time would prove me right and the smug sons-a-bitches that ignored me would be proven wrong.

Despite the fact that Lt. Jones commended me for my suggestion that we violate Title 15, it was one of the few times that my custodial advice was acted upon. Other ideas, such as my repeatedly arguing that deputies should be allowed to carry recording devices inside the jail, were ignored or shot down to peals of derisive laughter in the briefing room where the brass had assembled. "Are you joking?" one lieutenant asked me. "Do you really believe we want subordinates recording what we say in here?"

Like I could give a shit.

The fact remained that I'd done my homework. Such practices would be legal in most areas of Odorama Central save for attorney room and penitent-clergy settings (and if they had been allowed in the case of the latter, then a certain famous ex-football star might today be doing his richly deserved sentence for the double murders he had committed—and the culpability for which he had yelled out his confession to another former football star-turned-pastor visiting him in the jail). In short, I thought that some objective recording of events would prove invaluable.

As it stood, we were having to rely solely on our ever-diminishing credibility to validate our every action and inaction, such as when deputies had one version of events, and the civilian staff another, regarding a use-of-force incident in the facility's medical wing.

That law enforcement agencies had a history of excluding high IQ candidates was something of common knowledge. Such episodes did little to deter me from the belief that at least LASD's promotional mindset was similarly constituted and I'd truly been lucky in skating on the psychological exam.

As my every suggestion got knocked down in MCJ's version of conversational whack-a-mole, I spent most of 1993 in petulant supervision of the 4000 and 5000 floors on night shift, and celebrated the New Year watching *Dick Clark's New Year's Rocking Eve* on my pocket television while sitting on my ass inside the Jail Investigations Unit. More and more I wondered: *Why fucking bother?* So what if I didn't buddy up to administrators and kiss their collective asses? The suggestions I'd made deserved consideration even if I didn't, but when it came to judgment and initiative my alleged superiors lacked either.

Once again, I found myself courting distractions, indulging in petty vices and working out on duty whenever possible. This protest did not prevent me from being ever vigilant for one sworn enemy: Lt. John Wieselscheiss, who could recite the Department Manual verbatim but didn't have a novel thought in his head, could be counted upon to make his 5:00 a.m. rounds in a bid to catch me or one of my peers fucking up.

Frustrating his every effort was one of the few highlights I had during this period.

Part of me was intrigued at my inability to get things done on the Department. After all, college professors had taught me the academic hazards of indulging in any real novelty of thought, and my ability to regurgitate their spoon-fed pabulum was the stuff decent GPAs are made of. That same cagey couching of opinion served me well enough in the Sheriff's Academy, where a degree of conformity and uniformity was expected.

I'd long since come to know the hazards of not adhering to the party line and that the exhibition of fearlessness or initiative outside of matters of life or death could tempt ostracism. Dissent was fine, but only in the abstract.

The reality was that the Department was an organism that would expel foreign bodies to preserve its homeostasis. Those who deviated from script found themselves expelled from the Academy, 86'ed out of custody, banned from patrol and barred from promotion.

Thus it was that men who had no trepidation at pulling over carloads of armed men proved reticent to speak candidly in offering in-house dissent.

I realized that for all my ideals, I was not markedly different. In trying to make as few waves as possible while appeasing the need to speak my mind, I'd saddled myself on a marginal career path. There was no way in hell I would ever insinuate myself into a position to make the changes that I wanted to make.

I wondered if I couldn't be like some judge who cannily orchestrated appellate court rulings in order to curry favor with a president and gain appointment to the highest court—then legislate from the bench as he saw fit.

But I couldn't. Part of it was a desire to abstain from Dad's art of bullshitting to get what he wanted. I wanted people to genuinely know what I believed and why. I could prostitute myself academically without problem. There, I was part of a transitory and anonymous population whose works were evaluated through some paradigm, assigned an arbitrary grade, and tossed.

Cosigning the bullshit of others? No.

That did not mean the Department wasn't changing. A certain fidelity might be expected of its working parts, but when external pressures—such as self-proclaimed community activists, members of the clergy, politicians, litigants, and the news media—brought their considerable forces to bear upon it, the Department proved quite adaptive. Already I could see how incidents such as Rodney King and the Department's Arco-Narco scandal (wherein members of an elite narcotics team, including a fellow Class 213 graduate, were taken down for skimming, extorting, and stealing money during search warrant services) had affected everything from the Department's operating budget to its policies and morale. The Department had changed more in a couple of years than it had the entire preceding decade.

Among those changes were force policies, both for patrol and custody.

On the one hand, there were more options on the less lethal weaponry front. On the other hand, there was an unspoken expectation that such options be explored before deadly force was employed. It didn't matter that failure to deploy deadly force might have resulted in an officer's death, either. There were more and more incidents where deputies had deployed deadly force and been fired for doing so—only to get their jobs back through civil service hearings.

The insult was multifold. The involved deputy was stigmatized; the termination set an inhibiting precedent for other deputies; the deputy would be re-hired only to retire on stress. Such had been the outcome for shootings in Lakewood, Century, Firestone, Ladera Heights, and other LASD jurisdictions.

I saw such incidents as political concessions by an upper echelon still hell-bent on placating the implacable, this time by making sacrificial offerings of its personnel. It seemed as though Sheriff Block had adopted a "shame on them for putting the Department in the spotlight" attitude whenever a shooting became controverted.

For the moment, I was immune to all of this. Indeed, while the Department was transitioning to the 9mm Beretta as the standard issue sidearm, I was able to continue carrying my preferred wheel gun (it was easier to clean and slightly more evocative of the wild west). All I had to worry about was that the force used on my floors were within policy and could pass muster under the evaluative eyes of outsiders.

This was not as easy as I'd hoped, given an environment wherein lieutenants and others seemingly saw many of the sergeants and deputies as rife for some manner of vicarious implication that would liberate them of the bars on their collars. The way I saw it, things at Men's Central Jail generally went according to plan, despite the fact that the facility was under-staffed with a horrendous ratio of inmates to deputies.

But then Captain Phil Scarpelli and Lt. Lawrence Muirhead would pull some sergeant aside and express concern about force issues, such as the number of pepper spray incidents on the 3000 floor.

We sergeants tried to explain the realities of working the floor; that deputies destined to encounter varying degrees of resistance from particularly obdurate segments of the jail population, such as gang and diminished capacity modules, were thereby obligated to overcome said resistance for their own welfare as well as that of other inmates. That their failure to do so tended to find shit spiraling out of control otherwise.

Such explanations did not satisfy the lieutenants who convened a meeting to discuss the perceived problem.

Accommodating us with a bar graph detailing the exponential increase of pepper spray incidents relative to the decrease of force incidents, the brass openly speculated that deputies were becoming promiscuous in their deployment of Scovilles. (Yep, such are the means by which the hotness of chilis and the like are measured. I suspect that somewhere is a family crest adorned with a smocked sadist putting pepper on some poor bastard's tongue.)

That there'd been a marked increase in the number of pepper spray incidents was not exactly counter-intuitive. When the nature of a use-of-force option is reclassified to a lessor means of problem mitigation, people are going to use it. At least they weren't going over the top of inmates' heads with flashlights or executing Bruce Lee kicks to their groins.

One would have thought this an improvement by any objective standard. After all, our wards weren't displaced Peace Corps volunteers, or people whose sole concern was the welfare of aquatic mammals. We were dealing with people for whom violence was the lingua franca of both the streets and their home away from home.

Nonetheless, we assured the brass that we would try to keep things in check.

By any objective standard, the deputies' interactions with the inmates were overwhelmingly professional. Certainly, it wasn't anything that approximated Abu Ghraib.

Even those deputies for whom I didn't hold any particular affection handled themselves well for the most part—at least when I was around.

I did notice an increase in the number of force incidents on my floors during my days off. This, I interpreted less as a matter of abuse than an increased willingness to interact with the inmates when a more favored sergeant was around.

I may not have been hated—nobody ever vandalized my car or otherwise fucked with me—but I sure as hell wasn't one of the boys either.

Outside of being denied certain positions, my inability to be accepted as "one of the boys" had always been perfectly fine by me. Nobody would ever find me in an Arco-Narco line-up. Even Temple Station fuck-ups could not implicate me in their peculiar sociopathology. They may have, for a time, deluded themselves and others, but I was among those not shocked upon hearing that they'd been found dirty for authoring falsified reports, planting evidence, and assault under the color of authority. Several other deputies constituted a small crime ring among themselves, stealing credit cards from people they'd stopped. Even horndogs that I might otherwise have some empathy for did shit-stupid stuff that I would never have even contemplated. Fired or prosecuted for their transgressions, the actions of these men affected me in ways good and bad.

That guys who'd always acted like they were something they weren't—better cops than I—were now being punished for what they actually were—thieves, bullies, and rapists—afforded me an agreeable sense of schadenfreude.

But that was a self-serving silver lining. The bottom line was that the actions of these idiots and sociopaths reflected on the whole of the profession, endangering its practitioners by feeding into the whole "corrupt cop" mythos.

And while there were many great custody deputies—a vast majority, in fact—it was also true that the idiot representation was much higher in custody than on patrol. For every bad apple that had cleared patrol training, more had tripped up along the way. Often, this had been in their first post–Academy assignment in custody where they'd been busted for abusing inmates, selling contraband, and insinuating drugs into the jail.

To the degree that my particular shift or floor had spared me with having to deal with such morons, I was appreciative. But the longer I was there and the more precipitous the drop-off in hiring standards became manifest, the more I knew it'd be a matter of time before some immature deputy would fuck up royally and somehow I'd be made to pay for it on some front, if not civilly, then professionally.

I wanted out.

9

Middling Management

My ass might have been stuck in custody, but it seemed my heart had never really left patrol.

I was surprised at how anxious I was to return to patrol as a sergeant, given how equally anxious I'd been to get out of it as a deputy. Something inside me felt as though some hard acquired and invaluable truth had slipped away somewhere along the line, and I worried if I wasn't falling prey to that "be careful what you ask for" thing all over again. Why would I want to return to something I'd campaigned to escape from? Was my otherwise vaunted memory really that bad? Or was I simply to be pissing and moaning no matter where I was assigned?

I realized that for all my pessimism, some part of me was optimistic that things might be better if I worked in a different capacity—sergeant—and at a different station. There was some basis for my hope. After all, I'd enjoyed working the Hall, both my stints at Biscailuz, and most of my time at Temple. It was only the station politics that'd been my bugbear.

And so I began lobbying to get to a station on the east side of the county. My first stop was at Walnut Station with its commander, future Undersheriff Lenny Waldo. He acted like someone had put the lips to me.

At least I'd had some prior contact with Industry Station's Capt. Marcus Nakamura when he was a lieutenant at Biscailuz while I was an off-the-streeter—a tidbit that I was conscientious enough to mention during my interview. Whether or not it put me over the hump or not, I can't say.

But I did make the transfer list to patrol.

And much like I'd hoped, things started out promising enough as Sam Shimano and I were reunited, with Shimano once again mentoring me.

After spending my first day at Industry getting familiarized with the nuances of the station and the role of watch sergeant, Shimano introduced me to life in the field as 140S ("One-Forty-Sam" translated as Industry Station field sergeant: 14 denoted the station number and "Sam" was the phonetic that corresponded with "sergeant").

Within minutes of leaving the station, Shimano ran the license plate of a family van.

"Looks like the Brady Bunch ride," I mused.

"Yeah, but Greg and Bobby have shaved heads."

The van came back stolen. I was impressed; and later, after the suspects were booked, asked Shimano if such felony arrests always came so easily at Industry.

"That's only my second in two years," he laughed.

Not counting one off-duty arrest I'd made while at SIB, that was still at least two more than what I'd made in my five years out of patrol, an absence that proved damnably apparent on multiple fronts.

For one, the deputy's daily worksheets were no longer done on paper but on the monolithic Mobile Digital Terminal that now dominated the passenger compartments of our patrol vehicles. With so many state-of-the-art bells and whistles, the MDT intimidated the hell out of me and I had to pat my familiar Smith and Wesson Model 15 .38 revolver on my hip for comfort.

That I'd retained my trusty revolver this long was owed to my intra–Department transfers not accommodating my training in the use of its replacement, the Beretta 92F 9 mm semi-auto. Out of 8500 sworn personnel, I was among the last of a breed. Curious Industry deputies paraded around me like I was some kind of dinosaur, occasionally tapping at the thing on my hip and asking, "What the hell is this?"

It was a revolver, as old school and romantic a wheel gun as to be found in this day and age.

And as far as I was concerned, the longer I could dodge the Beretta, the better.

Once Shimano had covered all the bases and figured it was time for me to sink or swim on my own, he signed me off training, an emancipation that spared me worry. (It seemed that no matter where I was on the Department, I was always destined for some goddamned training or probationary period, eventualities I'd come to dread since my SIB fiasco).

From the get-go, I felt pretty optimistic at Industry, although there was some initial temptation to act on every brainwashing mechanism I'd been exposed to in supervisor's school. At one point, while dealing with a suicidal numbnuts threatening to jump off the roof of a building, I even asked some deputies to see if they could find a mattress for him to land on. Then asked myself: *Really?*

Soon enough, I was letting my own intuitions guide my actions.

Whereas life as a custody sergeant had been predictably sedate— the occasional riot notwithstanding—life as a patrol supervisor offered no shortage of things to keep me busy.

As watch sergeant, I'd occasionally conduct briefings (if the field sergeant was too busy), assign vehicles and radios to the next shift, walk facility and jail checks, and handle whatever else popped up on the station radar. The rest of the time, I was apt to be performing CPR on deputies' reports, or answering the telephone.

"Industry watch sergeant's office, Sgt. Scoville speaking. How can I help you?"

That scripted offer of assistance could find me dealing with just about anything under the sun, including people who wanted their refrigerators cleaned out, mail brought in, and trash cans emptied. Plumbing requests were not uncommon.

That these calls got routed to me was initially befuddling. But when I braced the desk on the issue, I was told that this was how things were done. If someone didn't like the answer they'd gotten from the desk, they were to be transferred to the watch sergeant. This was not the way we did business at Temple, but then as Marvin Gaye once said, "Mercy, mercy me. Things aren't what they used to be."

Maternal concerns were at least understandable. Often, they would come from a mother worried that her son was being harassed by deputies because he looked like a gang member, but wasn't.

I never understood this perspective, and made it a point to ask the caller why they didn't do something about the kid's appearance instead of calling up the station. My parental concern would be less about some cop stopping my child, but whether or not an actual gang member might mistakenly identify him as a member in good standing before pulling alongside him and asking that most loaded question: "Where you from?"

Because for all the talk of precipitous police shootings, *that* was when the shots were most apt to ring out.

Inevitably, the caller would say she understood where I was coming from, but the lack of commitment in her voice told me loud and clear that she wasn't going to do anything about it.

If most of our constituents were ultimately apathetic about changing things for the better, I figured that there wasn't much I could do to placate them either. Many that I dealt with were second and third generation gang affiliates; others didn't want or have cause to do anything with us, unless it was to have us come over to change a father-in-law's diapers. Our demurrals were usually followed with a timely reminder of who paid our salary. Some deputies were known to offer a nickel rebate.

My main mission was to just get along with the people I worked with and protect those who were protecting everyone else. If I succeeded at that level, I'd be ahead of the game (particularly given my mercurial disposition).

To that end, I tried to run interference on behalf of the deputies as much as possible. If people wanted to call and bitch about the deputies, I'd give them an ear; if they demanded to see a supervisor in person, I was there. Almost invariably, by the time our interaction with one another was concluded, they'd reconsidered their postures on the offending deputy and concluded I was the bigger asshole.

I could live with that. After all, I had been.

Now that I was back in a radio car as often as not, I was able to see how much things had changed during my time out of the field.

One of the first things I noticed upon my return to patrol was a more generalized disrespect for its practitioners. Be it Joe Citizen or Gabriel Gang Banger, people were more open with their hostilities. Whether manifested through facial expressions, the tone of their voices, their choice of rhetoric, or overall demeanor, there was no mistaking the contempt many held for us.

Naturally resentful of being held liable for a debt I'd not incurred, I found myself hard-pressed not to justify their conclusions: *Oh, you think I'm an asshole? Well, far be it from me to prove you wrong...*

Even on this point, I generally proved chicken shit in every sense of the word. Still, extracting any pound of flesh was apt to be sublimated on some asshole whose sole threat was to my physical safety. Other, more sentient creatures, received their own brand of amnesty, if only because I didn't want any more complaints in my personnel jacket than absolutely necessary.

Weeks went by, and I familiarized myself with who the local street gangs and their affiliates were (one needed an NFL flow-chart), where the biggest problem locations were (Bassett, Valinda), and the best local eateries that popped (gave free food). Despite an expressed opposition, I was sent to Beretta training and transitioned to my new sidearm. If I remained somewhat intimidated by the semi-automatic, I'd at least begun feeling comfortable in my role as a patrol supervisor.

Already I'd earned the respect of some deputies, the opprobrium of others, and was probably considered neither here nor there by most as I only worked the one shift, thereby minimizing contact with most assigned to the station. Whatever else, I felt much more at ease than I had at Men's Central Jail. Patrol deputies tended to be more mature, particularly given the amount of time many had spent working custody. Whereas I'd been fortunate to make my first station in seven months, some deputies were having to wait four years and longer, particularly to an in-demand East-end station like Industry.

As far as the brass went, my failure to appear at a station meeting in the first month—an honest-to-God oversight—pissed off Captain Nakamura. He never quite warmed to me after that, and it was obvious that my absence had not impressed others in the station command either.

Not that I was destined to be wild about some of them in any event. My naturally defensive nature made it easy for me to write more than a few off as type A personalities bucking for rank, or sour-pusses with no joie de vivre. God forgive the occasional mix and match, because I wouldn't.

Thankfully, these were in the minority. For the most part, I liked the lieutenants and my peers, most of whom possessed a sense of humor and didn't take themselves so seriously. It was nice to be among people who were more concerned about getting the job done than determined to be liked, or disliked, by the deputies.

Industry Station's jurisdiction offered few surprises. I'd grown up in this east end of the San Gabriel Valley. My childhood in Valinda, one of the unincorporated County areas within the station's boundaries, had given me enough first-hand experience with the Hispanic gang demographic to give me some idea what I was in for. As a child, I didn't appreciate their predatory instincts, particularly as it was never a one-on-one affair. It encouraged a certain racism, and among us white kids it was common knowledge that if "you fight one bean, you take on the whole burrito." A friend and I would get in a fight on the playground and the ensuing brawl would be like the ending of *The Wild Bunch* all over again, with the Mexicans kicking the shit out of both of us. Later, by the time I reached Temple, my racism had abated and, if anything, I had a better empathy for what the Hispanic demographic had to deal with on the peer pressure front when it came to street gangs. This allowed me to get along pretty well with locals on both sides of the law, some of whom had christened me "The Loco Gabacho."

But whereas the gang-related hostilities associated with my childhood of the sixties and seventies involved little more than the occasional knife or baseball bat, succeeding decades had seen the violence increase in both frequency and intensity. That this period roughly coincided with the whole MPAA thing and a plethora of films featuring Peckinpah-like choreographed violence was something I am still waiting for sociologists to look into. But suffice it to say where gunplay had once been the exception, it had since become the norm when it came to interspecial hostilities.

The first drive-by shooting I'd ever heard of had taken place my senior year of high school. A classmate, Carlos Valvodino, had been shot and killed while sitting in a vehicle less than a mile from my house. Neither he nor his friend, who was also wounded, had any gang affiliation. Both had been nice guys, and the act seemed so fucking stupid and anomalous that I couldn't imagine it happening again.

But it did, and with such increasing frequency that drive-bys became so commonplace within Los Angeles County that within a decade hundreds of inner city youths were killed every year in drive-bys.

"Where you from, vato?"

"What clique you with?"

"What's your name, homie?"

Just as one might today want to haul ass at the first syllable of "Allahu Akbar!" in a food court, a similar tack was advised when hearing any of these unwinnable questions. I'd heard that a visitor from Tucson was standing in East LA when, in response to such a question, answered "Arizona"—which coincided with the name of a local street gang. At least his injuries had not proved fatal.

That could not be said of many others, though. Intended victims, proficient in the arts of hyperkinetic contortionism and haul-ass, might evade an ambush only to have a bystander shot and killed instead. Such a tragedy accounted for more than one momentary lull, as when a member of Eme (the Mexican Mafia) lost a loved one in a drive-by gone wrong and decreed that shooters were expected to walk up to intended targets thereafter.

Short-term gang prohibitions aside, there wasn't much that could be done to stop the tide of violence—not with the synergy of cops increasingly coming under public and media scrutiny. The more that cops attempted to intervene and stop prospective players, the more they entertained pro forma allegations of racism. As the demographic shooting black youths to the tune of 400+ a year mirrored that of the victims, jamming Asians and whites just to keep up appearances would have been a waste of time and constrained resources.

One example drove the point home: After the drive-by killing of a small child, Altadena Station deputies were tasked with hitting gang members hard in hopes of preventing a second shooting.

It lasted one weekend.

County supervisors got one too many complaints, then told the deputies to stand down and the shootings continued.

If you were to examine my personnel jacket, you would find no mention of Shepherd and me saving the man's life in Duarte. Nor would you find any documentation of other things that perhaps warranted some level of acknowledgment, both good and bad.

Sometimes things just fell through the cracks. Some supervisors were more conscientious about documenting "Aw, shits" and "attaboys" than others, a posture most often attributable to some asshole in the equation.

Shepherd's denied recognition on the C.P.R. incident was simply a matter of his being collateral damage.

When the fire captain called to advise of our rescue of the cardiac arrest victim, the person on the other end of the line had been a Temple supervisor that I absolutely hated and who assiduously returned the favor.

Ernie Hoferschwein had also been a thorn in my side from the time our paths first crossed. But while it seemed that his mission in life was to give credence to the assertion that short people were mean because they were closer to hell, my primary grievance was my personal conviction that he'd crashed into my Porsche 924—yes, a piece of shit, but *my* piece of shit—and driven off the station parking lot.

In keeping with my nature, I communicated my suspicions to him in the same parking lot where the incident had taken place. This precipitated an exchange of mutual "Fuck yous," and my transfer request for ELA station.

The captain called me into his office and asked what was up. I told him.

"What would it take for you to stay?" he asked.

"The guarantee that this particular sergeant will never handle anything of a supervisory nature relating to me, up to and including saying, 'Hi.'"

"You got it."

And no words were exchanged between the sergeant and myself from then on.

However, the fact remained that the conclusion of the fire captain's call also marked the conclusion of anything more being said of our rescue. Again, I'd gotten what I'd asked for: The sergeant had not dealt with me in any supervisory capacity over the matter.

Hoferschwein ultimately ended up leaving the Department under murky circumstances, including domestic violence issues. The last I heard, his residence was an officer safety hazard hit in nearby Arcadia: "Former LASD SEB with numerous firearms and K9s. Supervisor to respond to location incident to any calls to location."

Thankfully, most of my Temple supervisors had been better than that.

Formally, and informally, they often took the time to run interference on my behalf, calming the aggrieved nerves of would-be complainants and smoothing ruffled feathers.

While Helbing had given me a wonderful foundation with which to work upon, sergeants like Randy Maxwell had taken the time to further enhance the documentation of my reports to ensure their not only getting filed but successfully prosecuted. They were quick to acknowledge good work, and a compliment from an old timer like future Homicide Sergeant Peter Mondale ("You gave the best crime broadcast I have ever heard in my entire time on the Department") could find me floating on air for days thereafter.

But as much as I loved attaboys, my natural inclination was to obsess on the negative and my experience with Hoferschwein was no exception. Not that his example was without its saving graces. Hoferschwein served as a reminder that while I could be a moody loner, I was not wholly responsible for every interpersonal problem that came my way: There were bigger—at least figuratively speaking—assholes in the world. Dodging them in the workplace might not ever be in the cards.

But if you braced the motherfuckers and let them know you weren't going to be victimized by them, you might be able to work around them.

At some level, all of this—the good, the bad, and the indifferent— had been filed away in my memory. The cumulative effect of all this data was a growing vision of what I wanted to be as a supervisor.

One reference point was Sergeant Gabriel Rieser.

That Rieser was hardly my biggest fan at Temple Station had been obvious. I was a little too loose for his tastes and he struck me as being wound a little too tight (yes, stress cadet me saw him as too tight). As Sergeant Rieser was, for a time, my evaluating supervisor, this could have been a problem.

But Rieser proved painstakingly objective in evaluating my work performance. While he never gave me an "Excellent" rating, he invariably gave me a "Very Good" evaluation, which was what I felt I deserved. If, as I suspected, he found me immature and my sense of humor suspect, no one would have gleaned as much in reviewing the annual evaluations he'd prepared of me. I came across as dedicated and squared away— which, whatever my in-house shenanigans, was how I liked to believe I came across in the field. That is, when I wasn't goofing off.

Rieser's example had long since been filed away, and I'd long since made a vow that as a sergeant, whatever my personal views of my subordinates were, I would evaluate them on their merits as an employee, be it civilian jailer, community service officer, dispatcher, or deputy sheriff.

Industry offered up all manner of deputies, both likable, and not. But whether or not I liked them, I wanted to be fair with them and as their annual evaluation was in many cases the most tangible evidence of a deputy's work history and their assignment standing, I went out of my way to give them what I truly felt they objectively warranted and documented my justifications accordingly (not every supervisor was so disposed, including one who'd simply copied the narrative of one employee's evaluation and pasted it onto another's, changing the name but forgetting to alter the gender).

But it wasn't just a desire for fairness that drove me to take extra time in documenting a deputy's assets. It was a growing awareness that sooner or later, that deputy might just need some documentation that spoke favorably as to their character.

That the profession was changing was no news flash. Already it was more untenable to be a cop than when I'd signed on.

Nothing had so changed the field as the Stacy Koon Jazz Ensemble—Timothy Wind, Theodore Briseno, and William Powell on batons, and Koon himself on the Taser—having beat the shit out of a certain dusted idiot. Improv was fine when it came to comedy and music, but when it came to use-of-force incidents it always translated to a fuck-up. Ever since the Rodney King fiasco, LAPD and the whole of law enforcement had been on the defensive.

While there was general consensus as to the public's take on the King incident, within the profession there remained those who felt the incident wasn't excessive. Some noted that during the pre-video footage portion of the arrest, King had attempted to take a CHP officer's sidearm and should have been shot then and there. I wasn't there, and have mixed feelings on the incident. I condemned Rodney King for acting as the catalyst for what would ultimately result in the deaths of many people, but also the tactics that were used. LASD deputies—having accustomed themselves to such techniques while working custody, which their LAPD peers had not—would have employed a swarm takedown of King much earlier, obviating the need for any objectionable use of force or footage thereof.

Still, there was not a law enforcement administrator who was not affected by the drama, and long before the verdicts were read deputies at east end stations, such as Industry, were waiting on the eastbound I-

10 for trucks laden down with stolen property from the riots. Force policies had been changing. Bean bag shotguns, the Arwen 37 (a cylindrical launcher that fires 37 mm non-lethal rounds), and Tasers were joining pepper spray and PR-24 batons as less lethal options being deployed in the field.

Other things were in the works too.

Under the Police Assessment Resource Center (PARC), the sheriff's department had implemented a Personnel Performance Index system as a means of identifying prospective problem personnel (i.e., abusive and/or racist personnel). This "early intervention database" provided a systematic recording of data relevant to incidents such as uses of force, shootings, commendations, and complaints regarding LASD personnel. It also tracked the progress of administrative investigations, civil claims and lawsuits, and Pitchess motions that were handled by the Department.

Theoretically, it was actually a decent idea, and probably an overdue one too.

But certain pathways are paved with good intentions, and I could see how more than one deputy could find himself Hell-bound given the manner in which the tracking was being done. Such data was finding itself insinuated into employees' personnel files and evaluation; at one point, there was a list circulating throughout the Department of those deputies with the highest number of PPI entries.

Little attention was given to the shift, unit of assignment, or the deputy's mission—just the raw numbers of how often he or she had used force or been alleged some impropriety. Already, deputies' fears that this tracking system would come back to bite them were proving warranted.

To my mind, it was just one more inhibitor to proactive policing. I didn't want to be an accessory to the cause by hamstringing some deputy's career by saddling him with a half-assed personnel evaluation form. If a deputy wanted to transfer to a choice assignment and was deserving of the consideration, I wanted the person considering his application to be provided some context for anything that might prove deleterious to the candidate's acceptance, so I labored over their evaluations.

But this worked both ways. Just as I wanted hard workers to be rewarded, I believed lazier employees should be held accountable.

While at MCJ, I'd examined one employee's time cards and found that he'd called in sick more than 60 times—the equivalent of three months of work days—obligating all manner of last minute schedule changes and the hiring of overtime behind his vacancy.

It was while I was working on his evaluation that the employee called in sick again. As soon as I found out, I called his home only to be told he wasn't there. Some telephonic sleuthing continued and I eventually reached someone who relayed a message to the employee: Call me.

The employee did and began to detail how bad he was feeling. I cut him off and told him I wanted a number at which I could call him back. He paused, then admitted to being in a Las Vegas motel room.

I put him on an "Improvement Needed" program with an eye towards getting him fired. From then on, any and all absences would require a physician's verification with the understanding that he would be at home unless hospitalized. The lack of any wiggle room and the understanding that any singular transgression would be grounds for automatic termination would prove insurmountable for the employee, and I figured it'd be a matter of time before his time with the County— or at least on my floor—was over.

To my great surprise, he not only cleaned up his act, but didn't call in once during the succeeding evaluation period.

At Industry, our paths would once again cross as he transferred in as a station jailor. He admitted being worried given our previous relationship, but let me know he was a new man. He proved it too.

His evaluations went from being "Improvement Needed" to "Outstanding."

That there were varying competencies among County personnel was something I'd realized almost from day one on the job. There were all manner of reasons for this. One was the employee's dedication to the profession. Another was their experience, or lack of it.

This was amply illustrated the night our sister station, Walnut, suffered a tragedy.

I'd been working on the umpteenth revision of a force document in the watch commander's office when I heard a Walnut deputy announce over the radio that he was rolling a fellow deputy to Queen of the Valley Hospital. Initially, I didn't put a lot of concern into it, figuring that the lack of a crime broadcast probably meant it was somehow related to a fender bender.

But then someone asked the nature of the deputy's injury.

"Gunshot wound to the head."

As Industry units blocked off intersections from the freeway to the hospital, I caught up with the black-and-white caravan as it pulled into the Queen of the Valley Hospital parking lot. The hospital staff was ready and hurriedly got the injured deputy, Sam Bell, into the emergency room and stripped him.

The deputy that'd transported Bell stood off to the side, his uniform shirt and pants soaked with his fellow deputy's blood from having lifted him into his unit.

Citizen accounts of what had transpired allowed deputies to piece together what had happened. How Bell had conducted a traffic stop on a 245 (assault with a deadly weapon) vehicle and detained a male occupant in the back seat of his patrol car when a second male on a skateboard came up behind the deputy and shot him twice in the head before freeing Bell's detainee. The suspect had since fled, but was believed to possibly still be in the area.

A complement of Industry deputies and myself responded to Walnut's jurisdiction to help as needed.

I'd been on long enough to have seen my fair share of deputy-involved tragedies and how adrenaline worked its magic on their fellow deputies. They could get fired up, pissed off, and hell-bent on finding the assholes responsible. But most of the time, they still kept their wits about them, their over-riding concern being to do right by the injured deputy.

But on this night, my fellow Industry deputies and myself watched as Walnut personnel ran around like chickens with their heads cut off, stepping on one another's radio transmissions, running stop signs and red lights without their emergency lights on, and generally acting like they didn't know what to do.

I told our units to stand down. As far as I was concerned, Walnut deputies could continue to do what they wanted and we would assist them as we would our own—by following the lead of whomever had their shit together.

I just hoped that the citizens of LA County didn't pay the price for the deputies' macho grandstanding.

It wasn't intra-agency hubris that found me dwelling on how differently Industry deputies would have conducted themselves. It was having seen them in action. This had been my first exposure to Walnut's personnel during a large-scale operation and it had not been a good one. I could only hope that it was an anomalous example of their discipline.

The episode was impactful. In all my time at Temple and Industry stations, I'd never seen such behavior, and it forced me to re-evaluate some of the arrogance that I'd been exposed to throughout the years.

One of my indictments against what I considered the "Firestone attitude" was: *So what if you work a fast station. Sooner or later, whatever happens at your station is apt to happen at pretty much any station.*

That it had been a defensive appraisal was as undeniable as the fact that perhaps I'd been wrong. Not all stations were created equal. Certainly, Avalon station on Catalina Island wasn't apt to entertain much in the way of Blood on Crip crime, or have its fair share of meth lab explosions. And if that was the case, then perhaps some stations did have a sharper learning curve than others, and perhaps did warrant greater respect than others.

In any event, Industry deputies had a higher exposure rate to adrenaline-inducing episodes than Walnut deputies. Perhaps, in doing so, they'd learned to better rein in their biological responses. I doubted that the Walnut deputies running around that night would conduct themselves in a similar manner if—God forbid—a similar incident happened again. Deputies might not be desirous of owning up to their mistakes, but they tended to be reflective enough to recognize them within.

Bell survived the shooting. His assailant, Michael Hardwick, was arrested. Odds are that unless you are on the Department, a relative to one of those involved, or live in the area, you're unfamiliar with their names. As opposed to, say, Michael Brown or Eric Garner.

None of this is meant to imply that our guys were infallible. While I would put the Industry collective up against just about any other, certain individuals could be counted upon to assert their … individuality.

One Industry deputy secured a found grenade in the trunk of his patrol car … handled two more calls … then returned to the station with his ride-along and parked his explosive-laden black and white in the parking lot. A few "WTF were you thinking…?" inquiries later, the patrol car and the watch commander's brand new Corvette that he'd parked next to were taped off and Arson/Explosives Detail en route. The Vette's owner paced in the distance, surveying the ministrations of the Arson guys and periodically casting a baleful glance in the direction of the careless deputy.

"If they end up detonating that thing and damaging my car..."

She didn't finish her sentence. She didn't have to.

Even otherwise squared-away deputies would occasionally undermine their reps through ill-considered shortcuts, such as the deputy so hell-bent on avoiding an end-of-shift hit-and-run report that he tracked down the suspect and transported him back to the accident site in hopes of getting a belated exchange of information between the involved parties.

I rolled on a possible suicide call and arrived to find a deputy leaving the location and waving me off with the assurance that the call had been initiated by an overly imaginative boyfriend and that the subject of concern was perfectly fine. I then asked the deputy if he had actually gone inside the location. He admitted that he had not. I accompanied him inside the residence whereupon I found a three-page suicide note in the latter stages of its composition.

I tried not to get too pious about any of this shit, as I liked goofing off as much as the next guy. Still, such incidents were filed away if only to prevent a pattern of negative job performance from arising.

And I didn't know of too many deputies who didn't have legitimate beefs when it came to handling crap. Last minute workloads on deputies who had the misfortune of working overlap cars were common. Deputies who couldn't get their reports read in the field were obligated to stay beyond the end of their shift on in-custody reports, lest some narrative deficiency result in a defendant's release.

Lazy deputies were not the biggest threats on my radar. Outside of the omnipresent threats posed by gangbangers, there were certain employees who concerned me, including some who should not have been on patrol training in the first place.

As Anthony Perkins attested, you don't have to be macho to be scary. The scariest employee I ever knew will here be referred to obliquely, as I don't know that she ever got the mental health assistance she desperately needed. Surely she had no business showing up armed for duty.

One day after she had complained about feeling physically ill, I told her to go home. Now, most deputies would have jumped at the chance. She looked at me as though trying to find the ten ring on my chest.

As unnerving as I found her to be, my compassion was reserved for her training deputies, each of whom at various times found themselves re-practicing their holster draws just to make sure they would be in the running if things suddenly turned south for them and their trainee.

One night, the station training sergeant and the trainee's training officer agreed to have a sit-down with her. As a precaution, they decided to make the meeting an "impromptu" one that would take place after the training unit had made an arrest—and the trainee had secured her sidearm inside a station gun locker. It was a prudent decision.

But as they discussed her questionable training status and her mood soured, the sight of her hand repeatedly gravitating toward the rear pants pocket of her uniform set off internal panic alarms: Did she have a backup weapon and was she going to pull it out here and now?

The training sergeant and training officer stared at one another with the same unspoken thought—*Am I really going to have to draw down on a fellow deputy sheriff?*

Through a genuinely impromptu master class on tact and diplomacy, they were able to defuse the situation and get the counseling session over with. The trainee ultimately transferred to another station while still on training and became someone else's problem.

Like Handleman, the presence of such employees offered a peculiar peace of addled mind to the likes of me even as they simultaneously stressed me out. So long as the Department was comfortable having their likes around, I figured my neurotic ass was at least safe on the employment front.

But then, the mere fact that I'd been on the Department for more than a decade now pretty much shored up my ever worrying about getting fired. So long as chiefs and commanders were continuing to get drunk behind the wheel and crash their rides, extort sex from subordinates, and still promote up the food chain, I figured that by any objective standard I was less of a liability.

And liability was the Department's number one concern.

Nothing so messed with the organization's homeostasis as civil lawsuits. For years, the Department had a policy of settling what it deemed nuisance suits out of court, paying off would-be litigants to avoid the hassles associated with going to trial.

There were problems to this short-sighted practice.

For one, the Department's tally of force-related payouts only ballooned and served to undermine its defense when it did come time to fight a civil suit ("You've a history of paying out monies for abuse cases, don't you?"). For another, many of those latter lawsuits would result in huge dollar losses, such as one involving a Samoan wrestler and her family who walked out of court with millions of dollars in the aftermath of a party that'd gotten out of hand.

While bean counters could shuffle things around—and did—the bottom line was that monies lost came out of the Department's operating budget, an impact affecting everything from the hiring of new personnel, to the acquisition of new equipment and training.

Desperate for fresh personnel and increasingly hard pressed to get rid of those it had, the Department continued to lower the bar on multiple fronts (e.g., lowering hiring standards; sending suicidal employees to patrol). Out-dated or over-used equipment became mainstays, and I'd find myself wheeling and dealing with some poor deputy as to which dilapidated patrol car he'd end up taking into the field.

Personnel of all ranks were increasingly shuttled into short-term assignments irrespective of whatever workloads they were already entertaining. Station detectives would find themselves working a day or two each month back in patrol.

Nobody was unaffected and I began referring to ourselves as the Pauper Police.

Mitigating lawsuits became a focal concern on the Department, which proceeded to train its personnel in a bid to foster cultural sensitivity, diminish instances of sexual harassment, and avoid hostile workplace lawsuits.

Lest they fall on the radar of the growing numbers of opportunistic lawyers determined to exploit what they perceived to be the County's deep pockets, I expected deputies to likewise keep themselves out of trouble. My interests weren't entirely altruistic—depending on their transgression and my proximity to it, they could vicariously implicate me in the proceedings.

This found me conducting all manner of supplementary training seminars at station briefings. Generally, the audience was sympathetic;

most of the time I was preaching to the choir. Deputies knew what was being put onto their backs, but they also knew that going to work with an occasional reminder freshly in mind didn't hurt either.

What did hurt was the one-two punch of lost civil suits and their attendant policy revisions.

Deputies were increasingly fed up by what they saw as ever increasing expectations without commensurate pay and benefits. By the mid–nineties, many were opting to lateral to other agencies with better pay and benefits—which only added to the Department's problem.

Between those who'd moved elsewhere, retired, or were fired, as well as a diminishing backfill between a constraining budget and lack of qualified candidates, the poor bastards who remained found themselves multitasking like never before.

As one of those multitasking bastards, my collateral responses expanded to accommodate supervision of the jail, an ever increasing number of employee evaluations, and—along with Evan Lidstrom—the obligation to work as the station watch commander damn near as often as I did my sergeant position.

The wearing of many different hats took a toll, but not as much as what I perceived as a zeitgeist of defensiveness within the profession.

Every year, new and often drastically different policies were formally handed down from on high. Vehicle pursuits were cancelled with ever increasing frequency and foot pursuits damn near verboten. Use-of-force reports were more scrutinized and more than once I'd made revisions on some investigation at each state of its review so that it eventually came back pretty much in comport with its original form.

No less taxing was what was being informally communicated through the Department's changes. Concurrent with the Department's downsizing of just about every investigative unit of import was its doubling the size of its Internal Affairs Bureau. No one could mistake its message or priorities: We are more concerned with policing ourselves than policing the streets.

This would have been an understandable posture if every station had the reputation of Rampart. But they didn't.

The longer I was on the Department, the more the prospect of being sued weighed on my mind. I was hardly alone in my thinking, and I often wondered how many a distracted cop's mindset had factored into their on-duty death in inhibiting them from taking a necessary shot. With time, I would find that in all greater likelihood that it was doubtlessly a reality, given conversations with other officers who had survived shootings.

In house, such concerns affected my ability to deal with female deputies with the same degree of candor that I did their peers. Some of my worries were warranted.

Once, while eating a sausage, I had a female deputy purr at me, "I bet yours is bigger" (she was wrong) and I prudently refrained from comment. Later, she filed a sexual harassment complaint against another County employee.

It wasn't as though I didn't have other incompetent or highly suspect deputies to stress me out. But I was more aggrieved with simple collateral responsibilities: dealing with whatever problem or melodrama might assert itself in the secretariat area, the desk, or the jail; making sure that in-service rosters reflected the names of those who'd called in sick at the last second, then calling those same people back at home to verify that they were; and assigning radios and rotating their batteries in the chargers.

I was still expected to write my employees' evaluation reports and handle whatever other collateral responsibilities I might be tasked with at any particular moment. If an employee backed up and banged up a car, injured himself by falling down the stairs, got punched by an inmate and/or punched an inmate, or otherwise used some other manner of elective force, I was obligated to make the appropriate documentation (often to the point of redundancy given the number of different forms required of the same incident). On those occasions when a certain pock-marked lieutenant saw fit to leave his office to watch his son play baseball in Glendora or otherwise goof-off, I wore two hats.

All this, of course, took place irrespective of where I might be in the handling of my usual watch sergeant responsibilities.

As watch commander, I was obligated to conduct my facility detail checks, handle incoming complaints and media inquiries, review and approve deputies' arrests of felony suspects, supervise the entry of evidence into the watch commander safe and its ledger, and monitor any important incident such as a vehicle or foot pursuit or containment operation.

The uniform could prove as much an obstacle as a means to establishing a dialogue. Nowhere was this more evident than when it came to dealing with the mentally ill. As the sight of an authority figure was hardly the kind of thing to assuage their concerns, I made it a habit to appear as non-threatening as possible.

It wasn't as though hospitals didn't have less lethal incapacitators with which to deal with their wards, and figuring that they hadn't served them well in dealing with some deranged soul, I'd try a different tack.

On the one hand, my job had afforded me all manner of supplemental training to what my one-time major—psychology—had given me. A natural empathy—thanks to my own paranoia, psychic connectivity, hypnogogia, and bouts of precognition—helped too.

Still, I'd always been more than a little amazed at how many times I'd rolled to places like La Puente Mental Health and accomplished what their own professionals had failed to do in calming a mentally disturbed person down. I wasn't the only one who was taken aback that a uniformed authority figure could diffuse a situation without deploying a less lethal use of force. But then I usually entered the equation feeling some immediate kinship with the soul in torment. *You're scared? Distrustful? I get it—me too. You've got reason to be fearful—even of me. But while you might not like what I have to say, I won't lie to you…*

However successful I was in dealing with the psychologically compromised, my success in dealing with straight-up assholes was an iffier proposition.

Sometimes I enjoyed the exchanges, and never more than when some college kid would start getting in my face. What's the most universal lie a cop is apt to encounter?

"I know my rights!"

Bullshit.

It amazed me that people so disrespectful of the law were often the first to invoke its protections. Anarchists, gang members, drug dealers—you name it, they were quick to cite whatever amendment came to their addled minds irrespective of any actual import it might bear on the matter at hand.

True, the pond was as small as it was shallow, but all the more reason not to put up with their shit. Even as principled a Berkeley hater as I will think twice before challenging one of its law professors to a legal debate. But when it came to some kid finishing his general credits at

Mt. San Antonio College, I wasn't going to tolerate his lecturing me on the law.

The non-prescription abuse that I was subject to (i.e., taking too much shit for my own good) extended to in-house confrontations too.

There's a marvelous scene in *North Dallas Forty* where John Matuzak chews out a coach, noting, "Every time I call it a game, you call it a business. And every time I call it a business, you call it a game."

It was the same talking out of both sides of their faces thing that at times found me feeling as absolutely bat-shit crazy. I wasn't in the mood to calm anyone down at such moments, including myself.

In 1995, I began experiencing problems with my hands. I had always been troubled by weak wrists, but I would alternately experience excruciating pain or numbness (I'd be able to stick my hand under boiling hot water and not even feel it).

Tests were run and I was put on a light duty desk assignment. Eventually diagnosed and treated for bilateral carpal tunnel syndrome, I was back in the field relatively quickly.

Still, I had to work with my hands. I'd fucked up on the home front too, what with my computer game playing. But the amount of writing I was doing as a sergeant was really exacting a toll.

My April 22, 1995, journal entry detailed my typical day during this time.

"This was the shift: A gang sweep at La Puente Park (discarded weapons on the grass in their wake); a pepper spray on a 51–50 in Hacienda Heights; Bill Galvan talked another 51–50 out of jumping off a roof; I got flagged down inside a RadioShack by a trio of Black strong-arm robbery victims; a bomb threat at the Olive Garden; two vehicular 245's at Home Depot, etc."

A 51–50 is the state's Welfare and Institutions Code for people who have mental health issues. All of this entailed some manner of documentation, even if it was just on the mobile digital terminal in our patrol car. But it was often more than that.

Still, I was not exactly being put in harm's way all the time. The same could not be said of specialized units working at the station.

One Thursday night, Operation Safe Streets Bureau, the Gang Enforcement Team, and Special Enforcement Bureau conducted a buy/bust operation at the corner of Laura Avenue and Valley Boulevard.

One of the buyers apparently recognized the macadamia nuts that they'd sold to him for what they were. He returned to the location and registered a complaint with a gun. They killed him, but not without considerable expenditure of ammunition: 16 rounds and two hits.

Industry Station has always had its fair share of gang activity. One year it eclipsed East Los Angeles Station for gang-related homicides. These were largely inter-gang issues, with most of the victims being from the shooters' rival gangs.

But that changed early in 1997 when we experienced a severe surge in murders.

Whatever the catalyst was, things escalated quickly with both sides—blacks and Hispanics—incurring fatalities. Suddenly, we had 11 homicides in 14 days—a mere night's shift in Chicago, but damned noticeable at home. It got to the point where trainees had multiple 187s under their belts, and any time a "shots fired" call went out, everyone knew what they were rolling on before they got there. The only question to be answered was which side had gotten the upper hand. The sides this time were blacks and Hispanics.

One of those deaths occurred on a Sunday afternoon in Rimgrove Park. Unaware of the racial hostilities taking place in the area, a 16-year-old black kid and his uncle had gone to the park to shoot some hoops. For some 40 minutes, they did so under the gaze of Hispanic gang members occupying some nearby bleachers. Suddenly, one of the gang members got up and approached the two on the court and opened fire. Though wounded, the uncle was able to find refuge in a park restroom. His nephew fell where he'd stood, shot in the chest.

The last thing the young man saw was my ineffectual presence standing over him.

The boy's death had such an impact on me that upon returning to the station the first thing I did was check all data systems for some criminal history on the boy. But there was nothing in the Juvenile Automated Index Number or anything else I could find. The boy had absolutely no criminal history or gang affiliation.

With most gang-related homicides, any emotional reaction was blunted by the knowledge that the victim had somehow played a role in his demise; there was the promise that some karmic justice had been at play—more than one deceased gang member had been wanted for murder at the time of his own.

But that was not the case here.

I was pissed off.

Though I was not yet a parent, I knew that if I was and had been made aware of the ongoing racial hostilities, I'd have made damned sure that my son would not have been on the court that day.

That night after I got home, I got on the phone, dialing numbers until well past midnight. I spoke with various bureaus on the Department, petitioning each to go to the news media and let the public know what was going on.

"It's the only thing that's going to prevent the murder of another innocent child on our streets."

My pleas apparently fell on muted ears. I knew that at some level they heard me because they apparently recognized the danger of such candor and told me to stand down.

Despite admonishments to let it drop, I considered contacting the news media myself. But the only way I could do so without getting completely fucked over would be to do so anonymously. Besides, I'd already tilted my hand and suspected that once contacted by the news media for verification of my assertions regarding the racial hostilities, journalists would get nothing more than a Bratton-like reply by those in power. That would leave me looking like an alarmist Chicken Little.

Thankfully, the players were arrested and the race killings stopped.

At least, within our jurisdiction.

The Department had bigger fish to fry, namely making sure that it didn't generate sexual harassment lawsuits.

Increasingly, it seemed that the Department's training curriculum was being devoted to peripheral concerns. Part of it made sense. I'd read that fully a third of such lawsuits in LA County involved law enforcement agencies. Something had to be done.

My problem was with what was being done about it. Long established social norms and practices were suddenly being deemed offensive with civil penalties attached. It didn't matter how entrenched one's belief system was, or how objectively warranted another's offense to it might be, everyone was expected to stop on an ideological dime and execute a 180.

This seemed wildly counter-intuitive to my spirit-of-the-law sensibilities. Where was the give and take, the reciprocal empathy and tolerance that allowed for a transition period and genuine discussion, perhaps even debate?

For whatever reason, it seemed like I was always one of the first to get immersed in whatever our current trend of supervisory training the Department had to offer. Most of it, I could do without. Not in a practical sense, but in a philosophical one. There was some cultural mainstreaming of ideas that I'd always bridled against: affirmative action, alleged equal opportunity proceedings that contradicted more meritocratic proceedings.

But in doing so they were helping to foster a new dogma, a new set of rules that I bridled against.

It was still fine to make fun of people, so long as it was the *right* groups of people. Even my heathen ass could see that Christians were increasingly getting screwed over when it came to their belief system, and the cultural elite's posture was one of "my rights trump yours."

And cops were among them.

In any event, I found myself in another lecture being taught about sexual harassment and its multitude of permutations, both intended and not.

Freshly indoctrinated, I returned to work and regurgitated what had been spoonfed me the day before, leaving no ambiguity as to the Department's seriousness on the matter and my dissatisfaction with it. Nonetheless, I was satisfied that I'd fulfilled my supervisorial responsibilities and that those in attendance had been duly edified of the Department's newfound intolerance.

And no sooner did I walk into the locker room than I found myself staring at a pair of 38DD's adorning the inside of Jorge Velez's locker. I pointed at the centerfold.

"You might be well advised to take that down, Jorge."

"You're kidding, right?"

An overwhelming wave of self-disgust was enveloping me just then.

Jorge and I had worked around one another long enough to have indulged in the usual male banter and for me to be saying something like had to be a joke, right? Frustrated, I complicated things further.

"No, I'm not," I said. "I'm ordering you to take it down."

"What?" Jorge was slack-jawed between incredulous syllables. "Why?"

Why indeed.

There'd recently been an undercover operation at MCJ wherein the Department had hidden cameras in the men's locker room and part of me wouldn't put it past the Department to do the same here, just to get my ass for dereliction of duty. Up to now it wouldn't have found anything along those lines on me. But now it would. Rather than give Jorge a well-deserved explanation, I simply told another deputy who'd attended the briefing to fill Jorge in then stormed out feeling like a hypocritical ass.

That was the least of my worries.

Later, I found out what had happened between Jorge and the deputy to whom I'd attempted to delegate my responsibilities.

"What was that about?" Jorge had asked.

"I dunno," the deputy replied. "Maybe he's gay."

Over the next few days it'd become apparent that I had fucked up royally and abdicated my responsibilities as a supervisor. If only I'd taken the time to explain the reasons for my request, I'd have saved the deputy some well-deserved resentment and myself the ensuing headaches. As it stood, I'd impressed some as a dictatorial and possibly gay asshole who'd taken offense at a goddamned titty shot. Most of all, I'd violated the tenets of my conscience.

The following Monday, I went into the captain's office and explained my posture, letting her know that in a world that offered no shortage of things which I found infinitely more objectionable than a pair of well-developed and surgically augmented breasts, I just didn't want to be policing the men's locker room or anywhere else for something someone might find offensive. I did not promote to become an arbiter of offensiveness and would henceforth resist the role unless somebody made a complaint known or pasted a *Hustler* centerfold atop the station doorway.

And that latter one might prove iffy.

Godfather wisdom decrees that justice denied becomes justice subverted. I still wasn't entirely sure what was viably ethical in a world of vacillating practices, but sure as hell knew what comported with my sense of fairness.

Years of having witnessed all manner of varying disciplines just within the Department's confines had sensitized me to such matters and even my atheist ass could see where certain Christians were increasingly persona non grata on the social, political, and professional front. Hell, even Christmas greetings were becoming an endangered species.

Incensed at all manner of needless aggravations, I created my own web page wherein I vented on life's piss-offs.

This bit of personal initiative was long before the advents of MySpace and Facebook, and marked me as something of a frontiersman on the cyber front, as well as a target for those who didn't like what I had to say. The latter made a point of making their feelings known to the Department which, in turn, would come around hinting that maybe I should take the page down.

But I felt secure enough about my first amendment rights to continue indulging them. Along with my refusal to acquiesce came the intimation that I might actually change the focus of my diatribes—hitherto committed largely to media bias and events involving outside agencies—and really give the Department something to legitimately sweat about. Things like its ongoing practice of promoting chiefs and commanders on the heels of their getting busted for DUIs and hit and runs, or how some female sergeant had supposedly blackmailed some of the upper echelon into getting LAPD to drop possession charges on her sister for fear of her releasing compromising sex tapes involving their own.

Perhaps nothing helped more than my captain, Laura Herlihy, who suggested that the page be made an obligatory read for those interested in the Department or law enforcement. Each time the Department backed off. The sole concession that I ever made was a cropping of my uniform picture to conceal any clear nexus to the Department.

Perhaps the problems associated with my page accounted for the Department's continued resistance to my recommendations that it start its own web page. To my addled mind, it would be a perfect conduit to its constituency, a means of providing timely notifications on events taking place in LASD's jurisdiction. It would also provide a forum for Q and As with the public, serve as a supplemental means of educating citizens about the laws that protected them, and act as a catalyst for an ongoing dialogue with the public. In the meantime, the Sheriff's Information Bureau was fulfilling its role as inoffensive gatekeeper, but hardly living up to its name.

It would be years before the Department would create its own website. In the meantime, other police agencies created their own and LASD's once sterling reputation on the trailblazing front suffered.

Even if part of me resented the Department's reticence to engage on the cyber frontier, another part of me got it. The internet and its denizens were largely tabula rosa in the Department's eyes and maybe it was a prudent call to let others lead the cyber charge so that it could vicariously profit from the cautionary parables they afforded.

But my paradigm was that one of the biggest problems associated with law enforcement was the lack of palaver between law enforcement and those with whom it interacted. To me, this new medium was just another means of exchanging ideas, opinions, and information. I knew that my willingness to talk with just about anybody about anything was enough to mark me as a nonconformist, but also believed that sooner or later the conversations were going to take place, and the longer they were put off, the more volatile those chats would be.

That, coupled with my naturally nosy nature, was enough to find me playing audience with just about anyone, irrespective of their race, creed, ethnicity, or religion, so long as they were willing to talk. Practically, this pretty much boiled down to those with whom I was allowed to interact within the scope of my duties.

So while I didn't have much say in picking the demographics of victims, suspects; strangers, or co-workers, I generally liked talking to people one-on-one. Occasionally, this posture allowed me to get close to some with whom I perhaps did not have a whole lot in common outside of the profession.

Deputy Pat Hastings was such a person.

For years, Hastings's sexual preferences had been the subject of idle speculation among his peers. Not once did I ever hear it mentioned in a negative context, just a sincere "Do you think…?" kind of thing. More than once, I had seen women act a little gaga over the guy to no discernible profit. Oh, he was nice enough to them, but I could never tell if it was just the kind of adolescent cluelessness that I had possessed as a teenager whenever a girl showed some interest in me, or if Hastings was genuinely disinterested.

But around the time of his father's passing, Hastings came out of the closet and not through matters of his own accord. He had found himself in the kind of dire emotional crisis that required specialized intervention. The first deputy to show up to help him was his partner, David Braun. Braun—who sported a Confederate flag tattoo and was probably even more right to the likes of Attila the Hun than I—was Hastings' best friend on the Department and his strongest advocate.

In the aftermath of Hastings' crisis, Braun was known to say, "I don't give a shit if Pat is gay. He's my partner and I love him."

Theirs was a unique dynamic, with one good-naturedly referring to the other as a "breeder," and the other returning the favor with, "cock-sucker." But nobody could deny the fraternity they shared with one another.

Like Braun, I had an affection for Hastings, whose compassions were routinely manifest towards those he came in contact with in the line of duty. But while Hastings was unfailingly polite and empathetic when circumstances permitted, he could be also counted on to take care of business. He was respected and liked by most at the station.

I'd come to regard our relationship as one of friendship as well as of supervisor-subordinate. I knew this could get my ass in trouble, but figured what the fuck?

Candid conversations between the two of us were a given. One of these chats took place during the training day when Hastings and I had gone to lunch together. The gay lifestyle was the topic at hand and the conversation eventually drifted closer to home with an in-house incident Hastings had found objectionable, a joke made by a fellow sergeant at the previous year's station Christmas party that'd been punctuated with a pejorative for homosexuality.

"Now wait a minute," I said. "Are you telling me this as a friend, or as a supervisor? Because if it's as a supervisor, I will have to document it."

"No," Hastings replied. "I've already brought it to the station's attention and it's been documented and an investigation started. I just wanted to get some things off my chest and see what you thought about it and how I should handle it."

Through my readings and conversations with other gay individuals,

I'd come to the opinion that most wanted nothing more than just be treated like anyone else, with no special privileges or concessions made. And it was with that paradigm in mind I offered the following counsel.

"Just suck it up," I said. "If he didn't mean anything by it then the worst that could be said was that he was insensitive to your presence. Nothing was apt to come of it, and nothing probably will come of it."

I truly believed that too.

But I was wrong.

What I had not expected was getting absorbed into the investigation as having been a party-after-the-fact transgressor. Internal Affairs sat my ass down and asked why I hadn't forwarded a formal complaint on the employee's behalf.

I explained the totality of the conversation I'd had with Hastings and my understanding—given what had been communicated to me by him—that any documentation on my part would only be replicating work already initiated by others and therefore a waste of the County's time—and mine.

While I was eventually exonerated for not having filed a formal complaint, I was found to have been "insensitive."

For this, I was given a punitive day off.

It was only as a matter of principle that I took exception to getting a punitive day off. The fact of the matter was that I was increasingly taking time off without pay.

An unfortunate run of luck at Caesar's Palace—wherein I'd won four thousand dollars in the two hours it took me to acquire a gambling habit—and my growing resentment towards the day-to-day bullshit of dealing with martinets and B.S. policies found me taking off to some local Indian casino with increasing frequency.

Despite the fact that my wrists continued to bother me, I was determined to do some sideline writing, starting with a story for Comic Book Marketplace. Its publisher, Gary Carter, liked what I sent and gave me carte blanche to write about anything that appealed to me.

For several years, I'd been buying and selling comic books, and at one point had acquired more than half of the top fifty most valuable silver age comic books, most of which were sold to pay off the debts incurred at the blackjack table trying to expedite my County retirement.

So on top of aggravating my carpal tunnel with Department documentations and impotently beating the shit out of the green velvet lining the gambling tables, I was now writing market reports and other comic-related articles. And even if the pay wasn't much, my having received subsidization as a writer had given me some level of validation. John Updike I wasn't, but someone had thought enough of my product to pay me for it and that was what mattered.

Optimistic that the iontophoresis treatments I was receiving for my inflamed wrists was helping, I considered pushing the envelope and doing something for a law enforcement publication. But what should I write about? What could I write about?

It was about this time that the president of the American Civil Liberties Union, Nadine Strossen, participated in a panel at the San Diego Comic-Con. I asked her if she'd be willing to be interviewed for a law enforcement publication. She said she would.

Cool, I thought. I have a story!

Now all I had to do was find a magazine to print it.

I bounced the idea off *POLICE* magazine's Devon Helm. To my surprise, he proved receptive to the idea.

April 12, 1998. Easter Sunday.

In the last hour of my shift, a "417—man with a gun" call came out. Twice it was unacknowledged before Brad Higgins gave an ETA of four minutes.

At the station desk, I contacted our dispatcher, Daryl Richmond, who gave me a quick rundown.

"Suspect threatened to kill the informant and her family last night," Richmond reported. "Tonight, he's at her house with a gun."

Something told me that this wasn't going to be one of those 417 calls that ended up with the safe recovery of a B.B. gun, or the detention of an elderly gentleman wielding a suspicious cane.

It had been shaping up to be one of those days. I had nearly shot a dog, helped talk a suicidal guy into coming out of his hiding place (but not out of trying to kick out the back window of the patrol car), and just left the scene of a deputy-involved traffic collision.

The caller was certainly a believer. She was crying and begging for someone to come and stop the armed man threatening to kill her, her 18-month-old daughter, and the rest of her family.

As I rushed out of the desk area, I dished off my unfinished accident reports to the watch commander, for the first time actually looking forward to being able to finish them later.

Over the radio, I told Higgins to wait at Alderton Avenue and Valley Boulevard, down the street from the victim's house. Deputy Duane Miller and I picked up one another's unit at Old Valley Boulevard and Valley Boulevard and rolled the rest of the way in tandem. Sirens blaring, rotators slicing the night, our black and whites were blocking traffic for one another, leapfrogging until we reached the designated corner.

The Aero Unit was down, so we turned onto Alderton Avenue with our lights blacked out and hoping for the best. Streetlights on Alderton were sparsely distributed; most were out of commission, having been shot out by locals. If there was a saving grace to the insulating blanket of darkness, it was that the gunman might have difficulty seeing us. Of course, we wouldn't be able to see him as well as we'd like either.

The pitch of the night confused the issue and made determining the actual house we had been called to more difficult. We got out of our cars to discuss our options.

Half of us had our portables on frequency 8. Those of us who didn't could hear Daryl Richmond updating the call over the tactical frequency: the suspect had armed himself with a rifle. Within seconds, another update came out: the suspect was attempting to break into the house.

As dispatcher, Richmond had a way of communicating urgency without inspiring panic. It was in the manner that his voice took on a simple but serious "that's the way it is, folks" tone. And because he used it sparingly, it had the desired effect. We knew the shit had hit the fan.

It would be another couple of years before active shooter protocols would enter the profession's parlance, but we knew what we would have to do within the small window of opportunity afforded us. If we were to stop him before he got inside the house and started shooting, we'd have to make an aggressive approach.

I directed Deputy Charles Mata and his trainee to create a containment one block east of the location. Meanwhile, I told deputies Eddie Bernal and Jeff Deerborn to cover the south side of the front yard as Higgins and I approached the front of the location.

Over "L-Tac" frequency, Richmond informed us the suspect was on the "right" side of the house. As good a dispatcher as Richmond was—and for my money he was the best in the County—his telling us this didn't help us much. Was the suspect on the right side of the house as seen looking *in* from the street, or as seen from the inside looking *out*?

But Richmond only relayed that which was being communicated to him by the law enforcement tech, who in turn was only relating what was being told to her over the phone by the informant.

And the informant was giving her *bad* information. Bad information that was about to have implications for Higgins and me.

Crouching our way past barred windows, spray-painted curbs, and graffitied garage doors, we neared the southeast corner of what we believed to be the victim's property.

My gun was out and the safety was off. I'm sure Higgins' was too.

It was quiet.

Too quiet.

I've seen enough Walter Hill movies to know what to listen for on a violent break-in: the sounds of wood splintering ... stained glass shattering.

But I heard nothing. Nothing to suggest there was a break-in occurring, or that we were even at the right house.

Higgins and I paused and looked at one another, each thinking the same thing: Which damned house is it?

The yard of the house in front of us—surrounded by wrought iron fencing with concrete pillars at 6-foot intervals—was a blanket of darkness. Scurrying along the sidewalk, using the slender pillars for cover, Higgins and I made our way to the edge of the driveway.

As quietly as possible, I crouched next to the pillar nearest the driveway. I reached up and tried the gate: Locked.

I pulled my hand away from the gate. Before I could turn back toward Higgins, the silence was pierced by the sound of a shot and the darkness was interrupted by a bright amber flash. I felt something pepper my left leg. The first thought that crossed my mind was: *Well, we've got the right house.* My second was: *I've been shot.*

Simultaneously, Higgins and I came up over the tops of our respective pillars and returned fire. I wasn't overly optimistic about our chances of hitting anything. My eyes hadn't adjusted to the darkness, and the only thing for us to go on were the subsequent shots from the suspect's gun. Nonetheless, that's what I aimed for, raising my sights just a bit above the muzzle flashes in the hopes that I might get lucky and hit the son-of-a-bitch in the head.

Save for his first shot, I couldn't hear the suspect firing. I could only hear the short, staccato bursts of our Berettas. Our first volley was immediate and synchronized, our first and last rounds indistinguishable from one another.

When we finished our first volley, we ducked behind the protective columns again.

I felt the beating of my heart against my hopefully bulletproof vest. "I'm hit," I told Higgins.

"Can you move?" Higgins' speech was rushed. But then it was always rushed. No hint of panic. I told him I thought so, so we decided to move for the cover of a Camaro that was parked along the curb in front of the house. Laying down cover fire as we ran, we dove behind the car: Higgins by the trunk, me by the driver's door.

Again, we rose and fired our third volley toward the amber flashes. To my mind, these were not panic-induced shots. I was carefully placing my rounds given the circumstances. My gun didn't seem to jump as violently as at the practice range.

Higgins saw the man moving into the yard, but I didn't, despite the fact that I was straining desperately to do so. So many concurrent thoughts: *Where are our fellow deputies? Where are our rounds going? How badly am I hurt?* But one thought eclipsed all others: *Just where is this son-of-a-bitch?*

How many rounds I'd fired, I didn't know, but I did know that most of my clip was gone. In preparation for engaging the suspect again, I dumped my first clip and reloaded.

Higgins asked again if I could move. For the first time, I glanced down at my leg. It was saturated with blood, but I still didn't feel any pain. I nodded.

Higgins took off first, and I started after him. He ran past the first patrol car parked in the street a short distance behind the Camaro and got clear to a second patrol car parked beyond it. But my left leg was wobbly, like the wheel of a shopping cart that steers of its own volition. Hobbled, I couldn't keep up with Higgins and stopped behind the first patrol car. I couldn't hear anything coming from the yard, only the voices of deputies yelling, "He's still firing!" Now this might seem to anyone else a statement of the obvious, but it was greatly appreciated by me. I still couldn't hear the suspect's rounds.

This may have been the first time I'd ever been shot at, but I'd been present at shootings before. I always had a tendency to lose my hearing in such situations. Massad Ayoob, a firearms and law enforcement training expert, describes this condition as "auditory exclusion," a phenomenon wherein the body wills itself to tune out certain sounds. Armed with this knowledge and my County-issued Beretta, I was afforded some peace of mind. Try as I might, I still couldn't hear the suspect's gunfire, only the deputies' cries and Higgins cajoling me to keep up.

Fortunately, I wasn't experiencing any other sensory impairment, save for the agreeable absence of pain in my lower leg. And while I would never have an adequate estimate for how long the firefight lasted, I did not see things as speeding up or slowing down.

Except me.

Crouched behind the trunk of the patrol car, I was content to stay there. I felt calm, and was willing to take this fight to the son-of-a-bitch.

But Higgins wouldn't have it. He darted back out from cover as I started towards him. Seeing that I was having a hard time of it, he reached out to help. I felt his hand take hold of my jacket collar. As he pulled, I went ass over teakettle into the street. My world spiraled and I lost my bearings. At that moment, I felt at my most vulnerable.

Just as the suspect raised his gun to finish us off, Bernal squeezed off two quick shots. Then Deerborn opened fire, and Bernal took advantage of Deerborn's fire to draw a better bead on the suspect. He fired two more rounds and the suspect's silhouette dropped and disappeared into the darkness. Their cover fire not only caused the man to duck, but apparently marred his aim as well. Higgins and I ran back past the second and third patrol cars, where Deputy Dillon Paulson met me.

Several deputies gathered around me. I directed them to establish a containment and to pay particular attention to the side of the house and the rear yard should the suspect attempt to flank us.

Crouching down for cover (I was becoming increasingly familiar with the bumpers of our patrol cars), I examined my pants leg. The blood was heavier. Paulson later described it as looking like "wet black velvet." But as I wasn't "pumping out," I knew the suspect hadn't hit an artery. I felt a strange calm and a sense of relief at how I'd performed under fire, and immediately recriminated myself for having a screwed-up sense of priorities.

I also couldn't believe what Higgins had done. Actually running from a position of cover to save my ass. Given the object of his efforts, some might question the wisdom, but none could question his gallantry. I was indebted.

Higgins requested paramedics. Sheriff's Radio Center asked how "the wounded deputy" was. Higgins responded, "He's okay—for having been shot." He then told me to get into a patrol car. Check that: He ordered me. I said, "No, I'm the only field supervisor available." On this matter I lost out, and the deputies herded me to the back seat of Paulson's car. My insubordinate subordinates. God bless 'em.

Only later did I realize my debt to the others. As Paulson rolled to the hospital, I gave thanks to the suspect's poor aim, to the man who built a well-constructed fence, and to my partner, Brad Higgins.

I looked again at my pants leg. Multiple holes. Nothing big. Keying the mike of my portable, I told Miller—who was still at the scene ram-rodding the containment—that I thought the suspect was armed with a shotgun. It sounded like the coordination was going well. Erroneously believing I'd switched to L-Tac, I asked that no one notify my family regarding the shooting. The Sheriff's Radio Center dispatcher advised that my desk was 914-N (i.e., notified).

More than one cop has survived a firefight, only to get wracked in a collision while en route to the hospital. So it was to my considerable relief that Paulson got us to the hospital in one piece. As he pulled up to the emergency room, I asked him to roll down the rear window so I could reach outside and let myself out. He did, then hurried around to my side to help me out. He draped one of my arms over his shoulder, then we walked past two attendees holding a wheelchair. As we passed through the emergency room doors, I embarrassingly realized the wheelchair had been meant for me.

The staff motioned us into a cubicle. I half-limped/walked to see what was behind curtain #1 (screaming kid); curtain #2 (disoriented female); before settling on curtain #3 (empty bed). I hopped onto it and they immediately had me disrobe. I was relieved to be wearing clean underwear; moreso that I didn't soil them with anything other than blood.

The nurses started examining my leg. There was a series of small holes on my calf and two more higher up on the back of the thigh. They cleansed the wounds, asked what happened, hooked me up with an IV, and give me a tetanus shot when I wasn't looking.

Meanwhile, Paulson was on the phone, talking with the sheriff, the watch commander, the chief, the watch sergeant—anyone who happened to call. Eventually, he dragged the phone into my cubicle and I called Judy.

I told her what had happened, then talked to Dad. His voice broke a little and I emphasized that I was fine. Judy called Stacey, who was celebrating Easter with her family. Despite rolling from 15 miles away, she beat them to the hospital.

Four vials of blood in a tray: Where'd that come from? There was a lot going on, and the distractions kept my mind off the cleaning, swabbing, and lotioning that was going on. A man brought in a portable x-ray machine and took images of my lower leg.

The captain called from the command post. It wasn't even 9:30 p.m. yet. How the hell did she get there so quickly? I told her not to come to the hospital. Her presence was needed at the scene.

Judy and Dad finally showed. She was crying; Dad was anxious. Still, he was calmer than I expected. Later I found out it was because Paulson had done a good job of being attentive to him, assuaging his fears.

The sheriff and Chief Byner showed up. The last time I saw Byner was when I spoke up at a station patio briefing against some new Department edict that disadvantaged the deputies. He looked and acted the same: a born politician.

I couldn't think of the last time I saw the sheriff, but I knew he looked better the last time we met than he did on this night. His health and candidacy problems had taken a toll on him.

Ill at ease with the two men, I was content to have my mood be mistaken for self-consciousness at the attentions being paid me. And to some degree, it was.

I gave them a "just the facts" debriefing of what happened. Block looked confused, like he didn't know what to say to me or my family. Some part of me blamed the man, but why or for what I didn't know. I knew I didn't like him.

The doctor said that it was probably birdshot that'd taken up residency in my lower body. He said it was not likely to cause any problems and didn't warrant surgery. Most of the pieces would work themselves back out.

Armed with this information and a new pair of crutches, I told the sheriff and the chief that I just wanted to get the hell out of there. They nodded. Their response was something between "we understand" and "we do too." I wasn't surprised. Their parting handshakes were as requisite and sincere as their introductory efforts.

After signing my medical release forms, I received painkillers, antibiotics, and good-natured kidding about setting off metal detectors in airports. I thanked the hospital staff and Paulson and made my way to the parking lot.

My former training officer, Lynn Helbing, was waiting for me outside of the hospital. He'd been at home when his daughter, Sherry, called and told him I'd been injured. It touched and surprised me that he would roll from home to visit me. I gave him a brief rundown of what happened. He looked at my leg and shook his head. "I've never been shot," he noted. "Been sued, but never shot." We all cracked up at that. I've never been sued. I think I'd sooner get shot.

The first thing I did when we got in the car was to switch the radio to KFWB, whose tagline was, "You give us 22 minutes, and we'll give you the world." Sure enough, the shooting was the top story. The reporter gave a skeletal sketch of the incident and identified me by name. I was surprised at how quickly my name was released. He added that the suspect had retreated into the house where he took ten people hostage. As the incident drew on, I slowly receded from the limelight, and the focus turned to the suspect and his hostages.

For most of the drive home I remained quiet, wondering just how and why Higgins and I survived, and what the outcome of the ongoing hostage crisis would be.

When we got home, I listened to the concerned messages of friends on the answering machine, then turned on the television. The shooting was the top story on every channel. I tried to tape some of the channels, but my lack of sophistication with the recording equipment meant that I missed most of them.

Mark Porter called from Queen of the Valley Hospital. He was shocked to find that I'd already been treated and released. I was too, especially as several news broadcasts were reporting that I was still in ER in fair condition.

When I removed my shorts, I saw blood on the back of them. Upon closer examination, I also found a hole in them. Seems the bastard got me in the ass too.

My leg was tender to the touch and I didn't want to put any weight on it, but otherwise it didn't hurt. Stacey applied more antibiotic lotion on it and mixed me a strawberry daiquiri. We watched an action film with Michael Rooker as a cop exchanging a shitload of rounds with a bunch of bad guys. Stacey asked if I was okay with it.

"Yeah," I said. "At least he's hitting what he's shooting at."

I continued to obsess about how this situation would end. My worst fear was that by failing to take the suspect out, we we'd left him the opportunity to carry out his intentions. Not knowing if I would get a wink of sleep, we went to bed as Special Enforcement Bureau and the Crisis Negotiations team continued working through the night to get the suspect to surrender.

I eventually went to sleep at 4:00 a.m. With the light on.

Upon waking, the only dream I could remember concerned black-jack tables in Vegas. Outside of "taking a hit," I didn't see it as a metaphor for gambling with my life and figured this boded well.

Waking up after getting three hours of sleep, I listened to a voice message from Deputy Don Fielder. The suspect surrendered. There was no loss of life and no additional bloodshed. I was relieved.

Nine hours after the S.O.B. shot at us, he was in custody.

Friends and family continued to call. My cousin Bob jokingly found my actions suspect.

"What you won't do to get days off. I figure that if our girls can get a 50 percent retirement for sexual harassment, you're good for a 70 percent stress retirement, easy."

While that might have been a future concern, I was more stressed at the prospect of Monday-morning quarterbacking and what the Department's take on our actions would be. Sgt. Dick Weaver assuaged my fears, saying, "Sometimes you have to load your balls in a wheelbarrow and take care of business. From everything I've heard, you guys did a great job."

Stan Southern, a psychologist with Employee Support Services, called to schedule the requisite psychological debriefing. Homicide detectives called to arrange an interview.

I called the captain and ended up speaking with her secretary, Jan Turner, who told me that in the 26 years she'd been at the station, only two on-duty deputies had been shot: two sergeants, both killed. I was third-time lucky.

The only person luckier than me was Higgins, who thankfully wasn't hit when he left the safety of cover to help me. I talked to Higgins. He didn't like the emphasis I placed on the word "luck." He said we made our own luck by conducting ourselves in the manner we did.

I wasn't about to argue.

It wasn't just gratitude that kept my mouth shut. I genuinely believed that Higgins' argument had merit: We did the best we could given the circumstances. We didn't roll over and play dead. We acted as a team—no separation of partners, no dilly-dallying around.

Still, I was having trouble dealing with how the hell we came out of it. It might not have risen to the survivor guilt of Ira Hayes, but the whole "salvation of the agnostic" thing had me wondering: *Why*?

This philosophical introspection worsened when Homicide showed up.

I had heard of, but never met, detectives John Black and Bob Carolla. Black was a legend on the Department, his reputation cemented when he shot and killed the man who'd assassinated his training officer seconds before.

Introductions were exchanged. I could tell they'd both had a very long night. Their eyes were red and droopy, yet alert, and their voices were scratchy. Black went through a series of suspense-inducing tests of his Sony recorder. Finally satisfied that our words could be taped for posterity, he began the interview.

There was no coaching going on, but I could tell by their demeanor that I was in good hands. I glanced out the window. Birds were picking at the feeder beyond. *Life goes on*, I thought.

The questions—perhaps by design—were phrased somewhat as they would be in court ("Can you tell me where you were working on April 12?").

I told them what I remembered, which at the time wasn't much. I could only explain my frustration, drawing an analogy to some arbitrarily edited film footage that played out a fragmented scene. Gaps and holes of various duration. Initially, I could only recall our first volley: I simply didn't remember firing on the run and couldn't recall firing from behind the car.

Still, what I gave them was an honest and reasonably accurate synopsis of events.

Black put his notes and recorder to the side and leaned forward while Carolla stretched. They said that from what they'd been able to find out, we all did a great job. Black told me we were exchanging fire with a man armed with an AK-47 from a distance of maybe 30 feet.

This floored me.

The suspect, Rick Estevan, was 6'2", 250 lbs., and 34 years old. A third strike parolee with nothing to lose, he'd shown up at the location with an arsenal: the assault rifle, a shotgun, a .357 magnum, and a .45—all stolen. Three additional clips for the AK-47 were laid out on the front lawn. Loaded for bear, he almost got a few of us.

Apparently, he was loaded too. Eight empty beer cans littered the front lawn where Estevan drank and contemplated the night's pending festivities.

Black said that because we engaged the S.O.B., his primary target—the girlfriend—was able to escape. In fact, she was lying a few feet away from us throughout the firefight. Black believed that once he lost his primary target, Estevan's resolve to kill the remaining family members diminished. He estimated the suspect fired between 8 and 11 rounds.

I was appreciative of what the Homicide detectives had said and done, and saw them out. I felt better.

Marcia Barton, the crisis negotiator who dealt with Estevan over the phone throughout the night, called. She said the first time they threw the negotiations phone into him, he threw it back out. When he eventually decided to talk, Barton had to downplay the number one concern to Estevan's addled mind: my injuries. He kept saying that he knew he shot a cop. Barton said, "You don't know that. He might have been shot in the crossfire by another cop."

Estevan, whose capacity for delusion had already been manifest in regards to the girl's affections, found appeal in this speculation. His optimism grew when he heard a television reporter say that I'd been shot by a shotgun. "I never fired a shotgun!" he asserted. "I fired an AK-47!" The guy was grasping at straws, anything that might keep him from going to jail forever, and Barton wielded those straws like a carrot before a starving horse.

By nightfall, I was completely beat and went to bed early. I was just about to fall asleep, right at the edge of Slumberland, when suddenly

Mr. Sandman popped a flare and I saw the bright amber flash again. Suddenly, I was wide awake. I eventually went back to sleep.

With the light on.

I thank Barton for her efforts and the phone call. I slept easier knowing the S.O.B. didn't kill anybody.

Captain Herlihy called as I got ready for my psych appointment. I'd heard that the sheriff jumped on her case for not having responded to the hospital while she was maintaining the command center at the scene. I let her know that his actions pissed me off, and she certainly had no apologies to make.

At the shrink's office, I found a book on coping with shootings. It chronicled the effects of officers' deaths on friends and families, as well as the psychological and physiological responses for cops who have survived duty-related shootings: post-traumatic stress disorder; drifting in conversations; recreating the incident; revisiting past incidents; playing "what if?," "if only," and "why?" games. After a few minutes, Dr. Southern came in and introduced himself, then led me back to his office.

Dr. Southern's office was user-friendly: two immobile (but padded) chairs faced the doctor's stereotypic recliner. No couch.

He reviewed a questionnaire I'd filled out in the waiting room. After digesting the information, he asked if I was doing okay. I liked his tone, his tact. It wasn't, "Are you having difficulty?" or "Are you experiencing problems?" He simply wanted to know how I was doing. I told him I was fine. Increasingly, I felt self-conscious. Not at speaking to a shrink, but for occupying his time. I felt like a survivor. I felt lucky. Still, I was grateful for the occasion, and took advantage of it.

I ran down what happened to the best of my understanding and recollection. He was already familiar with the case to some degree, having responded to the scene the night of the shooting. He related some kind things the deputies had said about me. I even got the (perhaps mistaken) impression that he respected me. We had a good conversation, and I was candid in my responses to the situation, both at the time and in its wake. I let him know that my readings had helped. He eventually concluded that I was doing fine.

I didn't mention that my ballistrophobia—fear of being shot—had not been cured.

We then kept my appointment at Queen of the Valley Hospital. The therapist, Ron, gave me a thorough massage and probing and for the first time since the shooting, I felt genuine pain. He gave me more salve ointments and scheduled me for a follow-up.

Stacey drove me past the shooting site. A couple of men were in the driveway attempting to resuscitate their washer and dryer. I introduced myself as the appliance assassin. He seemed pleased to meet me, but didn't extend a word of thanks. His mind was on his dead machines.

I looked around and could see where a bullet struck and fragmented a portion of the wrought iron gate. This must have been the round and shrapnel that struck me. None of my anticipated fears or reactions occurred: no sweats, no palpitations, no shakes, no dryness of the mouth. Our trip down memory lane was over.

Whatever else, the number of hits on the washer and dryer vindicated Higgins' and my shooting. It also explained why our shots weren't more successful as the suspect had moved and hidden behind the appliances as he engaged us.

Duane Miller called and asked why we did it. He reminded me that I once said that our lives were never worth taking such risks. He seemed upset, as though he bought into what I'd said—and I hadn't. Perhaps, he just misunderstood me. Perhaps, he understood me too well.

During our chat, he inferred that there'd been some negative takes on the shooting. I asked from whom, but he couldn't—or wouldn't—say. I called Lt. Ken Smoot, but a fat lot of help he was. I told him some of the innuendo I was hearing was more stressful than the shooting.

"You and Happy Harry—the glass is always half empty," he said. "Things will never be better for you with that attitude."

I wanted to say, "You're right. Because I'm not afraid of pissing off my alleged superiors any more than you are intimidated at being insensitive to your subordinates." I bit my tongue at this, and regretted my restraint even more when I talked with Higgins later.

On the morning following the shooting, a deputy was in the watch sergeant's office with Higgins and Smoot when he idly wondered how long Higgins had to schedule his appointment with the shrink.

Smoot had replied, "Why does he have to go? He didn't hit anything."

Higgins responded quickly with a (figurative) shot on Smoot. "How many times have you been ambushed by an AK-47?"

Smoot acknowledged, "You're right. About the only thing I have to sweat in the watch commander's office is paper cuts."

The following Sunday, I kept the Sabbath holy by showing up for work for the first time since the shooting.

Throughout the day, Will Halpern and I handled several informal debriefings.

When I walked out the back door of the station after my shift, I found myself standing near my car in civilian clothes feeling vulnerable. I felt like a target.

At work, I started to feel self-conscious at the inquiries on my leg: People wanted to see it for themselves. I declined all requests (including the captain's) and contemplated going home and performing various acts of self-mutilation to warrant their sympathies and appease their curiosities.

I acquired a litany of (hopefully) affectionate monikers. Lead Leg, Wounded Knee, Hopalong, Eileen (I Lean), Ironsides, Tiny Tim, and Lead Catcher.

It all reminded me how close I came to being nicknamed Ahab.

I was surprised at how relatively little impact the shooting had left on me. But then, I was surprised at how well I'd conducted myself during the shooting.

This was no bragging point—simply the acknowledgment that I'd often wondered how I'd respond during a shooting. Now, I knew. That is, I knew how I would react to that particular shooting on that particular night.

The fact remained there were hundreds of officer-involved shootings every year and mine had just been one of them.

Thinking of similar incidents—the Long Beach, Mississippi, shooting that occurred shortly after ours; the Riverside incident wherein two officers were killed after stopping 75 yards away from the location—I couldn't help but feel extremely fortunate that we'd survived. That should be our priority—to survive and go on and do our job and do honor to the memory of those officers who were less fortunate.

Life at Industry Station afforded all manner of stranger-than-fiction affairs, situations that would have strained a dramatist's credulity.

During a containment search for a burglar, Deputy Mitch Thieleman opened the rear door of a van to find a suspect hidden under a blanket. Just as his hand grabbed the unseen man's head, Thieleman heard a gunshot and felt something slam against the palm of his hand. The burglar had stuck a gun into his mouth and fired. The bullet had come to rest at the back of his skullcap. Thieleman said it felt like he'd barehanded a Nolan Ryan fastball, and the beet red circle in his palm looked like he had.

During a search for a serial arsonist, two deputies spotted a suspect and jumped out of their patrol vehicle to confront the man. This precipitated a knock-down, drag-out fight that found the three men rolling in the street. However, the car had remained in gear and drifted towards the trio, gaining momentum as it rolled. One of the deputies was out of harm's way, but the other wasn't and at the last second rolled out of the car's path. The suspect was struck by the car and killed.

As much as I liked Temple and romanticized my time there, I'd long since concluded that, as a group, Industry deputies were more squared away. Temple exposed its deputies to a broader array of societal transgressions than some of the faster stations, but there was no disputing the fact that Industry was busier.

Industry was also more experimental with how to deal with its crime problems. At one point, it had an illuminated life-size image of an actual sergeant placed atop the roof of a shopping market in the hopes that it would prove an inhibiting deterrent to car thieves and purse snatchers. In reality, we received complaints from citizens for encouraging a false sense of security among the store's patrons and the cardboard cutout was taken down.

More successful, for a time, was Pat Rolman.

Pat was a dummy deputy. Decked out in a uniform shirt and helmet, his high-density foam torso could be found propped up behind the steering wheel of a patrol car parked along Valley Boulevard in a bid to slow down speeders. He was effective, too, as morning commuters hauling ass to work could be seen slamming their brakes in deference to his roadside presence.

Monday through Friday, Pat would be shuttled to a busy traffic spot by a Community Service Officer (C.S.O.), then picked up later in the day and returned to the station.

While the C.S.O.s weren't too enamored with Pat, he was about as low maintenance a Department entity as they came and rarely generated complaints, save for when some elderly citizen would register a grievance over his refusal to roll down his window and address a question.

Still, Pat proved to be more popular than his real-life counterparts and was often the odds-on favorite for Employee of the Month.

But one day a C.S.O. had forgotten to pick up Pat and he went missing. Hours later his torso was found abandoned in a field where someone had deposited a quiver of arrows into his chest.

Pat had been assassinated.

We'd have had a funeral for Pat, but it wasn't in the Department budget.

You can beat people, take them to jail, even shoot them.

Just don't tow their cars.

Few things in life will make a grown man break down and cry like impounding his ride. And while towing cars was a routine aspect of patrol, working traffic enforcement meant you quickly found yourself on a first name basis with the local tow truck drivers.

Between vehicles that had been in accidents or used in crimes, we were always towing cars. If we were citing a driver for being unlicensed, we were required to take his ride. Like everything else, occasional discretion came into play. If some gal showed up, had a license, a good attitude, and a cooperative husband in the back seat of the patrol car, we might just let her take the car, especially if she had kids and plainly had had enough of hubby's shit.

As watch commander, I had to listen to motorists make cases for getting their cars out of impound. And they really had to make a damned good case. Only the most mitigating of circumstances called for amnesty, for a couple of reasons.

First, it was an indictment of the deputy's initiative in impounding the vehicle. Most deputies, recognizing civil repercussions for arbitrary stupidity, generally refrained from indulging in it, which meant that in impounding the car in the first place they'd most likely made sure to dot their I's and cross their T's.

Second, there was no ambiguity about the law. For the vehicle to be impounded, it had to have been used in the commission of a crime. The majority of the time, those petitioning the vehicle's release were culpable of nothing more than driving without a license, or driving on one that'd been suspended or revoked. In either instance, they were effectively saying "fuck you" to those motorists who'd not only gotten and retained their licenses, but were likewise paying car insurance for the privilege. It was from the unlicensed demographic that we got many of our hit and runs and people who gave false information to those motorists with whom they'd collided.

Suffice to say, I didn't sign off many such requests.

When off duty, I generally tried to put on blinders. I didn't have a ballistic vest, radio communications, or backup. Back in the day, I didn't have a cell phone with which to call a police station. Far too often a defendant arrested by an off-duty officer was acquitted by a jury of his idiot peers, thereby leaving the officer vulnerable to a civil suit. It just wasn't worth going out on a limb.

All the same, I would occasionally fuck up and do the right thing, and had I received official recognition for every off-duty activity I'd initiated, my personnel folder would have been substantially thicker than it already was.

The first off-duty incident I'd ever found myself involved in occurred while I was working custody at the Hall of Justice.

I was watching TV at my parents' home when I heard the corralled horses two doors down getting agitated, followed by the sounds of breaking glass and screams.

I grabbed my five-shot revolver and off-duty badge and ran down the driveway to the street. Two doors down, I saw several men smashing the windows out of a neighbor's house and trying to get inside. In the middle of this, a man stepped out and fired a shotgun in the direction of a car that was stopped in the middle of the street.

The situation was fluidly chaotic and I had no idea who the good guys were. I figured my primary concern was the guy with the shotgun and aimed at him.

"Drop the gun!"

The man didn't comply, but he didn't fire at me either. Instead, he ran back towards a third house and disappeared (later, I found that he was another neighbor who was trying to scare the attackers off).

The suspects ran back to the car and jumped in. I waited curbside while others called the Industry Sheriff's Station.

Shortly, a black and white rolled down the street. The driver deputy hit me with his spot lamp and I held my off-duty badge aloft while keeping my revolver at my side. Through his driver's window he motioned me to approach.

But as I did, I saw that his passenger deputy was fairly climbing over him to get a shot at me. He'd never seen my badge and, having fixated on my sidearm, considered me a threat—the driver deputy had never communicated his observations to the passenger.

Fortunately, the driver deputy calmed my would-be killer and I was able to give a description of the suspects, who later turned out to be three childhood friends, one of whom had stabbed and killed his mother years before and had been released after completing his stint with the juvenile detention system.

The incident was enough to lead me to think twice about getting involved in shit lest I get my ass shot.

And yet time and again I would find myself dealing with situations that would somehow involve me. Even something as innocent as a shopping expedition with Stacey would suddenly become a detour to the Twilight Zone.

We were walking through a shopping market when I heard a commotion in the next aisle. As we walked past it, I looked down and saw a woman cowering up against the shelves, her face reddened and makeup smeared with tears. A black man holding her by the arm glanced in my direction and immediately upon making eye contact asked, "What the fuck are you looking at?"

An obviously drunken asshole, seemed an apt enough description but I kept my mouth shut.

The man turned his attentions from the woman to me and quickly closed the gap between us, cussing and challenging me the entire time. "You want some of this, motherfucker?"

I silently cursed the woman's dating standards, and myself for having glanced down the aisle. But I kept my mouth shut and didn't say a word. Alas, my silence apparently only emboldened the man, as he kept yelling and threatening to kick my ass. Finally, he took a swing at me.

I was armed, and didn't want to get in a fight over my weapon with this asshole. But for all intents and purposes, that was what I was in for and I figured I'd stop this fucking mess as soon as possible.

LAPD had prohibited the carotid restraint hold in response to public outcry—a number of suspects had died as a result of its use. But LASD had recognized its efficacy as a less lethal tool, and suffered no qualms about pandering to the public at the expense of deputy safety. Just as important, they taught us how to use it correctly, and to make sure that pressure to the carotid was released as soon as the subject lost consciousness.

I squeezed the sides of his neck with my bicep and forearm and he passed out. Laying him face down, I then positioned myself so that I was partially atop him with his right arm torqued as far up behind his back as possible. He came to seconds later, just as pissed off as when he'd gone off to Little Nemo Land.

"You motherfucker! I'll kill you!"

"You'll shut up and lie perfectly still, or I'll break your fucking arm!"

And so, we stayed like that, him cussing me out the entire time while the red-faced woman waited nearby. The man's friend also stood by, offering some sage advice, "Don't fight with the officer, dude." West Covina cops arrived shortly thereafter and took the man into custody.

On another shopping trek with Stacey at the Puente Hills Mall, I stopped to use a public restroom. A short, stocky man hurriedly rushed out of a stall and left without stopping to wash his hands. Glancing in the stall, I saw tissue paper strewn about the base of the toilet and suspected that he'd been using the restroom for something other than its intended purpose.

This was initially of no concern to me, but eventually I noticed the stranger from the restroom apparently following us throughout the mall. Any doubt was removed when he followed us into a bookstore and then to the rear of the store. Stacey was perusing a row of books while I feigned interest in a book at the end of the aisle, keeping a vigil on the stranger out of the corner of my eye. Suddenly he bent down and his hand shot down and brushed against Stacey's ankle, causing her to jump.

The man stood up and attempted to run away, but I grabbed him.

"No!" he cried. "Please let me go! I have to leave!"

I'd noticed something in the man's hand as his inverted palm swept by Stacey's foot. Holding onto his wrist, I pried his clinched fingers open to find a then state-of-the-art micro camera.

I detained the man pending the arrival of a sheriff's deputy who took him into custody.

The stranger turned out to be a commander in the U.S. Navy. That he was using government technology to take upskirt photos of women was apparently frowned upon by the Navy and he pleaded *nolo contendere* on the charges.

Fucking brazen pervert.

There were other instances, such as when a man mourning the DUI-related fatality of his son got drunk himself and did a hit and run on my car. Or the time a former neighbor, in the throes of AIDS-related dementia, showed up naked and smashed out the windows of our condominium before holding us all at bay with a large glass shard.

Regardless of the event, I was usually able to get someone safely detained for the police, save for a couple of other hit and run capers where the suspects fled on foot.

But then there were those occasions where I was a party to the proceedings from the get-go. And on these matters, more than a few of the entries would not have been favorable in nature—largely because of the role my unfavorable nature played in them.

Ironically, it was just such an incident that helped get me back on track in a most unpredictable manner.

I showed up for work one day and was told our latest station captain wanted to see me. Walking into his office, I found him perusing a memo. As he was obviously ignoring me, I spoke up, saying that it was my understanding he was expecting me. The captain acknowledged me, then resumed his reading.

Leaning against the doorway with my arms crossed to emphasize my own dismissive attitude, I waited impatiently. A lieutenant entered the room briefly, was told the document read fine, then left. The captain and I were alone again. Volatile situation, that.

I didn't trust our newly promoted captain. I'd worked with him at both MCJ and during his previous stint at Industry. Each time he'd been a lieutenant. But now he was a captain, one that some people thought quite a bit of. But all I could remember were uncomfortable moments, such as when he'd once looked inside my Yoshinoya lunch bag and said, "Jesus Christ! What is this stuff? No wonder you're so weird!"

He'd clipped the last sentence, realizing that perhaps he'd been more candid than he'd intended. Surprisingly, it hadn't hurt my feelings that much at the time; rather, it made me chuckle.

On this day, when the captain finally spoke he did so without hesitancy.

"I received a memo regarding an off-duty incident of yours that occurred a few days ago," he said. I recalled the incident. Another motorist and myself had exchanged mutual "fuck yous" before heading to a nearby California Highway Patrol Station that proved to be of little help to either of us. The captain put the memo aside.

"Why haven't I received one from you?"

His tone suggested a certain joy at having me at his questionable mercy. My defensive reaction was … defensive.

"Well, that's typical of the Department's chicken-shit way of doing business." I asked, "Why don't you just write my ass up now?"

It wasn't the smartest thing I'd ever said, and it pretty much set the tone for what followed.

"Shut up with that smart-ass attitude!" the captain yelled. "Sit your ass down!"

"No, I'm content to stand."

"Do you have a problem working under my command?"

"I don't like, respect, or trust you," I replied matter-of-factly. "But other than that, I can work with you."

"Well, I don't care if you don't like me. People don't have to like one another. They can come, do what they get paid to do, and go their separate ways at day's end. But if you can't trust me, then I can't have you working for me because I can't have a person working for me who doesn't trust me."

"Then if you want me to put my transfer in, I will."

"Fine. If you have a problem with me, we'll get you out of here."

By now, the adrenaline was coursing through my veins so powerfully that my legs began to feel wobbly. Reluctantly, I took up the man's offer of a chair.

"I'm not normally one to be picky," the captain continued. "But if that's the way you want to play it, then what are you doing coming in at ten minutes past the hour?"

Business as usual, I thought, but refrained from volunteering as much. It was the first time I'd censored myself during our conversation.

"Look, why don't you just relieve my ass of duty right now?"

"For what?"

"Stress."

"Stress? What have you got to be stressed about?"

"I have a litany of things I'm stressed about, and this is just one more chicken-shit thing I've had to worry about since you came back to the station. I notice that the Department's really good about documenting negative stuff and filling your personnel jacket with crap that can come back and bite you in the ass later. But when it comes to acknowledging the good you do, it's curiously lacking."

That I found him particularly culpable was about to become apparent.

"When you were out here in the field as a lieutenant," I continued, "you were present on multiple incidents wherein I was the on-scene supervisor, including one where there was a murder suspect holed up inside a house. You called the suspect on a cell phone and tried to talk him into surrendering, but couldn't get him to do it. But I did.

"Or the time we had a shooting with multiple people dead or wounded that was itself followed by a deputy-involved shooting. I'd supervised the initial call-out, coordinated multiple crime scene containments, walked the duty and area commanders through the incident, and left everyone—including yourself by your own admittance—with a damned good impression about how the incident was handled. Each time you told me that I did a great job handling the situation. But did you ever document one of them? No."

I went on down a list of opportunities where he might have been as vigilant in writing me up as he was in documenting my being late, including a time when a judgment call on my part "probably resulted in lives being saved" (the captain's words at the time, not mine).

The captain made his first overture of being conciliatory.

"Maybe you're right, I should have written something along the way."

"And then you come back to the station. At your staff meeting, you went down the list of station supervisors and when you came to my name, you rolled your eyes like, 'I know about *this* one,' thereby obligating the lieutenants to defend me in my absence."

"Well, I did know about you. I worked with you at Central Jail, and I remember that force incident involving you and Sgt. Cross."

That was when I realized just what'd been coloring the man's impression of me all these years. It involved a custodial use-of-force incident near shift change that wasn't handled appropriately.

And blame rested squarely on both my shoulders and those of a sergeant from the previous shift. The captain continued.

"Don't you think I have the right to ask how my employees are doing?"

"You have the right to ask without editorializing the matter by rolling your eyes. The fact that more than one lieutenant—lieutenants who respect me and what I do here—brought the matter to my attention should underscore the fact that you were out of line. Now, in light of all this shared history, would you trust you if you were in my shoes? Would you think that you had my best interests at heart?"

"Maybe I did make some arbitrary judgments on you," the captain admitted.

"It'd be disingenuous of you to say that if you'd been dealt with in this manner all this time, you wouldn't have felt the way I do. I mean, are these actions consistent with someone who has your best interests at heart? Whatever else, I've not lied to you. And whatever my feelings about you, I've not said a negative word about you to anyone here at the station. I try not to say anything about anyone that I wouldn't say to their face."

During the next 90 minutes, we cleared the air on multiple fronts and I found the captain more empathetic than I would have expected. I also realized that I was not without my share of culpability for the man's impressions of me. Still, when all had calmed to a relative peace, I could see that the captain retained some valid concerns about a particular supervisor: Me.

There was a brief pause in our conversation.

"So what happens now?"

The captain's question was rhetorical, but I answered nonetheless.

"I don't know. I will say that if you're willing to let me work here, I want to. This station has the best morale of any on the Department, and I'm not anxious to leave it. But at the same time, I don't want to continue feeling vulnerable all the time. Would you be willing to have me work for you? The question is: Can you trust me?"

"This is how much I trust you."

And with that, the captain tore up the damning memo.

Dammit, there's never any Kleenex around when you need one.

As there was no shortage of things I could be taken to task for—insubordination, failure to document an off-duty incident, conduct unbecoming an officer, late for work, drama queen—I knew then that he was putting his ass on the line for me too.

As it was, I worked for the man for a few more years, during which he actually gave me a coveted position. He eventually promoted, then retired.

While working Temple, I'd find myself inventorying some hype's inner arm scars, searching for some fresh puncture wound and asking myself, *Just what the hell am I doing?*

That same thought had kept me company while chasing some suspect down a dark alley. It rode shotgun when I'd pushed the pedal to the metal to beat the descending barriers of a railroad crossing. It was right there every time I'd conducted a search of a darkened building in search of an outstanding suspect.

But lately such contemplations had taken a more macroscopic scope: Just what the hell are *we* doing?

The more I studied America's so-called war on drugs, the more sickened I felt by it. If it was a war, it was one we were seemingly hell-bent on losing; certainly, we weren't allowed to win. For all the "Just Say No" campaigning and DARE and SANE Programs (the LAPD and LASD anti-drug abuse programs, respectively), America had a fixation with sticking stuff up its nose and in its arms and nothing was going to change it.

I'd long ago forgone citing for marijuana possession, having relegated the matter to the "spirit of the law" side of things. That it had once been a felony was beyond me; I wondered to what extent its prohibition might actually be racially motivated. I didn't know how many people had died because of pot use, but was willing to bet many more had gone tits up behind cigarettes and alcohol. The whole thing struck me as intellectually disingenuous, ethically ambiguous, and conducive to the whole slippery slope that found law enforcement personnel scouting properties like real estate agents in a bid to see which would make their narcotics forfeiture efforts most worthwhile.

It was the saprophytic nature of law enforcement that intrigued me, how our profession profited by the malfeasance of the world, and how much was added to or deducted from it according to other variables—taxes, crime rates, and the usual Compstat fudging.

But as the years passed, I saw something else taking place—a synergy between what Americans were willing to tolerate and what they weren't willing to finance. It didn't matter if the polarity was counterintuitive and contrary to every Maslowian predicate—it was what it was. People would sooner insulate themselves with their iPads and cocoon themselves in their homes than venture elsewhere. And if those who did go out and about got victimized, then caveat emptor. The smart money was at home, and at home it would stay.

It followed that law enforcement funding came to be in commensurately short supply, with the past decade having been a particularly rough patch. As a result, those on the front lines had cause to worry about cutbacks, layoffs, and the lack of pay raises. That there would be a corresponding diminution of respect and support for our profession was something I'd long intuited.

The more I worked in the field, the more I saw the results of this. Waffling ran up and down the Department food chain. Means and agendas that were at cross-purposes, and unreasonable judicial expectations were entrenched realities of law enforcement. But they didn't have to be, and candid discussions about them would go a long way to removing their threats. Might some feathers get ruffled along the way? Absolutely. But fewer people would die or be otherwise victimized.

But rather than possibly offend some constituency, it was easier for law enforcement administrators to leverage the problems onto the backs of their line personnel and citizens who didn't always recognize what was in their best interests.

And so it was that I noticed a growing evolution in all manner of Department policies. Foot and vehicle pursuits were increasingly subject to supervisor intervention; even the initiation of one could be grounds for days off. It was a given that force policies were changing too. What once required a verbal notification to the watch commander now required all manner of documentation. Deputies were getting fired for deadly force incidents, only to get their jobs back through civil service before taking well-deserved stress retirements.

Whatever else, none of this was impacting the upper echelon, who'd promulgated political expediencies, made the requisite sacrificial offerings on the badges of others, could be counted upon to get into DUI crashes, and still be promoted.

But that's the way it is when you're a squirrel at the top: It's hard to show some balls when you're always insulating your nuts.

In my early days on the job, I thought my fellow cops and I would be conducting our enforcement of the law with the kind of blindfolded neutrality affirmed of Lady Justice.

But long before Bill and Hillary, Bernie and Weiner, I saw that the financially well off and powerful were not only different, but received a different brand of justice too.

Transgressing celebrities, judges and political elites might get some token wrist-slapping, while the poor bastard caught with a dime bag in a flop motel room could count on the full weight of the justice system being brought to bear upon his scrawny ass.

With each passing year, I'd found my perspective on our drug laws changing. Some of it was selfish. I'd grown tired of paying visits to the homes of childhood friends only to have their parents or siblings ask if I was there to bust them. It seemed stupid that I couldn't continue my associations with them simply because they'd been convicted of violating some narcotics statute.

I was increasingly for legalizing, or at least decriminalizing, the self-medicating protocols of our long-haired counterculture types. I figured that they'd be less of a pain in the ass if they were suffering less pain themselves. I suspected that things would change for the better on the drug war and elsewhere, and increasingly wanted to be an agent of change, too—part of the developing zeitgeist within law enforcement that advocated for more commonsense enforcement while being more aggressively attuned to defending the profession.

As I saw it, those laws that were objectively defensible—the *mala en se* types—should be aggressively enforced and no apologies made. And if someone died in the proceedings, then as Sheriff Peter J. Pitchess had once observed, "It is truly tragic that the deceased put things into motion that resulted in his death."

If the nascent "let's decriminalize drugs" part of me was irritated at the sight of LASD's Special Enforcement Bureau deputies—the best of the best—lined up alongside red carpet galas with blinders to the full-bloomed pupils of celebrities parading by, I was even more aggrieved at the profession's inability to adequately defend itself against proliferating allegations of institutional racism.

These rampant abdications found me second-guessing my career choice early on. But that was part and parcel of the problem—it wasn't just a goddamned job, but my fucking *career.* I had invested a considerable amount of time, sweat, and energy into it and could see myself eventually contributing in some manner greater than my current capacity.

If I was still occasionally beating the steering wheel on the drive home, it didn't change the fact that I was in it for the long haul. And whatever my growing reservations regarding the powers that were, I still respected the line cop. Hell, if anything, I admired him all the more for recognizing what he was up against and still plugging away at it.

But my own efforts were increasingly token in nature.

I still saw myself as a pretty honest cop. And yet the more wiggle room there was, and the more things fell away from the black and white of crimes universally recognized as such, the more I found myself taking advantage of it.

Wiggle room was to be found just about everywhere.

Outright stealing never much appealed to me, and outside of time and the usual clerical crap—paper and pens—I have never taken something that belonged to another.

Did I have the opportunity to misappropriate things belonging to others?

Thousands of times—incident to every residential or commercial door I found open, every burglary I investigated, every car I searched, every detainee's wallet inventoried, and every decedent's home whose care was momentarily entrusted to me.

Fear of getting caught might have been an inhibiting factor, but my hesitance to violate the laws I was enforcing was mostly in keeping with a desire to limit my hypocrisies.

That said, the brain can get acclimated to the varying degrees of deceit, so that the more you do, the more you can do. The syllogistic reasoning employed within the profession was not remarkably different than that of the clerics of old: The ends justify the means.

But if a cop's thumb was pressing on Lady Justice's scales, at least its owner, nine times out of ten, had honest-to-God good intentions. Not only did I figure I was one of the nine, but I could do much worse than applying some of John Stuart Mill's arguments to my evolving concept of how that might be achieved. As part of a societal collective, I really didn't want to screw anyone over. I wanted to do the right thing.

But long before I'd come along, the profession's practitioners had learned that doing the right thing could gain the wrong results, so that practices were increasingly nuanced.

If a disproportionate number of minorities ended up on the wrong side of the cell bars and accusations of racism followed, everyone from prosecutors to police administrators would come up with new means to justify the numbers. Aside from necessary inclusions of race data into just about every logging mechanism available to us, we were given all manner of convoluted excuses to insinuate into every arrest narrative and courtroom testimony.

If it wasn't lying, it was at least narrative embroidery.

March 2, 1999. Almost a year after the Easter shooting, Estevan's trial started. Jeff Deerborn, Brad Higgins, Dillon Paulson, Duane Miller, and I sat in the D.A.'s office and discussed the case. I was surprised to find out new facts about the shooting.

I learned that Higgins and Deerborn were shoulder to shoulder at one point when they saw movement on the other side of the fence. They both debated firing, wondering if it was the suspect, as the info being relayed to them over the radio indicated the girl was still in the house. But Higgins held off, and they soon saw the girl's hand reach over the fence. They told her to get over as quickly as possible.

Deerborn later said, "Thank God we didn't shoot her. That would have bothered me."

"Not me," said Higgins.

Inside the courtroom, the girl was testifying on the stand that she was never afraid during the incident and didn't know why we were there in the first place. The D.A. later played the 911 tape of her pleading in a terrified voice for deputies to hurry because Estevan was trying to get into the house to kill them. She then testified that she didn't care if I got shot or if any of us got shot—that's what we were paid to do.

The jurors rolled their eyes and the defense attorney said she probably buried his client with that one. While her statement turned me off, I took a Malcolm X posture on the matter: by any means necessary. If it took suffering her asinine sentiments to garner sympathy from the jury, so be it. I felt like all we did was interrupt an act of social Darwinism. Of course, we didn't get to choose whom we rolled to help.

Talking with Miller at the end of the day, I admitted to feeling like an idiot.

"Why would you?"

"Oh, it's not that we did anything that was embarrassing. But if I died and went to heaven or hell or wherever my destination lies and found out what I'd been killed over, then I really would feel like an idiot."

In a pretty decent Rodney King impression, Miller asked, "Can't we all just get along?"

"If we could, we wouldn't be here."

I did a fine job giving my own testimony until I explained to the courtroom how Higgins had gotten ahead of me and doubled back from safety to drag me back to cover. I didn't blubber, but only because I kept my mouth shut for several excruciating seconds that might have been as difficult for the jurors to watch as it was for me to endure.

The judge kindly gave me a cup of water.

I resumed my testimony, explaining what happened at the scene up to the time I was transported. I was noticeably humbler on the stand, less confrontational than in the preliminary trial. I didn't want to alienate myself from the affections of the jurors.

The judge thanked me for my testimony.

During the sentencing phase of the trial, I was given the opportunity to read a prepared statement about how the shooting had impacted me. In my speech, I described the parallels between Estevan and myself. We were roughly the same age, raised in the same community, and may have frequented the same movie theaters throughout our childhoods. Yet our lives took decidedly different paths that brought us together on that Easter evening. We'd made decisions along the way that would affect not only our own lives, but the lives of others. That I had chosen a profession with the intent to help people while Estevan had chosen avocations that led him to be a third-strike felon and attempted murderer should leave the jury with an obvious choice.

Mr. Estevan, in my opinion, had intended to kill someone that night. If it wasn't his ex-girlfriend, it was going to be a cop. It didn't seem to matter to him. The worst part of Mr. Estevan's behavior was the fact that he lay in wait for us as we approached the house. He knew exactly what he was doing and did as much as he could to protect himself while he assaulted the police.

The following Tuesday, I called the D.A.'s office to ask about the outcome of the trial. The girl I spoke with pulled up part of the transcript on the computer. "We the jury find the defendant in the above described case guilty on counts one and two: guilty of 245d P.C., Assault with a Deadly Weapon on a Peace Officer, a lesser included offense…" She said that it was difficult to discern the rest, but he'd also been convicted on counts three and four, which were filed as 245 as well.

My heart sank somewhat. Estevan had been convicted, but not on either attempted murder charge. I thanked her and hung up.

I felt numb. I knew that time heals all wounds, but I hoped it would give me some sense of perspective.

I had great difficulty understanding that the jury would have found him no more culpable if he'd swung at me with a crow bar. Perhaps, they needed greater sanguinary evidence. Maybe I should have had my pants booked into evidence, given a little more show and a lot less tell.

I knew what I'd like to have happen. I wanted to see him put behind walls, enclosed for time immemorial. To have that whole "Cask of Amontillado" thing done with him.

The next day, District Attorney Danielle Miller called to set me straight on what actually happened. Apparently, the girl in the D.A.'s office had read to me from the wrong transcript.

Estevan had been found guilty of attempted murder of a police officer with special circumstances (on me); attempted murder of a police officer (Higgins); assault with a deadly weapon (Deerborn and Bernal), as well as multiple counts of residential robbery, burglary, terrorist threats, possession of stolen weapons, and more. In short, he was convicted on 16 of the 17 felony counts.

On April 15, he was sentenced to 160 years.

The formal review of our Easter shooting had become one protracted, nightmarish affair. After passing scrutiny by Internal Affairs, the case went to the commander with input from Captain Buckley. Lt. Ron Olofsson's elliptical descriptions about what had been discussed behind closed doors immediately aroused my suspicions. I was a little stressed and pissed about the continual Monday-morning inferences, although to my face everyone seemed highly supportive of the actions we took.

I thought about how carefully Olsen had chosen his words. It sounded to me like he was saying that the commander and captain did a good job of "defending our actions." Like I was supposed to be grateful! What the hell was there to defend?

I wish someone had the balls to come out and tell us what and where we did something wrong, because they sure as hell hadn't come out and told us that we did anything right. Having read the criteria for the Medal of Valor criteria, I thought we are all deserving, Higgins in particular.

While the Department is notoriously vigilant in documenting shit on us, it is curiously lax when it comes to favorable recognition.

But when it came to the shooting? Not a word of thanks, good job, way to go, or jack shit. Even the damned shrink failed to called back in six months. Everybody treated the whole affair as an afterthought.

During the conversation, Olsen did mention that special recognition had been given to Higgins—as it should have been. When asked what the word was on any *official* recognition, he said that, yes, something should be formally given.

Then he asked if I would help write it.

Help him write it?

I was pissed. The whole thing had been written up and submitted by Will Halpern a year ago, only to be shit-canned by a lieutenant whom I routinely butted heads with ("too flowery" a description of the shootout was the explanation given).

Now the whole awards thing was being resurrected as an afterthought?

Thanks, but no thanks, I said.

Unknown to me, Olsen had picked up the ball and submitted the Medal of Valor recommendation. The awards committee convened, reviewed the incident, and unanimously approved it.

On the day of the Medal of Valor ceremony, Stacey and I got up early and drove to downtown Los Angeles. Our arrival was delayed, thanks in part to the convergence of Lakers fans who had descended on the area for the Lakers parade. I didn't know to what extent I should resent the Lakers for winning the NBA championship, or the Pacers for simply protracting their own agony. I do know that I was disappointed that our humble little fête was going to be impacted by the festivities honoring a bunch of mercenary jocks.

Nonetheless, we arrived at the LA Mart before most of the honorees and special guests. While the exterior of the building wasn't much to look at, the interior was quite impressive, and I was grateful to the Barkley for hosting it.

As more people arrived, I began seeing faces that I had not seen for years—many I could have happily gone years longer without seeing. I was thankful that two of the guests scheduled to be seated at our table were absent: Commander Nakamura and Captain McGowan. It was enough that I'd seen the commander at the grievance hearing on Monday.

Mom and Dad arrived with their friends. I could tell that Dad was nervous, but proud. Stacey looked radiant in her seventh month of pregnancy.

After a couple hours of rehearsals, a Torrance dance troupe kicked off the ceremony with a routine to the song "I Need a Hero." Halfway through the song, we marched onto the stage. As the dancers took their bows, we were applauded then returned to our seats with our guests. There was a nice prayer that honored cops while also beseeching for God to give criminals a change of heart, and failing that, a change of address.

Veteran actor James Whitmore read the narratives of each scenario that garnered the Medals of Valor. Ours was the last scenario and presentation made. Stacey later asked if I felt self-conscious at the many times Mr. Whitmore read my name. I told her yes, but that didn't mean that I found it any less agreeable. I was more worried about stumbling on the podium or knocking my head against the sheriff's when I bent to receive the ribbon around my neck.

After the presentations, we assembled in the foyer for group photos. Some of the deputies were asked to speak to the media. They canvassed the deputies for those who had Spanish surnames, and of those, who could speak Spanish to speak with *La Opinion*. I noticed that they were apparently disinterested in speaking with us despite the fact that we had saved an Hispanic family. But then, they probably would not have appreciated what I had to say.

All in all, it was a very nice day. Still, I was conspicuously aware that the vast majority of people within a five-mile radius—some 250,000 of them—were more concerned with honoring the Lakers. At some level, I resented it.

The next morning, I checked the *Los Angeles Times* and the *San Gabriel Valley Tribune* websites. The *Times* had a brief piece on the ceremonies, but did little to explain what had been honored and why. At least, they got my name right.

That's more than I can say for the *Tribune*, who only saw fit to mention Anthony Turbin (of all people!).

It was not for worry. I knew that they'd more than make amends the first time I screwed up big time.

Towards evening, David Stein stopped by the office and told me something that had happened during my days off. Apparently, someone had plastered flyers throughout the facility with the words "valor" and "courage" written on them, followed by the Webster's definition of each. Below this, they gave an example of how the words were defined in Industry station, something along the lines of "deputies get shot at and run screaming into the night."

Captain Buckley was furious. Starting with the 10:00 a.m. briefing and finishing with the 10:00 p.m. briefing, he made his feelings known to Industry deputies. He offered another word, as well as its definition in his book: "cowardice."

He cited the anonymous author of the flyers as a prime example. He suggested that anyone with any questions concerning the validity of acknowledging those involved with the shooting should come to his office.

I really appreciated his efforts. Still, I wonder if he may have inadvertently done more harm than good. Even those whose eyes had not happened upon the flyers—including me—were now at least aware of them.

Still, I do know that I would have done far worse had I been there on either of the two days. I felt somewhat self-conscious in retrospect as he had stopped by the office earlier and we'd spoken for several minutes without his giving any indication of what had happened. I wish I had known. I would have thanked him. Better late than never.

I suspected I knew who the author was, but remained unsure of his identity and his intentions. It may have been an innocent joke. It may not have been. It may have been payback for some of the attitudes allegedly projected by some of the Medal of Valor recipients. I hated to think that it was merely an objective appraisal of the night's festivities.

Bernal and I discussed both the flyers and the medals. He confirmed some of my suspicions regarding the take of many deputies regarding the medals—that they'd been passed out like candy.

With our shooting, there was a perception that some recipients had profited by riding the coat tails of those closer to ground zero. More than that, a large number of deputies believed that the Department had been overly generous in its acknowledgments of incidents at other assignments. As disheartening as the flyers were, the judgments being passed on those incidents that had occurred at other LASD assignments were harsher, with critics charging that the dangers inherent to some had been amplified in their documentation.

In the years following our awards ceremony, the numbers of medals awarded diminished substantially. Those that were so acknowledged were less apt to be criticized for it.

For my part, I was confused and hurt. Had I been seeing nothing more than the pissing and moaning of a bunch of jealous malcontents or the genuine disappointment and disillusionment of people who have grown resentful of the politicization of the award ceremony? Part of me could empathize with the naysayers. It was difficult not to acknowledge that the Department was putting some recipients more in the limelight than others. Often, it proved a peripheral participant to the incident in question.

While indulging my latest funk-induced introspection, I divined some creative inspiration: The story of a man who gets a medal but feels undeserving of it, and therefore feels he must do something to earn the right to keep it.

That this was not autobiographical is readily asserted.

There was an insecure and immature part of me that liked receiving such formal acknowledgments. Moreover, there was a part of me that was all too anxious to receive the medal. Whether or not I deserved it was for others to decide. I considered it compensation for things I should have been acknowledged for, but wasn't (and yet how thankful I was in not being held culpable on many a transgression for which I was no less responsible). In personally inventorying the physical and emotional injuries incurred on the job, no offense had been more harmful than the occasional backstabbing by a fellow employee.

Aggrieved, I thought about writing a rebuttal flyer but concluded that it would do more harm than good.

But while part of me wanted to keep my mouth shut in the belief that it would speak better for me, another wondered: But then who speaks for the other deputies maligned?

Brad Higgins could have run off "screaming into the night" but he didn't. Instead, he doubled back to rescue a fellow deputy, who was not content to further engage the suspect, but was resigned to it. But one does not engage in a tug of war with his would-be savior. I was, and am, grateful for his heroism. Bernal and Deerborn likewise could have run but they, too, elected to stand their ground and provide cover fire for us.

The identity of the person culpable for the flyers was never made known to me. There was only one thing of which I was certain.

The author was not at the scene on the night in question.

10

Cultural Sensitivity, Terrorism, and Doing More with Less

There's no way to rule innocent men. The only power any government has is the power to crack down on criminals. Well, when there aren't enough criminals, one makes them. One declares so many things to be a crime that it becomes impossible for men to live without breaking laws.

—Ayn Rand, *Atlas Shrugged*

For a time, I thought about transferring to another station, possibly back to Temple. But Evan Lidstrom gave me some advice.

"There's going to be assholes everywhere you go," he noted. "Why go out of your way for them?"

And so it was that I decided to keep them commuter friendly.

When it came to assholes, there was some representation among the deputies. But their constituency was so small and so obnoxious that nobody else liked them either. Lacking social or political clout, they rarely proved a problem for me.

Lieutenants were another story. Even if they were largely disliked, they nonetheless had rank and could make one's life miserable. None drove me more bat-shit crazy than Jim Clerc.

I'd always thought the man would have done well at Sheriff's Information Bureau. Not that he was particularly photogenic but he did have enough political ambition to put everyone else at the Bureau to shame.

Our paths had first crossed at Temple, but only briefly and even then with hardly a word between us. I took note of his complete absence of a personality and suspected that his had been a painful adolescence.

So while I didn't know the man, I at least had enough compassion to want to be civil towards him.

There'd been no overt hostility in our limited contacts with one another at Temple and so I felt comfortable enough to say "Hi!" to him as we'd pass in the long corridor connecting MCJ to Transit Services Bureau. My salutation was met with a dead-eyed glare of Duraflame intensity. We were the only two in the echoey corridor, so his point to make it known that I was beneath acknowledgment was all the more conspicuous.

Really? I thought. *You get promoted to lieutenant and suddenly you're King Shit?*

When my moment of *what the fuck?* wonderment had passed, I made a mental note to never say another word to the asshole unless my duties obligated me to, a commitment our separate assignments at the time made easy to keep.

But now we were at Industry and often working the same hours. As such, there were occasions where I had to discuss everything from subordinates' uses of force to employee injuries to the times I'd checked the jail during a given shift. I fulfilled these obligations with as much neutrality in my voice as I could muster.

This, for the most part, wasn't as difficult as I'd imagined it would be.

My compassion for him had long since died, replaced by the certainty that the bullying he'd doubtless endured as a teen had probably been deserved, and was destined to be sublimated upon others for the remainder of the bastard's life. I'd once heard a judge take into account the tragic circumstances a convicted serial killer had endured growing up. He expressed sympathy for the boy the killer had been, but contempt for the man he'd become. That pretty much summed up my take on Clerc, a man I wanted desperately to take on, circumstances permitting.

There was one problem. He would never avail me a forum in which to confront his miserable ass. Others with more limited faculties could be counted upon to give me an excuse to open up with both barrels, and disabuse them of the notion of ever trying such shit again. But Clerc was cagey enough to never denigrate me, or challenge me on things easily rebutted.

That it wasn't my style to be a snitch made him comfortable enough

to delegate tasks to me, like dishing off his watch commander responsibilities while sneaking away to watch his son play baseball. I never
objected as I was all for anything that put distance between us. But while
he saw no problem indulging his familial pursuits, he begrudged my
actual pursuits on duty.

After I'd gotten in vehicle pursuits on back-to-back nights, he
chewed me out.

"You're supposed to be supervising," he'd told me in the watch commander's office. "Not out making arrests."

Fine, fucker, I thought. *No sweat off my balls.*

And so I stopped. Just one more nail in the coffin of my proactive
policing career.

To my knowledge, he didn't bear me any more ill-will than he did
others at the station; certainly, he never tilted his hand at anything I
might have ever done to offend him, save for occupying a position one
tier below his.

And that might well have been enough.

The fact was that Clerc didn't show much use for those he considered beneath him; namely those who were below his rank. There were
exceptions—he knew what he could get away with and with whom based
upon their political affiliations on the Department.

When it came to dealing with higher-ups, he could be as star-struck
and fawning as any teenage girl. Nobody excelled more as an ass-kisser.

But his nature was also so patently obnoxious, and his agenda no
less transparent that his upward ascent on the Department remained a
mystery soluble only by the notion that his personal library was stocked
with 16th century tomes on dealing with the devil. He was as insensitive
and anal-retentive an authoritarian as I have ever seen or could imagine.

One autumn, I got sick and for most of one week, my temperature
was over 102 degrees; the nine hours' sleep I got on the fifth day eclipsed
the total of the other four. The entire time I lay in bed, unable to find
any position or medication that allayed the fever or soreness that
plagued me. I felt like I was living some hype's lost weekend, sweating
and experiencing delirium tremens.

After finally seeking treatment at an urgent care center, I was given
a diagnosis of double pneumonia.

Two weeks later when I returned to work, the first thing Clerc said to me wasn't "How are you?" or "Glad to see you're better," but "You didn't turn in your audits for October."

Fuck! The bastard knew I was out sick.

Such were the reasons I relegated Clerc to his own taxonomic status, *Homo Culus*, and loved it when his name came up and another deputy referred to him as "that no-good, no personality Green Bay-loving asshole." I hadn't even known he was a Packers fan, but it fit.

Despite his own penchant for going outside of the area and being inaccessible, he found it necessary to keep tabs on me on the radio.

"Are you rolling on this hot call?"

"Yes."

"I hadn't heard you on the coordination."

"I was in the restroom at the time and didn't want everyone to hear the highly distinctive echo in the background."

He laughed. It was the single time he had exhibited a sense of humor.

My contempt for him wasn't because he wrote anything up on me. He never did. But then he never had any cause to. We were both too smart to give the other any ammunition.

I didn't hate him because he was void of warmth, or even civility. I hated him for his kind—and of his kind he was the worst I had to deal with on a routine basis.

There were others who could be counted upon to pay lip service to service-oriented policing while acting like total dicks to their subordinates.

But if some pencil-pushing administrator expected me to cite chapter and verse of the Department's policy and procedures manual, he was going to be disappointed; if he jumped in my shit about it, I got right back in his face.

As noted, Lt. Tom Wolanski had started to give me a ration of shit by wagging an imperious finger in my face and saying, "I'll tell you what you're going to do..."

"You're not going to tell me a goddamn thing until you lower your voice!" I yelled, my own finger darting right back in his face. "And you're going to speak to me with respect, or not at all!"

As his voice had been carrying, I had no problem making damned sure that anyone who'd heard him was no less privileged with my reply.

"Look, I didn't have the manual with me in the field," I admitted, knowing that my copy had been wedged in the trunk of my car and sharing space with an emergency blanket, road flares, spare tire, helmet, my gear box, all manner of Departmental miscellany—including cite books, various crime report forms, abridged and unabridged penal and vehicle codes, booking slips, and evidence bags—and other shit that I didn't want or feel the need to wade through to research at the time.

"But then," I continued, "I sure as hell knew that I had access to one here at the station and could review it for clarification on the matter at hand. I just figured I'd give you an update on the field situation as a courtesy beforehand. From now on, you'll be the last person I speak to on a situation until I make sure to have all my ducks in order!"

I never had another problem with the asshole.

In the fall of 2000, I'd successfully applied for a supervisor position in the Crime Prevention Unit that was housed in a modular building across the street from the station. The lieutenant I ended up working for was someone I already knew and liked and proved to be a joy to work for.

Unfortunately, the lieutenant ended up leaving the Department shortly thereafter for personal reasons and I found myself working for his replacement, a man whose overly-reserved nature aroused paranoia in those more accustomed to wearing their emotions on their sleeves, such as myself.

For a while, we worked to develop one another's confidences. While my attempts were largely unsolicited revelations of my family history, his were largely stories about how corrupt he thought Sheriff Lee Baca and many of the Department's upper echelon were. He spoke of the sheriff's ties with Asian gang affiliations, suspect campaign contributions, and favors extended far and wide to celebrities and other notables. He said that he had learned much of this while working the Asian Crime Task Force and that there was little doubt that things were not kosher within the Department.

A growing lack of affinity for the man at the helm—Sheriff Baca—as well as for his undersheriff, Lenny Waldo, made it all too easy for me to want to believe the lieutenant's stories, particularly as they echoed the sentiments by others supposedly in the know. This was particularly the case with Waldo, a man whose singular impression on me had been that of an arrogant blow-hard ass.

Still, if the heads of the Department were so corrupt and a plethora of anecdotal evidence so indicting, then why the hell wasn't anybody doing anything about it?

Part of the answer came soon enough, at least as it related to my lieutenant. And it boiled down to character.

It did not speak well of me that the sight of Lieutenant Tak Itachi hobbling down the main corridor of the station with his latest flare-up of gout could prompt a smile out of me. But any claims to the contrary would be bullshit, and that was one market I was content to allow him a monopoly.

Whereas my dad's bullshit was largely of the "in your face, tongue-in-cheek" variety—the kind that implicitly acknowledged itself as such— Itachi's brand was subtler. It ran the gamut from self-aggrandizing stories of "tuning up" (his word, not mine, but interpreted as "thumping") his fair number of detainees as a rookie of the year at ELA Station, to the various pieties he espoused as a supposedly devout Christian.

Nonetheless, I applied myself to the tasks at hand, which included getting the Emergency Preparedness Network (EPN) up and running.

The lieutenant and I had discussed forming a coalition of emergency services personnel with an eye towards putting on info-seminars to area residents. Local first responders—including Baldwin Park CHP, Irwindale PD, and LA County Fire—were brought on board and soon we were conducting presentations on fires, terrorism, earthquake preparedness and more.

These events were held at local venues, parks and firehouses and the like, and at a time of heightened civic awareness and involvement.

The terrorist attacks of 9/11 had changed people. They were apprehensive as to what kind of threats were looming and what they should do to prevent them; failing that, how best to deal with them.

We tried to answer their questions, with presentations on fire hazards, crime suppression and more. None proved more popular than one event held at the Industry Hills Palms Resort that featured seminars on a variety of terrorist concerns and drew hundreds in attendance. Topics ranging from suicide bombers to dirty bombs were candidly addressed by experts in the fields.

None of this shit was easy. Not all the EMS services involved were equally enthusiastic about the programs, nor could I blame them. This wasn't their baby; they'd been delegated the cooperation through their own higher-ups. And how much input would CHP have in a fire presentation after all? ("Yield to fire trucks or we'll ticket your ass!")

But while everyone was tasked with executing some aspect of our events, some were more conscientious about the enterprise than others. As the coordinator for these events, I occasionally had to crack the whip and call people out for miscues and get everyone back on the same page. This was largely accomplished during our monthly event planning meetings and intervening email correspondences, letting it be known that while I never wanted to embarrass anyone, I sure as hell didn't want to be embarrassed by not identifying lapses and addressing them before they became issues.

It paid off. Soon we had businesses anxious to be affiliated with EPN lining up to donate monies and goods to the cause. Emergency Preparedness Network funds soon eclipsed those of the commingled Crime Prevention funds creating a need for a separate bank account.

But someone higher up noticed that we had a five-digit balance in this new account and got pissed. Who authorized this? What were the funds being used for?

And the big parenthetical: How could we get our cut?

It was around this time that I passed both the written and oral examination for lieutenant. With the first two hurdles over and well on my way to earning pay commensurate to a position I was already performing on a routine basis, I simply had to wait for the results of my appraisal of promotability. Irrespective of any natural warmth shared between the lieutenant and myself, I was warily optimistic. I'd worked hard, deserved a decent score, and thought my religious supervisor would do right by his subordinate heathen.

Out of a possible 100, I was given an 85.

Eighty-five was high enough to insulate the evaluator from any accusations of sabotage while guaranteeing that the candidate would be out of the running. I confronted Itachi on the matter.

"I'm not happy with my AP rating."

"Well, it's what you received."

"I deserved better."

"I believe differently. I gave you as high a score as possible. There are only so many higher scores that can be given out at the station level and you know it."

"Yeah, and I also know I have been busting my ass here and for some time too. You're my supervisor. I expect you to advocate for me."

"You should advocate for yourself more. Not too many people downtown know you. Those that do…"

He didn't finish. He didn't need to.

If I was unhappy before, I was downright pissed now.

To have to campaign for something—to promote oneself through aggrandizement—turned me off. Any promotion that would require a concession to pride or conscience I would sooner deem a demotion.

And so I joined the latest fraternity of newly disappointed would-be lieutenants. I was hurting, but not for company.

Next to getting terminated, or demoted, one of the most demoralizing things an employee could experience was being denied a deserved promotion. The way I saw it, it wasn't a matter of my having failed to perform the job well or creating the requisite work foundation with which to supervise. Certainly, I had proven myself less a liability than an asset—which was more than could be said of others who ended up getting promoted. And of the thousands of field situations that I had supervised, not one had resulted in a lawsuit for the Department.

Nor had I failed to perform well on the written and oral portions of the promotional exam. No, it had boiled down to a phenomenon one lieutenant characterized as either being on the train, or not—and I had failed to squeeze my ass in there like some commuter at rush hour.

Itachi was right about one thing. There were only so many "high scores" to go around. It was well known throughout the Department that the folks in Region II were always going to be disproportionately represented when promotion time came around, as future felon Peter Tawagoto was known to take care of "his boys." Those of us in Region I would have to jockey for any leftover scores.

I may have been nobody's boy, but at least I was nobody's bitch.

In the spirit of misery loving company, I commiserated with a fellow non-conformist.

Henry Torosian had invited me to accompany him to an appeal of the Lieutenants Exam at the PPOA Conference Center. I considered going, less out of any personal outrage than for the dramatic fodder that stood to be heard. I settled for listening to Torosian.

As this had been Torosian's third time at bat, he was particularly frustrated. He had spent four years studying for the promotion exam only to discover that the whole thing was a farce, a carefully orchestrated charade by which the Department could handpick who they wanted to promote.

"Hell, just band the whole bunch and go through and handpick who you want," he lamented. "I don't care if I get asked to dance or not, I just want to be in the room and hear the music. I get tired of sitting in the parking lot in the rain."

Torosian said that he had a double misfortune in that not only did the civilian on his board fall asleep during his exam, but that the sworn member—a female captain—had downgraded him. Apparently, she had downgraded 14 of 15 applicants, the sole exception being a chief's aide.

Captains were going through candidates and handpicking those they wanted to hear. John Doron, another sergeant at Industry Station, had fared no better. A review of his oral exam scores revealed that the civilian board member had initially given him high marks which were then erased so as to be brought in line with the scores given by the captain on his board.

Torosian, who had been handing out the Department's Core Value Statement cards like candy prior to the exam, said the Department could take its fucking cards and shove them right back where they came from as they were all just a crock of shit anyway. He noted that the Department could do a good job of eliminating a good many political undesirables by eliminating the written portion of the exam, the sole objective portion of these exams.

Torosian concluded by saying that he was getting too old to be going through this needless aggravation. Too many years on. Too few opportunities left.

I felt bad for Torosian. Myself, too. I took solace in having learned a lesson from his experience. I knew that I'd done well enough on the written and oral exams to advance to the final round. The rest was a charade, so I decided to cancel the pursuit.

The bottom line was, if you weren't out aggrandizing yourself, then you sure as hell had better be doing it for somebody else. Such were the reasons why certain old school maxims—"It's not what you know, but who you blow"—still made the rounds. For all the lip service the Department paid to patrol being its bedrock, it just didn't give a shit about the man down the trenches.

Meanwhile, the sheriff's driver could be counted on as a lock to promote. The chief's aide too. The guy or gal at Sheriff's Information Bureau, as well—if he or she could dodge the occasional landmine.

The poor bastard out there doing battle in the street was destined to keep on doing battle—and running interference for the next newly promoted lieutenant.

It wasn't enough that Itachi had screwed me over on the lieutenant's exam. With the arrival of a former detective who'd returned to the station as a sergeant, word had it that Itachi was angling to place him in my spot.

Whether or not he'd intended it as part of his campaign to get rid of me, or was a simple act of cowardice, Itachi attempted to use me as a scapegoat.

The incident revolved around a second bank account that'd been created for the donated funds we'd been fast accumulating for the Emergency Preparedness Network. The area chief was looking over the station's financial records and happened upon the account.

"What's this?" he'd asked, aghast that the station had a new and suspect fund. "Who authorized this?"

He'd posed the question to both the captain and Itachi, both of whom suddenly acquired amnesia and said that they would ask the sergeant in charge—me—about it.

The only thing was, another lieutenant who'd been in the room warned me about the possible wrath that might be coming down on me.

I didn't understand why the chief had gotten his panties in a bunch in the first place and would have happily discussed the matter with him. It wasn't as though we'd solicited the funds—these donations had been ponied up by organizations that had faith in the Network and wanted to see it grow. As the last thing we could be accused of was creating a slush fund, the chief's concerns didn't bother me one iota. The failure of my immediate superiors to cowardly and connivingly own up to their responsibility did concern me, if only as it proved revelatory of their character—or lack of it.

No matter. I expressed my appreciations to my confidant and simply retrieved a copy of the written request to the branch to open the EPN account.

The one signed by the captain and Itachi.

Thanks to my station confidants, I was aware of other machinations at work. Whether or not the campaign was being orchestrated so much against me or on behalf of another was immaterial. The bottom line was that I was destined to be squeezed out.

I was pissed and determined to make a preemptive strike—by striking against coordinating any further EPN events.

I figured that this was fair game, as Itachi had seen fit to take all the news media credit himself, he might as well earn it too. Much of this was communicated through emails which became increasingly acerbic in tone (at least on my part). I was eventually told to vacate my locker. I did.

And moved my shit back across the street.

I don't know that I experienced much in the way of PTSD in the aftermath of my shooting, but there was no denying the sense of apprehension that accompanied me on my return to patrol.

That I was destined to once again essay the role of prodigal son was, I realized, a foregone conclusion. Deputies had been continually siphoned off from the Crime Prevention Unit until there'd been just two deputies, a civilian worker, and myself. Eventually, it would become a shadow of its former self with its daily operations seen by one community service officer. Collateral casualties included the Emergency Preparedness Network.

Whatever my feelings on the matter and the loss of community ties, the unit's demise was by any objective standard less of a transgression than the cutting back that had affected other units and bureaus as the result of the Department's budget crisis. Never before had the Department been so seemingly destined to be the Pauper Police.

I even realized that it really didn't matter what Itachi's agenda was, at least as it related to my going back to the patrol side of things. Even if the S.O.B. had loved me I'd still be back in the field. Still, I disliked the man as a matter of principle; namely, his lack of having any.

While the three years spent at the unit had ultimately proved little more than an agreeable enough distraction, it had at least insulated me from the prospect of ballistic interfacing and had afforded me some perks along the way (there had been no shortage of freebies and discretionary use of time).

But sitting in the sergeant's unit I would find myself entertaining mordant contemplations, wondering just how many cops had been denied promotions or reassigned from some choice assignment and had met their fate in patrol as a result of it.

My umbrella of resentments proved all-encompassing. I resented the fast-tracking of minority women—some of whom I otherwise liked—who were being promoted without ever having worked a day in patrol. Sent out for a three-month accelerated training program, they got their ticket punched and gravitated toward whatever administration position awaited them. I resented the good old boy network that had helped foment the Department's desperate and civilly extorted attempt to have women compensated for the opportunities denied them in years past. I resented affirmative action no matter who was profiting by it. Having lived in its shadow for four decades I'd gotten tired of wondering when they would just get rid of the fucking thing once and for all.

Most of all, I resented my own questionable and highly subjective principles. I wasn't sure to what degree they'd helped or hurt me in my Department movements, but figured that their biggest legacy might yet be getting my ass killed.

One night a call came into the station of a man brandishing a firearm at a local motel. Industry deputies responded and contacted the motel clerk and others who'd seen the man. They were told the man had been waving a BB gun, but that was about it.

Satisfied that there was no threat, the deputies walked up a stairway to the second floor landing. Approaching the occupant's door, they knocked.

Suddenly the man stepped outside, squeezing off shots from a gun. A deputy immediately returned fire. When the gunfire stopped, the suspect was down.

So was an Industry deputy.

The shooting happened on my night off and I watched coverage of the crime scene on the local news. Nothing in the initial coverage suggested any imminent danger to the life of the injured deputy. I called the station. The news was not good.

The deputy was Michael Aquino. I'd known him since we'd worked together at Men's Central Jail a decade before. He'd arrived at Industry shortly after me and had gone on to compete in the Police Olympics, taking a gold medal in bodybuilding. His was the kind of physique that was the subject of open admiration among young women and good-natured ribbing from envious deputies. Over the following week, it was that body that kept Aquino in the fight for his life.

Throughout, friends and loved one's kept a bedside vigil inside the hospital. There was an outpouring of love and prayers from the community. But in passing through both sides of Aquino's neck the bullet had done irreversible damage.

He died without ever regaining consciousness.

I attended the funeral. The sight of Mike Aquino, Jr., at his father's graveside devastated all in attendance and I sobbed all the drive home, clutching my son all the tighter that night.

The call that resulted in Mike's death and its handling was Monday morning quarterbacked and formally dissected by those at the scene and others whose positions obligated them to develop an intimate familiarity with it. Formally, critiques of the tactics involved were largely of the "consideration should have been given to..." variety.

But as time went by, deputies close to ground zero portrayed a less favorable image of what had happened in the moments immediately prior to and following the shooting. The wild west swagger that had accompanied the deputies' march up the stairwell—and following the incident, an immediate huddle off to the side between some deputies as Aquino lay bleeding—did not sit well with some of the assisting deputies.

The degree to which the criticisms were accurate I couldn't say. But they did cause me to reevaluate my initial support of the involved deputy, whose cocksure disposition had never sat well with me, but whose initiative in the field could not be questioned.

What was inarguable was that I would have handled the call differently. Not that the knock and talk would not necessarily have been given consideration, albeit with a different configuration of manpower on the landing.

But the fact that the suspect had turned off lights in his room as deputies arrived would have been enough for me to initiate a call from the lobby to his room, in a bid to have him come outside and talk. If he hadn't answered the phone or otherwise complied with the request, we might well have simply left, as no crime had at that point been committed.

None of this mitigated the culpability of the deceased suspect, whose suicide by cop was as cruel and stupid as any I'd ever heard. Responsibility for his death and Aquino's rested with him, as did the end of a second deputy's career, the deputy who'd fired his service weapon that night and ultimately resigned from the Department.

During my time at SIB, I'd stumbled upon a book someone had painstakingly put together. Pasted inside were news clippings detailing line of duty deaths since the Department's inception. That a couple of other long forgotten fatalities would eventually get added to it—indeed, I'd happened upon one that'd been missed—was no indictment on the archivist's efforts. Even the County's memorial wall at the Academy was continually being updated with the names of officers whose deaths had somehow not been earlier commemorated.

Those clippings had fascinated me, and I was shocked to find that the first two line of duty deaths had been no less than the County's first two sheriffs, both of whom had been shot and killed by wild west outlaws.

But among the felonious deaths chronicled were others, deputies who'd died through misadventures wherein fate alone could have been charged with malice. One had been killed in the Academy when a firearm with live ammunition had accidentally been deployed in a role-playing scenario. Another had been killed when a CHP officer's bullet ricocheted off the skull of an injured horse he was attempting to euthanize, and struck the deputy in the head. Other deputies died as the result of vehicle accidents, falls, and fires.

Later, I was able to use such insights in situations I encountered in patrol, such as when an Industry deputy dealt with a deer that'd been struck by a car and was lying in the roadway.

The animal posed a threat to traffic in both directions—thrashing around in a blind curve. The deputy asked permission to euthanize the creature. I authorized the effort, but with the caveat that he use a shotgun and aim for the heart. When I arrived on scene to find the deer's carcass riddled with bullets, the deputy explained that he'd forgotten to use the shotgun and used his Beretta instead. He had practically emptied his magazine trying to kill the deer, with the assistance of a telephone lineman who was equally ignorant of anatomy ("Try shooting it there … or there … or there…").

As terrible as I felt for Bambi, I was grateful the deputy hadn't tried shooting the animal in the head.

Seeing Aquino's young son at the gravesite was overwhelming and left me a tear-ridden idiot. All I could think of was what would happen to my own son if I was killed?

The thought branched off and got me thinking about other children, those whose mothers and fathers had been killed in the line of duty. How many deaths might have somehow been prevented? What tools could be brought to bear on a profession whose practitioners were availed varying levels of education, training, and support?

As I was still freelancing for *POLICE* magazine, I pitched the idea of an regular column wherein I would examine officer-involved shootings as experienced by the officers themselves. Similar profiles of OIS incidents and the lessons they afforded had been done before, notably by the likes of Massad Ayoob, Charles Remsberg, and others. But I wanted to capture the officer's perspective, in his own voice, as much as possible.

I'd anticipated all manner of resistance, not so much in-house— the editorial powers signed off almost as soon as I'd suggested it—as from the employing agencies. And it made sense. Statements by officers could be resurrected elsewhere, particularly in civil suits against them and their departments.

To that end, I decided that only those shootings whose investigations were closed and off any litigation radar would be profiled. Crime scene photographs would be requested, but not expected. Finally, not one word would go to print without the officer's permission.

I had an advantage going in. My experiences as a cop gave me empathy for their concerns and greater respect for both the difficulty of their job and the taxing nature of what I was asking of them. In many cases, they'd be re-opening old wounds, reacquainting themselves with things they'd just as soon forget. More than one would probably lose a good night's sleep over what was being asked of them.

I would not have asked if there'd been any doubt in my heart that other officers could profit by their experiences. I didn't want to just fixate on the pyrotechnics of the incident. I wanted to highlight a variety of concerns—the immediacy of the moment, any split-second adrenaline-enhanced inspiration, the political and social prices that were paid, and how the incident affected them and their families emotionally, or promoted changes in department practices and training, etc. Any of these factors could be brought to the forefront of the narrative depending on how the story lent itself.

Sergeant Rich Wilhelm took a leap of faith in being the point man in this experiment, and the willingness with which Wilhelm and his agency, Pueblo (CO) Police Department embraced the challenge was something I greatly appreciated.

None of this meant I could quit my day job, however much I wanted to. At the news that Sheriff Baca was coming to visit Industry Station and would be fielding questions, I submitted my own, including:

- Why do we need operations plans for conducting certain non-warrant, non–high risk searches?
- When will we see the next revised pursuit policy? Is the Department aware of any agencies attempting to challenge existing case law that has hamstrung us in our duty to protect?
- Why can't we issue deputies vouchers for disposable cameras to take to those less notable crimes wherein the taking of pictures is nonetheless obligatory? (As opposed to the less cost-effective practice of having sergeants shuttle cameras all over the county?)
- Why must we waste a lot of time taking third party complaints that don't involve possibly mitigating circumstances, e.g., those filed on behalf of a minor?
- In incidents wherein the evolution of a directed use of force and its justification are well documented on-camera, why can't we find a more streamlined manner of protecting ourselves (i.e., one that doesn't mean our having to make all manner of redundant documentation)?
- In recent months, we had a streamlined use-of-force form that was user-friendly while fulfilling the need for sufficient documentation. It has since been withdrawn in favor of a pre-existing form that is far more labor intensive. Is there any likelihood that we may see a more streamlined form in the future?
- As it stands, deputies document their respective uses of force as well as

any observations they may have had of force used by other deputies. Their documentations are then collectively synopsized by a sergeant. Why then must a watch commander then write what essentially becomes a redundant synopsis of the events? Is it not sufficient that if he finds the sergeant's findings appropriate, that he simply say as much?

- Historically, patrol has been lionized as the backbone of the Department. But I'd be curious to see the ratio of deputies and sergeants promoted from small unit assignments to those promoted from the field regions. Beyond that, there's been no shortage of anecdotal evidence of custody personnel getting A.P. scores equal to, and often exceeding, those of patrol personnel. Increasingly, it appears that it comes down to a good old boy system wherein reciprocal favors trump fieldwork.

- With the above in mind, and knowing the number of justified grievances filed behind the A.P. numbers, why not make the A.P. a "pass/fail" portion of the exam process instead of the artificial springboard it has come to be?

- For ten years, we've been told a streamlined check-off evaluation form will be made available for supervisors. When might this become a reality?"

Sheriff Baca addressed the promotional question, saying that I should get out more and make myself known.

None of the other questions were touched upon, or acted upon.

11

The Two-Step Paper Shuffle

One day, Lieutenant Alanna Auer had me accompany her to the empty watch commander's office. She looked like she could barely contain herself.

Closing the door, she sat me down.

"You're going to Detective Bureau."

I thanked her for the news. I'd been wanting to go to the Detective Bureau since I'd first heard of an anticipated opening. That I had the support of some of the D.B. guys, including the two sergeants that were already there, had encouraged some optimism, but nowhere near as much as the advocating that Auer had been doing on my behalf.

But shortly after my transfer in, it was apparent that Dave Johnson, one who'd lobbied for me, wanted to redefine the position that I was filling. While I'd appreciated his support, it didn't mean that I was going to be his lap dog and adhere to whatever agenda he had for me. The bottom line was that the D.B. lieutenant was my boss and so long as I was doing all right by him I was doing all right by me too.

That said, I was in charge of the operations end of things: Warrant service compliance, keeping track of detectives' work hours, sex offender registration, and working the occasional low-level crime with workable information.

I had only a couple of subordinates, and generally stayed out of their investigations. But if the sex crime investigator suspected a "victim" wasn't being candid, she'd let me know. I'd sit down with the person and, within a matter of minutes, could usually tell if they were lying.

It didn't take long to recognize a pattern. Some girls, faced with the prospect of dealing with a pissed-off parent for having been out too late, would fabricate a story of having been sexually assaulted. The allegation gave them an excuse for not being where they were supposed to be and evinced sympathy from their parents instead of anger. There were other reasons for filing such false reports, including some form of payback against someone.

Most of these "victims" were not flat-out sociopathic; they were just short-sighted in grabbing for a "get out of jail free" card. That they opted for such an out in the first place betrayed a lack of imagination, which was quickly evident when they started concocting the pertinent details of the alleged crime—what was said, the suspect's description, actions, etc.

If pointing out discrepancies in their stories wasn't enough to get them to drop the charade, laying a guilt trip on them usually did the trick. I'd tell them that in saddling us with this bullshit, they were obligating us to devote time to investigating it—time that could otherwise be spent on behalf of some girl who actually had been assaulted. Moreover, once the investigation was over, they could be prosecuted for filing a false police report. This was often the point they'd break down and confess.

That was about as interesting as it got working the Bureau, save for occasionally going out and assisting Johnson and his team on a search warrant service.

Not that I was complaining—at least, not as much as I had been. I had a cush job, was able to dress comfortably, and had weekends off. Still, it was perhaps the most boring time I ever had on the Department. I continually wondered if what I'd hemmed myself into after 24 years was what I really wanted to be doing.

Ironically, something non–Department-related would give me the opportunity for one last hurrah.

A job offer could be more than just a job offer—it could be at goddamned lifeline. And so it was with the case of *POLICE* magazine's offer.

Editor-in-Chief Dan Griffin had discussed the prospect with me before bouncing the idea off Publisher Leila Morris, and over an early dinner in Torrance she made it formal. They wanted to hire me and bring me on as a full-time editorial assistant. I'd be able to write what I wanted to write about, and do so in a manner I saw fit. They trusted my intuitions about the state of law enforcement and its practitioners and the need to get away from the usual politically correct pabulum that was increasingly being shoved down cops' throats.

Given the amount of free rein the publisher had committed, the promise of not having to deal with any more assholes with bars on their collars, and a salary that would offset a diminished pension that came with early retirement, I didn't hesitate.

"I'm in."

And with that, I was out of LASD.

Oh, there was still the formality of waiting it out till my twenty-fifth anniversary with the Department at which time my retirement benefits kicked in. But for all intents and purposes, I was gone.

If Lt. Art Garduno was as relieved as Ron Yasuda had been when I'd given notice upon going to work for Los Angeles County Sheriff's Department, I wouldn't know. But in hearing of my intentions to leave that same department, Garduno didn't shed any tears either.

"Well, okay" he said. "But I don't want you handling any more cases. I'll give you John Ness and you too can work the night car. Do whatever you want."

And with that I was back to being a cop again.

John Ness was a good street cop. I'd known as much for some time as I'd approved many an arrest he'd made and read his reports. I liked him, too, and we'd shared more than one late night telephone conversation about the state of the world.

He'd transferred to the Detective Bureau around the same time I did, and was as happy as I to be given the chance to work a night D.B. car with a partner.

He'd worked the car before, but alone. Our teaming up would allow for greater initiative as we'd be watching one another's backs and sharing the load. We agreed that, just as in my first stint in patrol, my partner would handle the booking while I wrote the paper.

We hit the ground running—literally. I got in my first foot pursuit in months, chasing a kid who'd rabbited on us from a bar and tossed a sawed-off shotgun under a car in the rear parking lot before I caught his ass going over a fence. On another evening, we passed a couple of gang members in a car who fled upon our making a U-turn to check them out. We got them detained and recovered a purse they'd just snatched from a woman. We got stolen vehicles and dope and for a moment the job felt like it had when I worked with Eric Shepherd years before.

But it was a different time. Ness and I recognized as much and didn't overstep our bounds. We both knew we were in the twilight of a profession and I was short-timing it. I didn't want to fuck things up by getting fired or prosecuted over something that in another era or place wouldn't have amounted to a hill of beans.

Still, it was the most I'd felt like a cop in years and by the end of our time together I almost resented the kindness Lt. Garduno had shown. I'd been given one more taste of patrol as I was on my way out the door.

I'd declined a retirement party, but an opportunity to goof off on County time was hard to kill. And so it was that a couple weeks later the Detective Bureau threw me a farewell fête on the station's back patio and dragged out some bewildered Law Enforcement Explorers to bid me goodbye.

My last day at work was spent turning my stuff into logistics and personnel, and picking up my retirement ID (with carrying concealed weapons permit indicated), reliving the same process I'd endured 25 years before, but in reverse.

I'd reconciled with my dad, retired from a job I'd grown to hate, and been hired by a magazine that wanted me and that I wanted to work for. Things were going smoothly.

I was fucked.

12

Life (and Death) After LASD

Three weeks.

That's how long my daily commute to Torrance lasted. Westbound on the 210 Freeway … Southbound on the 605 … Westbound on the 91 Freeway … hit some surface streets near Torrance and navigate my way to Challenge Way from there. It sounded pretty easy.

Except it wasn't.

As hard as it was on my car, it was even worse on my nerves. My publisher readily extended amnesties on my lack of punctuality—greatly appreciated. Having successfully pled my case to work from home, I gave away the Clint Eastwood poster that adorned my cubicle and moved out.

I knew that the company had gone out on the limb for me—I wasn't the only one who faced a long commute. But as I was the only one who was legally armed, it was probably a prudent decision on the company's part.

Still, I made a commitment with myself to make good on both the implicit promise of delivering well-written product, and on the explicit promise that I would attend annual editorial summits and whatever other periodic meetings were scheduled that required my attendance.

It was a small concession to make.

POLICE magazine was allowing me to explore facets of law enforcement I had not been able to explore before, and do so with a degree of impunity. If my liberally offered opinions offended someone, it might cost me a reader or two, but I wasn't apt to be fired or exiled to some gulag.

From the start, "Shots Fired" was a success and became *POLICE* magazine's most popular feature. Once Rich Wilhelm's story debuted and officers were able to see the magazine's intent with the column, they were more and more inclined to participate.

That the same could not always be said for their employing agencies was something I could never quite understand.

Given our contributing officers' often anxious desire to talk about their on-duty shooing incidents, and the magazine's policy that no shooting would be profiled until the circumstances surrounding the incident had been criminally adjudicated and the window of litigation closed, I found this a most peculiar parsimony on the part of the employing agencies. Could they not profit by lessons learned, or tactics validated, by other agencies?

The bureaucratic reticence pissed me off, and I sometimes wondered if there wasn't something that somebody involved in the equation was hiding. Such frustrations aside, the column was the one monthly obligation I could look forward to writing, even if procuring its next month's story was occasionally stressful.

While I often wished for more than the 2,000 words allocated me each month within which to describe and analyze an officer-involved shooting, I made do. Space limitations forced me to prioritize things; sometimes I would fixate on the evolution of the shooting itself—how it unfolded and came to some resolution. Other times, the manner in which the shooting had somehow become controverted or otherwise exacted a physical or emotional toll on the involved officer became the focal point.

On my way to profiling more than 100 officer-involved shooting incidents, "Shots Fired" won several awards and became imitated in the pages of other law enforcement periodicals. More importantly, it was acknowledged as having helped other officers to survive their own shootings.

That it would eventually prove a factor in my quitting *POLICE* magazine was about the only thing I hadn't anticipated.

Just before I retired, Dad had called me to reconcile after a two-and-half-year estrangement. He'd obtained some desperately needed psychological assistance for which I continue to be thankful.

But how unfortunate that our reunion would last only two and a half months—one-twelfth of the time we'd spent apart.

One Wednesday night in late October 2007, he had a heart attack. By Saturday, he was gone.

Part of me went with him.

I spent much of the next year barely even going through the motions. Somehow I fulfilled my *POLICE* magazine duties but spent most of my time in my room playing online chess games and doing Sudoku puzzles, things that kept my mind engaged in something other than grieving.

My sedentary lifestyle saw my body atrophy, precipitating a series of my own health issues, including a bout with a staph infection and recurrent stomach issues brought on by the toxic antibiotic that cured it. It seemed that each succeeding ailment had a domino effect so that I ended up dealing with a variety of gastrointestinal issues and stress and a deconditioned heart and belatedly paying for all my laziness and more.

In the middle of all this another tragedy hit.

My slow estrangement from my childhood friend Harold had been deliberate, initiated with a phone call I'd received from him shortly after my marriage. Harold had confided to having rolled over on his bed to see his mother in the doorway of his bedroom. In her face, he saw the devil.

"Dean, I mean it." There was no questioning the sincerity in his voice.

"I'm telling you, it was only love that kept me from killing her. I knew it wasn't her fault. But the devil was there. It was inside her."

Harold's shaky grasp on reality at the time found me wondering how long it would be before he'd see the devil in me and feel less inhibited about doing something about it. The way I saw it, my ongoing attempts just to keep my neurotic dad in check didn't allow me the opportunity to offer Harold much in the way of constructive support.

But now he seemed to be doing fine. He'd become active in a church, had moved out of his parents' home, and had been working at the same company for some time. He'd even done some dating. In July, we agreed to get together the following week for lunch.

But the week came and went and I'd forgotten to call him. Two days later, I found a message on my answering machine from his father.

"Harold's dead."

I called him back.

He said that Harold had apparently been chastised for some minor error at work and had gone home early. Two days later when he hadn't returned, his employers had requested a welfare check of his home. Police had found him deceased of a self-inflicted gunshot wound to the head.

Suicide had again taken someone from me and once again I was at a loss as to why.

Harold's death and concerns over my own mortality had me in a vacillating frame of mind. Part of me wanted to somehow do right by somehow honoring the memory of Dad and Harold and others that I'd loved and lost over the years lest every goddamn thing in my life seem a study in futility.

As much as I resented the idolatry of sports and their players, I appreciated the simple beauty of the game played. And as I saw life as a game, albeit a zero-sum game, I'd also seen it as something to be played as well as one could play it, given the natural limitations imposed upon the player. Even if you were destined to lose, you might wear down the base path a little so as to accommodate some successor's own sprint. Perhaps there was a lesson that might help another leg it out and make it all the way home.

Dad had, in his own neurotic way, helped me with mine. Harold, too, as had many others. There were all manner of better men and women who'd not been afforded the opportunities I had, and whose lives had been cut short for it. I could continue to lament the state of my health, or do something about it. Having seen the courage displayed by so many children dealing with imminent death, I figured the least I could do was get off my butt and so something to right my course.

I took up new hobbies like metal detecting and mountain biking, and came to genuinely appreciate the opportunity given me by Bobit Publications and *POLICE* magazine. I approached my work with renewed vigor. I tackled more arduous assignments, things that required a degree of research to which I was unaccustomed.

And at the back end there were rewards and awards. My health and self-esteem improved, and I received more and more recognition, both in-house and out.

Not that all recognition was good.

I strove in my feature stories, columns, and online blogs to be as honest and non-pandering as possible, and feedback suggested that most *POLICE* magazine readers appreciated the unfiltered candor. That it was occasionally spiced with some heart-felt expletive didn't seem to hurt either.

But then I knew that just because cops didn't have the latitude I did in speaking out on things didn't mean they didn't think the same kind of thoughts. In my latter years on the job, I'd recognized that there was a huge constituency of cops who just wanted to be freed of all the politically correct oversights and be able to speak their minds without fear of getting days off for doing so.

To that end, I was determined to avail them a forum in which to vent, to be able to call out chicken-shit administrators and pencil-pushing cowards and do so in indecorous terms if they so desired. And if an occasional and apt pejorative peppered the conversation, so much the better.

But nobody bats a thousand, and when it came to someone taking exception to my choice of words, it usually came down to polysyllabic ones.

One cop took exception to my having used the phrase "Damoclean Sword of law enforcement."

"While your English professor may be impressed, you should remember your audience, and stop trying to impress 'the great unwashed' with such phrases. I won't be reading any more articles written by Mr. Scoville. I frankly don't have the time."

Assuming he honored his promise, he never read my reply, tendered with a quote from H.L. Mencken: "Thousands of excellent nouns, verbs and adjectives that have stood in every decent dictionary for years are still unfamiliar to such ignoramuses, and I do not solicit their patronage. Let them continue to recreate themselves with whodunits, and leave my vocabulary and me to my own customers, who have been to school."

I added that he shouldn't let the door hit him in the ass.

Maybe I should have been more vigilant for that portal's proximity to my own.

13

Calling It Quits

Irreconcilable differences. Abandonment. Cruelty.

Nothing so contributed to my divorce from *POLICE* magazine as my inability to hold my tongue. The occasional aggravation—feature art work not being what I wanted, my boss exercising his editorial privilege where I didn't think it was needed, stories being killed owing to space issues—was something I'd learned to live with.

But I remained one to express reasonable dissatisfaction, and any alleged co-worker who went out of their way to frustrate me was apt to hear about it.

Usually, a single discussion was enough to get people on the same page. Anyone can make an initial misstep without everyone's panties getting in a bunch, so long as all parties were willing to work toward a common goal together.

Theoretically, that was the posture we Bobit employees had with the magazine's decision to produce podcasts of "Shots Fired."

When the idea had first been discussed, I was supportive of it. It would ensure a new audience and avail its existing base an alternative means of accessing its stories, and as "Shots Fired" had been my baby, my involvement with any of its various incarnations was presumed.

But from the outset I found that people were doing things without my input. Its inaugural production was depressing, the narrator's tone wholly inappropriate for the subject matter and offering anecdotal evidence on the hazards of getting what you paid for (i.e., free thespian labor).

Not that this was not a make or break problem—all we had to do was get a reader that knew what the hell he was doing and kick the Ted Baxter to the curb.

What wasn't fine was the continued policy of producing the shows without my input, and doing more harm than good. Given what I was hearing, first-time listeners weren't apt to be first-time readers, and my emails and phone conversations started getting sprinkled with words like "asinine" and "stupid" (thereby perfectly in keeping with the writer's penchant for describing things as they are, not how others would like them to be).

And so it was that what might have begun as ignorance or simple cluelessness on the part of the tech team escalated, with passive-aggressiveness morphing into outright hostility.

I skipped the passive-aggressiveness part and got down to business, emailing one of the primary instigators and apprising him of his lowly standing in my eyes before using the developing brouhaha as blog fodder for the *POLICE* magazine web site.

That the blog was quickly suppressed—taken off-line—was fine by me. The parent company had the right to do with work that had been commissioned and paid for as they wanted.

But the publisher then sent me a grievance-laden email wherein she took me to task for things that were apparently a source of both short- and long-standing resentments.

Most provoking was the following embedded paragraph.

"I expect a higher volume of material out of you. If you want to call your own shots, you're invited to become an independent contractor. We've restricted your CMS (content management system) and Facebook access because we don't trust you."

Even if her "my way or the highway" diplomacy and expressed lack of trust hadn't irked me, her next salvo pretty much sealed the deal.

"The fact that you have an 'agreement' to write what you want, when you want really has caused us to be in this position," she wrote. "You call the shots, then we cower. This is also a problem."

If it had been a problem, neither she nor Griffin should have agreed to as much on the front end. How difficult would that have been?

At least her full-blown vacillation was consistent, and asserted itself with her abandoning her support of me on this contentious matter.

I hadn't needed the job for some time.

And now didn't want it either.

I quit.

14

Post-*POLICE*

I went on to write a couple of things for other online sites, then pretty much called it a day, deciding that if after the better part of 40 years I had not mastered the art of getting along with co-workers and bosses, I might take a stab at something more autonomous—a memoir.

It chronicles not a long, hard climb to fulfilling career success, but a psychologically enervating trek to resignation. But the narrative is not without some value—my innumerable missteps offer a wealth of cautionary tales.

And yet I wouldn't trade the experience. For all the cognitive dissonance and repetitive spankings I endured, all the anal-retentive martinets I encountered, I did ultimately learn an invaluable lesson or two along the way.

A decade on after my retirement, word continues to wind its way back to me through the grapevine that my efforts were not necessarily in vain. Deputies, and even officers from outside agencies who had to run their arrests by me at the station, have forwarded their appreciations for whatever mentoring I'd done with regard to their investigations, arrest reviews, and report documentation. In other words, for being a useful link in that multi-generational chain of law enforcement mentors who labor to make sure all the I's are dotted and the T's crossed in the profession's peculiar apprenticeship.

Others, having promoted, have claimed to swipe a page from my book in routinely deflecting any animus from the citizenry away from their deputies and onto themselves.

As one never really knows how one comes across throughout life, this is heartening, particularly to someone who knows full well his own personality quirks.

Perhaps nothing has been more rewarding than hearing about how the officers' experiences chronicled in "Shots Fired" have been instrumental in helping other officers survive their own shootings, both in the immediacy of the moment and in dealing with the aftermath.

All that having been said, the most resounding truth today is that the practice of law enforcement is infinitely more difficult than anything I was ever exposed to. In an age where one can't watch the news or read an online magazine without finding a eulogy for a would-be cop killer, my sympathy for the poor bastards of the world leans increasingly toward the ones wearing badges.

Nothing fosters today's anti-cop zeitgeist more than the unfortunate advent of the Black Lives Matter movement, whose advocacies have proven dangerous to cops and citizens alike. The reticence of these agents of controversy to take an objective look at things, or review the findings of those who have, presents a great challenge to the profession. Harvard professor Roland G. Fryer Jr.'s study of officer-involved shootings, and his conclusion that no racial bias is involved, received hardly a mention in major news outlets. Yet inflammatory commentaries on shootings by less credible sources made headlines, led off the evening news, and helped to foment a bidding war for *The Hate U Give*, a reactionary novel detailing the officer-involved shooting of a young black person.

If cops indulged in the same kind of scapegoating being directed against them—and which they are accused of—they would be killing black civilians left and right, particularly as black males have, over the past decade, made up 42 percent of cop killers where the killer's race is known. But despite all the accusations and innuendo put out by "if it bleeds, it leads" media outlets, they don't, an irony that escapes their critics, who continue to fan the flames of racial outrage, resulting in ambushes like the ones in New York, New Orleans, and Dallas.

These media-driven ambushes result in the losses of men and women whose valuable contributions to society are well documented, which can rarely be said of their killers. The news and entertainment industries have blood on their hands, too. They have helped foster this anti-cop climate. Nobody holds them accountable.

Tragically, some officer deaths were preventable. At a November 2009 Thanksgiving gathering, Maurice Clemmons told his family and friends that he was planning to kill cops and children. He even displayed a firearm to prove the point. Several days later, he killed four Lakewood,

Washington, police officers as they sat in a coffee shop. In July 2014, Brian Fitch, Sr., told his girlfriend that he would kill a cop if he got pulled over. The next day, he shot and killed Mendota Heights police officer Scott Patrick and exchanged gunfire with other officers before being apprehended. In many cases, a shooter expresses his homicidal intentions ahead of time, and nobody does anything about it. When my dad's mental state began to decline, I entered a police hazard hit on his residence. I didn't feel comfortable doing it, but I would have felt worse if some deputy ended up paying the price for my negligence.

Epilogue

When it comes to law enforcement, it is the news media that most often controls the narrative. But occasionally, one of the profession will tailor their own.

This is mine. If its reflections are out of sync with those of others, so be it; and if my conclusions are wrong, at least I tried to achieve something on the page not afforded me at the beginning of my career: clarity and understanding.

Along the way, I did come to recognize a salient truth or two: Law enforcement as a profession is both vilified and glorified, yet rarely wholly deserving of either.

And if we cops don't see eye-to-eye, and are critical of one another's priorities and practices, then it's no wonder that those outside the profession don't know what to make of us. That vacillation can result in a kind of thin blue line between love and hate, as illustrated in the case of Scott Michael Greene, who wrote an email praising Iowa officers as "heroes" and expressing his love for them before shooting and killing two of Iowa's finest four days later.

Hopefully, I have courted neither love nor bullets, although I may have riled some former administrators (or perhaps inspired them to go write their own career reflections). If it will not strain the reader's patience, I want to drive home a few more points in closing.

The vast majority of my law enforcement peers were better than me, both as cops and as human beings. I have written about some of their virtues, but here offer my simple acknowledgment of the fact.

For all my atheism, hedonism, and prejudices, I placed a high premium on human life throughout the course of my career. I was respectful of others' feelings, so long as their reciprocating natures allowed.

Regarding racial tensions in America, my conscience (such as it is) is eased by the low bar society has set for itself. Let others follow the politically correct mandate of broad-stroking white heterosexual men as inherently evil racists, and foment scandals such as those at Duke and the University of Virginia. Let Barrack Obama use a memorial for fallen police officers as a forum to lecture on racism. Let the Tawana Brawleys of the world smear themselves in shit, if they so desire. I sleep OK at night.

When it came to conducting themselves ethically, some cops I worked with had considerably higher standards. Most were at least as ethical as I was. Those who weren't didn't last long. I believe this holds true now more than ever, given the ubiquity of cameras and other safeguards.

That said, I find it amusing that the profession continues to conduct psychological screenings of its aspirants, as any candidate's insanity should, in this day and age, be presumed. The more questionable aspects of my own mindset were often assets when dealing with others whose emotional stability was also in question.

Still, no one is more surprised by the length of my tenure than I. If I was a lousy fit, I was also an admiring one. I did not come into the profession with any particular agenda. My incentives were largely mercenary and my actions impelled by a secularist's intuition of right and wrong. Not surprisingly, I occasionally found myself at odds with others on both sides of the law who had differing viewpoints.

Indeed, I was so out of sync with the prevalent in-house opinions, that I can only see myself as having been an embedded pain-in-the-ass.

Was I resentful of opportunities denied and needless aggravations incurred? Fuck yeah. Still am. But I am comforted by the knowledge that I was able to conduct myself with adherence to my principles and values.

I once thought law enforcement to be a pretty haphazard calling. But then I realized that the same could be said of life.

Mine continues, with daily rewrites and little clue as to how it will all end (at least the guys who wrote *Casablanca* had some idea where they were going). If life as a retired cop turned writer hasn't promoted greater peace of mind, it sure hasn't detracted from it. And it's nice to think that after all the searching and chasing and fighting, at least I got that much.

And I finally found a motto I can believe in.

Be somebody's hero. Even if it's just your own.

Index